Simon Rogers is the editor of the
Guardian's award-winning Datablog
and Datastore (guardian.co.uk/data)
and a news editor on the paper,
working with the graphics team
to bring figures to life on the page.
He was closely involved with the
paper's groundbreaking decision to
crowdsource 450,000 MP expenses
records, as well as its coverage of the
Afghanistan and Iraq WikiLeaks
war logs. In 2012 he won a Royal
Statistical Society Excellence in
Journalism award; and he was named
2011's Best UK Internet Journalist by
the Oxford Internet Institute.

Facts are sacred

The power of data

Simon Rogers

faber and faber

guardianbooks

First published in 2013
by Faber and Faber Limited
Bloomsbury House
74–77 Great Russell Street
London WC1B 3DA

Published with Guardian Books
Guardian Books is an imprint of Guardian Newspapers Ltd

Typeset by Kari-Ruth Pedersen
Printed in Italy by L.E.G.O. S.p.A.

The right of Simon Rogers to be identified as author of this
work has been asserted in accordance with Section 77 of the
Copyright, Designs and Patents Act 1988

A CIP record for this book is available from the British Library

ISBN 978–0–571–30161–4

10 9 8 7 6 5 4 3 2 1

Contents

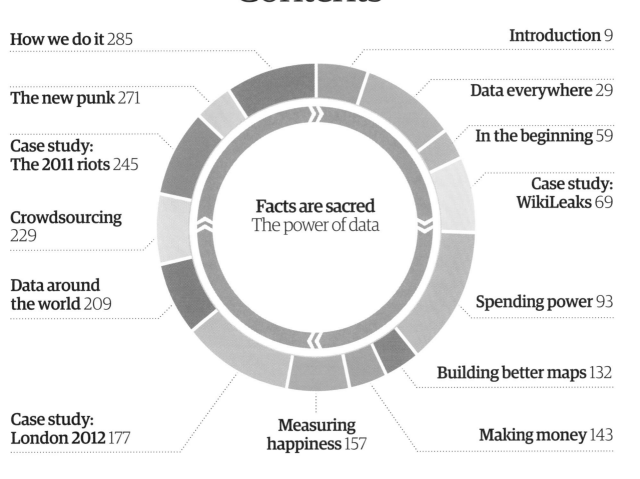

Facts are sacred
The power of data

Foreword

Data is spoken of as a new phenomenon, one of the information era, and one at the core of revolutionising digital industries, finance and commerce – but at its core it is little more than a term for the aggregation of facts.

As this, it is something that has been at the core of the Guardian for the full duration of its 190-year history, from a data table published on the front page of the Manchester Guardian's very first edition, to the quote from legendary Guardian editor C. P. Scott for which this book is named – that "facts are sacred".

The Guardian's Datablog, and its graphics, are the modern face of our approach to data, and the best of this is showcased within this book. From graphics explaining the economy or government spending, to background information on events, to in-depth analysis of huge news events like the UK's riots of 2011, data has been a core component of the Guardian's coverage.

As important to that approach is sharing the data we find and collect, and how we approach it, to allow it to be built on, analysed and improved by our readers. This has been at the core of the Datablog since its first post in 2009, and is as important now as ever it was – and this book is our latest contribution to these efforts. We hope it's one you find valuable.

Alan Rusbridger
Editor in chief, the Guardian

Chapter 1
Introduction

'Comment is free," wrote Guardian editor C.P. Scott in 1921, "but facts are sacred." He was creating his manifesto for the Guardian newspaper on its first century, a set of ideals journalists can still sign up to. "Fundamentally it implies honesty, cleanness, courage, fairness, a sense of duty to the reader and the community."

Ninety years later, publishing those sacred facts has become a new type of journalism in itself: data journalism. And it's rapidly becoming part of the establishment.

In 2009, when we launched the Datablog, all this was new. People still asked if getting stories from data was really journalism and not everyone had seen the godfather of data journalism Adrian Holovaty's riposte. It goes like this:

> **"Is data journalism? Is it journalism to publish a raw database? Here, at last, is the definitive, two-part answer:**
>
> **1. Who cares?**
>
> **2. I hope my competitors waste their time arguing about this for as long as possible."**

But once you've had MPs' expenses and WikiLeaks, the startling thing is that no one asks those questions any more. Instead, they want to know, "How do we do it?"

We wanted to show with this book how we do it. It brings together some of our thoughts about how data has changed our world – and what it tells us, expanding on themes that have flown across the Datablog since it started. It's not just a collection of stories; it's more like a manifesto for a new way of seeing things. In the past two years, data journalism has become our industry standard, our way of telling the big stories.

32,482

Number of records included in the indices of multiple deprivation, which are used by the government to measure poverty across England. Increasingly in the West, the problem is not too little data, but too much

Global warming
How observations are matching the scientific models

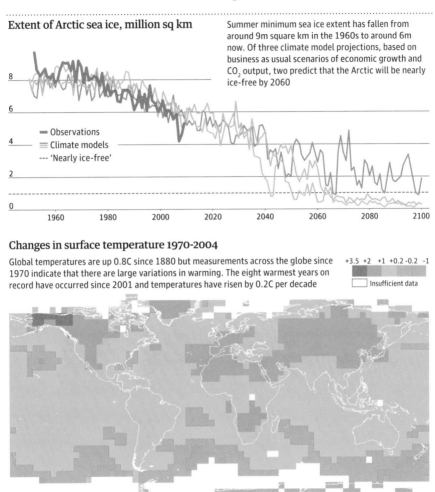

Extent of Arctic sea ice, million sq km

Summer minimum sea ice extent has fallen from around 9m square km in the 1960s to around 6m now. Of three climate model projections, based on business as usual scenarios of economic growth and CO_2 output, two predict that the Arctic will be nearly ice-free by 2060

- Observations
- Climate models
- --- 'Nearly ice-free'

Changes in surface temperature 1970-2004

Global temperatures are up 0.8C since 1880 but measurements across the globe since 1970 indicate that there are large variations in warming. The eight warmest years on record have occurred since 2001 and temperatures have risen by 0.2C per decade

+3.5 +2 +1 +0.2 -0.2 -1

Insufficient data

SOURCE: IPCC, MET OFFICE

It's not just about reporting and news organisations – data has become the hope for companies across the world, a potential source of revenue, either in exploiting it or in helping others analyse it. The divisions between what we do in the media and what happens out there in the rest of the world are breaking down – and data has played a huge part in that.

So we are not alone in this: every day brings newer and more innovative journalists, developers and entrepreneurs into the field, and with them new skills and techniques. Not only is data journalism changing in itself, it's changing journalism too. And the world.

10 things you will learn in this book

1

It may be trendy but it's not new

Data journalism has been around as long as there's been data – certainly at least since Florence Nightingale's famous graphics and report into the conditions faced by British soldiers of 1858. The first ever edition of the Guardian's news coverage was dominated by a large (leaked) table listing every school in Manchester, its costs and pupil numbers.

The big difference? Data was published in books, very expensive books where graphics are referred to as 'figures'. Now we have spreadsheets and files formatted for computers. Which means we can make the computers ask the questions.

The birth of infographics
William Playfair's charts

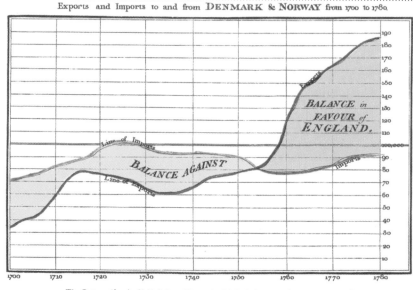

Exports and Imports to and from DENMARK & NORWAY from 1700 to 1780

BALANCE in FAVOUR of ENGLAND.

BALANCE AGAINST

Line of Imports

Line of Exports

Exports

Imports

The Bottom line is divided into Years, the Right hand line into £10,000 each.

William Playfair, a Scottish engineer and writer, published his Atlas in 1786, which featured 44 graphs, including this one. Playfair either refined or invented most of the statistical graphs we still use today

Eurozone crisis hotspots
Key measures reveal worst-hit economies

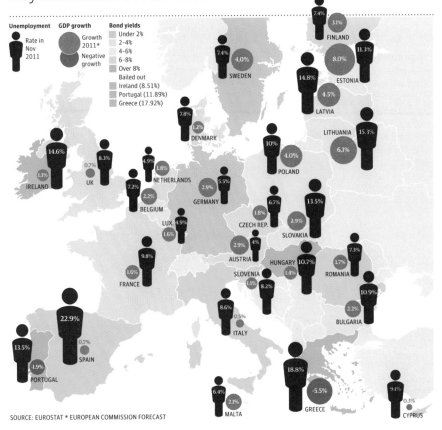

Unemployment
Rate in Nov 2011

GDP growth
Growth 2011*
Negative growth

Bond yields
Under 2%
2-4%
4-6%
6-8%
Over 8%
Bailed out
Ireland (8.51%)
Portugal (11.89%)
Greece (17.92%)

FINLAND 7.4% 3.1%
SWEDEN 7.4% 4.0%
ESTONIA 8.0% 11.3%
LATVIA 14.8% 4.5%
LITHUANIA 15.3% 6.1%
DENMARK 7.8% 1.2%
IRELAND 14.6% 1.1%
UK 8.3% 0.7%
NETHERLANDS 4.9% 1.8%
POLAND 10% 4.0%
BELGIUM 7.2% 2.2%
GERMANY 2.9% 5.5%
LUX. 4.9% 1.6%
CZECH REP. 6.7% 1.8%
SLOVAKIA 13.5% 2.9%
FRANCE 9.8% 1.6%
AUSTRIA 2.9% 4%
HUNGARY 10.7% 1.4%
ROMANIA 7.3% 1.7%
SLOVENIA 8.2% 1.1%
BULGARIA 10.9% 2.2%
ITALY 8.6% 0.5%
SPAIN 22.9% 0.7%
PORTUGAL 13.5% -1.9%
MALTA 6.4% 2.1%
GREECE 18.8% -5.5%
CYPRUS 9.1% 0.3%

SOURCE: EUROSTAT * EUROPEAN COMMISSION FORECAST

2
Open data means open data journalism

Now statistics have become democratised: no longer the preserve of the few but of everyone who has a spreadsheet package on their laptop, desktop or even their mobile and tablet. Anyone can take on a fearsome set of data and wrangle it into shape. Of course, they may not be right, but now you can easily find someone to help you. We are not wandering alone any more.

Data journalism is all about diverse sources. At the Guardian, being part of the news process means that we're part of the news desk (news organisations are obsessed with internal geography), go to the key news meetings and try to make sure that data is part of editorial debate.

7bn and beyond
How population levels will change by 2050

These UN population projections from 2010 show that across much of the developed West, fertility rates are falling and in some countries the population will actually fall by 2050. The big growers are Africa and Asia – with Europe's population falling by 41.7 million by 2050

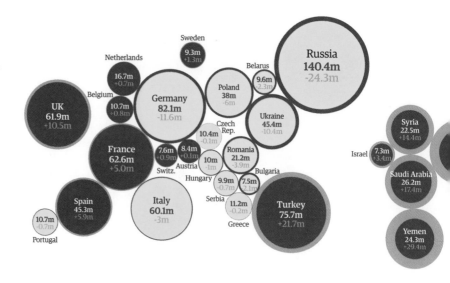

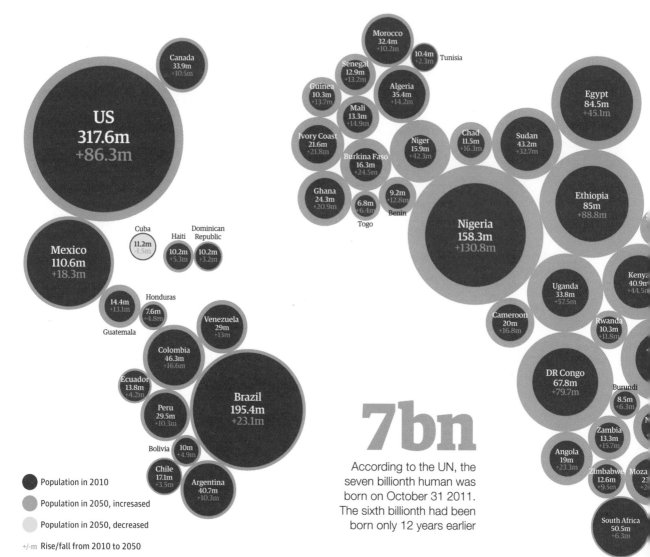

7bn

According to the UN, the seven billionth human was born on October 31 2011. The sixth billionth had been born only 12 years earlier

● Population in 2010
● Population in 2050, increased
● Population in 2050, decreased

+/-m Rise/fall from 2010 to 2050

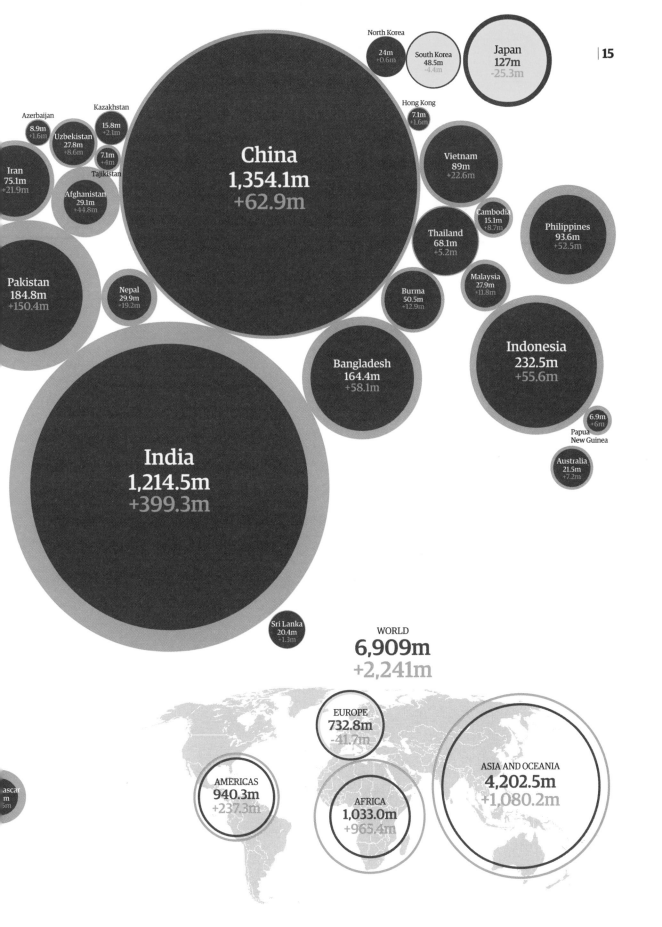

North Korea
24m
+0.6m

South Korea
48.5m
-4.4m

Japan
127m
-25.3m

Azerbaijan
8.9m
+1.6m

Kazakhstan
15.8m
+2.1m

Uzbekistan
27.8m
+8.6m

7.1m
+4m
Tajikistan

Iran
75.1m
+21.9m

Afghanistan
29.1m
+44.8m

China
1,354.1m
+62.9m

Hong Kong
7.1m
+1.6m

Vietnam
89m
+22.6m

Cambodia
15.1m
+8.7m

Philippines
93.6m
+52.5m

Pakistan
184.8m
+150.4m

Nepal
29.9m
+19.2m

Thailand
68.1m
+5.2m

Burma
50.5m
+12.9m

Malaysia
27.9m
+11.8m

Indonesia
232.5m
+55.6m

Bangladesh
164.4m
+58.1m

6.9m
+6m
Papua
New Guinea

Australia
21.5m
+7.2m

India
1,214.5m
+399.3m

Sri Lanka
20.4m
+1.3m

ascar
m
m

WORLD
6,909m
+2,241m

EUROPE
732.8m
-41.7m

AMERICAS
940.3m
+237.3m

AFRICA
1,033.0m
+965.4m

ASIA AND OCEANIA
4,202.5m
+1,080.2m

3

Data journalism is sometimes curation

Has data journalism become curation? Sometimes. There's now so much data out there in the world that we try to provide the key facts for each story – and finding the right information can be as much of a lengthy journalistic task as finding the right interviewee for an article. We've started providing searches into world government data and international development data.

The COINS database release in numbers

The government opens up its accounting books, 2010

3,298,513

items released in the first tranche of releases from the Combined Online Information System database, covering 2009/10

18,000

government spending items were released

24m

individual entries documenting where public money comes from, what it is spent on and whose pocket it ends up in

3,728

spends on consultancy by government departments

£1.8bn

spent on consultancy by government departments, up from **£1.5bn** the previous year

587

accountancy codes used

1,088

different bodies spend government money

4,855

individual spending programmes detailed

64

major departments in government covered by COINS database

The datasets are getting massive – 391,000 records for WikiLeaks' Iraq release, millions for the Treasury COINS database. The indices of multiple deprivation, which is how the government measures poverty across England, has 32,482 records. Increasingly government data comes in big packages about tiny things. Making that data more accessible and easier to do stuff with has become part of the data journalism process.

4
We're getting bigger datasets on smaller things

Data journalism is 80% perspiration, 10% great idea, 10% output. It just is.

We spend hours making datasets work, reformatting PDFs, mashing datasets together. Mostly, we act as the bridge between the data (and those who are pretty much hopeless at explaining it) and the people out there in the real world who want to understand what that story is really about.

5
It is 80% perspiration, 10% inspiration, 10% output

Traditionally, some of the worst data journalism involved spending weeks on a single dataset, noodling around and eventually producing something mildly diverting. Some of the best involves weeks of investigative data management before coming up with incredible scoops. But increasingly there's a new short-form of data journalism, which is about swiftly finding the key data, analysing it and guiding readers through it while the story is still in the news. The trick is to produce these news data analyses, using the tech we have, as quickly as we can. And still get it right.

6
It's not all long, complicated investigations

Religious tolerance
Social and political pressures on religion in 25 most populous countries, 2010

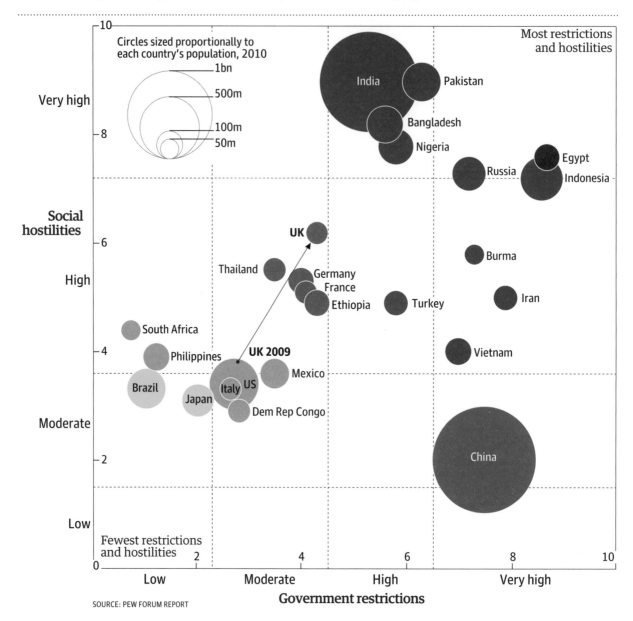

Circles sized proportionally to each country's population, 2010

— 1bn
— 500m
— 100m
— 50m

Most restrictions and hostilities

India
Pakistan
Bangladesh
Nigeria
Russia
Egypt
Indonesia
UK
Burma
Thailand
Germany
France
Ethiopia
Turkey
Iran
South Africa
Vietnam
Philippines
UK 2009
Mexico
Brazil
Italy US
Japan
Dem Rep Congo
China

Very high
Social hostilities
High
Moderate
Low

Fewest restrictions and hostilities

Low | Moderate | High | Very high

Government restrictions

SOURCE: PEW FORUM REPORT

160 countries where harassment or intimidation of specific religious groups took place, up 6% on the baseline study from 2006

The starting point for a heat map produced using Google's Fusion Tables online tools

7

Anyone can do it...

Especially with the free tools we use, such as Google Fusion Tables (pictured), Datawrapper, Google Charts or Timetric – and you can see some of the stuff our users have produced and posted on our Flickr group.

Good design still really matters. Something like our guide to the senior civil service (overleaf), or who knows who in the News of the World phone hacking affair – or even what happened when – work because they're designed not by machine but by humans who understand the issues involved.

8

...but looks can be everything

Whitehall's rarefied circles, 2011

This is the world of the senior civil service, courtesy of a list published by the government in 2011 naming every senior civil servant for each department. One of the largest units is the Efficiency and Reform Group in the Cabinet Office – driving the cuts agenda. It does not include staff working for agencies and junior staff within departments. At this end of the civil service, the rewards are high: the head of the civil service, Sir Gus O'Donnell, was paid almost £240,000

Cabinet Office
Cabinet Secretary & Head of the Home Civil Service **Sir Gus O'Donnell**
Salary **£235,000 - £239,999**
Civil servants in department **1,230**
Senior civil servants **216** (doesn't include head)
Number with minimum salary higher than prime minister **19**

Minister Francis Maude

- Knowledge & Information Management **1**
- Europe & Global Issues Secretariat **5**
- Honours & Appointments Secretariat **2**
- Constitution Group **5**
- Efficiency & Reform Group — Drives government's efficiency agenda **91**
- Joint Intelligence Organisation **2**
- Private Office Group **5**
- National Security Secretariat **8**
- Cabinet Office Communications **5**
- Corporate Services Group **1**
- Human Resources **2**
- Deputy Prime Minister's Office **2**
- Finance & Estates Management **3**
- Office of the Parliamentary Counsel **54** — Sir Stephen Laws, Chief Parliamentary Counsel **£225,000 - £229,999**
- Prime Minister's Office **17**
- Economic & Domestic Affairs Secretariat **8**
- Government Digital Service **5**

Foreign & Commonwealth Office
Permanent Under-Secretary & Head of the Diplomatic Service **Simon Fraser**
Salary **£180,000 - £184,999**
Civil servants **5,900**
Senior posts **119**
Salary bigger than PM **4**

Cabinet minister William Hague

- Europe & Global: Europe **20**
- Operations officer **17**
- Pol: Middle East & North Africa **13**
- Other Defence & intelligence **6**
- E&G: Africa **7**
- Europe & Global: Asia Pacific **11**
- Pol: South Asia & Afghanistan **9**
- Defence & intelligence: Americas **11**
- Other political **8**
- PUS office **7**
- Pol: Eastern Europe & Central Asia **4**
- UK Trade & Investment **3**
- Other E&G **2**

Department for Communities & local government
Permanent Secretary **Sir Bob Kerslake**
Salary **£170,000 - £1...**
Civil servants **2,650**
Senior posts **116**
Salary bigger than PM **2**

Wales Office
Director **Fiona Adams Jones**
Salary **£80,000 - £84,999**
Civil servants **60**
Senior posts **4**
Salary bigger than PM **0**
Cabinet minister Cheryl Gillan
4

Ministry of Justice
Permanent Secretary **Sir Suma Chakrabarti**
Salary **£180,000 - £184,999**
Civil servants **3,130**
Senior posts **171**
Salary bigger than PM **6**

Cabinet minister Kenneth Clarke

- Corporate Performance Group **49**
- Private Office **2**
- Her Majesty's Court Service (HMCS) **40**
- Tribunals Service **6**
- Justice Policy Group **45** — Helen Edwards, Director General **£160,000 - £164,999**
- Law, Rights & International Group **27**
- Office of the Public Guardian **2**

Scotland Office
Director **Alisdair McIntosh**
Salary **£80,000 - £84,999**
Civil servants **100**
Senior posts **4**
Salary bigger than PM **0**
Cabinet minister Michael Moore
4

Department for Transport
Permanent Secretary **Lin Homer**
Salary **£170,000 - £174,999**
Civil servants **2,080**
Senior posts **117**
Salary bigger than PM **2**
Cabinet minister Philip Hammond

Department for Environment, Food & Rural Affairs
Permanent Secretary **Bronwyn Hill**
Salary **£160,000 - £164,999**
Civil servants **2,640**
Senior posts **127**
Salary bigger than PM **1**

Cabinet minister Caroline Spelman

- Green economy & Corporate services **51**
- Chief scientific adviser **1**
- Secretariat **3**
- Food & Farming **30**
- Environment & Rural **37**

Department for Culture, Media & Sport
Permanent Secretary **Jonathan Stephens**
Salary **£155,000 - £159,999**
Civil servants **470**
Senior posts **43**
Salary bigger than PM **3**
Cabinet minister Jeremy Hunt

- Government Olympic Executive **19**
- Senior Management Team **17**
- Executive Board **6**

Her Majesty's Revenue and Customs
Chief Executive & Permanent Secretary **Dame Lesley Strathie**
Salary **£170,000 - £174,999**
Civil servants **75,340**
Senior posts **352**
Salary higher than PM **9**

Non-ministerial dept

- Permanent Secretary for Tax **24**
- Solicitor's Office **24**
- Other **8**
- Business tax **114**
- Compliance & Enforcement **52**
- People **19**
- Information Management **23**
- Finance **22** — James Ballingall, Deputy Director, Head of Assurance **£185,000 - £189,999**
- Personal tax **54**
- Benefits & Credits **11** — **£205,000 - £209,999** — Steve Lamey, Director General

Government Equalities Office
Director-general **Jonathan Rees**
Salary **£130,000 - £134,999**
Civil servants **120**
Senior posts **8**
Salary bigger than PM **0**
Minister Theresa May
8

Attorney Generals' Departments
Director-general **Peter Fish**
Salary **£120,000 - £124,999**
Director of Public Prosecutions **Keir Starmer**
Salary **£195,000 - £199,999**
Civil servants **9,500**
Senior posts **8**
Salary bigger than PM **4**
Minister Dominic Grieve
- Crown Prosecution Service **4**
- Attorney General **4**

Department for Business, Innovation & Skills
Permanent Secretary **Martin Donnelly**
Salary **£160,000 - £164,999**
Civil servants **3,940**
Senior posts **195**
Salary bigger than PM **9**

Cabinet minister Vince Cable

- Chief scientific adviser **6**
- Chief economic adviser **10**
- Legal, People & Communications **22**
- Shareholder Executive **19** — Stephen Lovegrove, Chief Executive, **£185,000 - £189,999**
- Ministerial & Parliamentary Support **2**
- Business & Skills **57** — Manufacturing, enterprise, economic development, information economy, further education — Philip Rutnam, Director General **£180,000 - £184,999**
- Knowledge & Innovation **12**
- Finance Directorate **13**
- UKTI - International **22**
- Market Frameworks **23**

200,43...
Civil servants work for major department... shown here

£142,500
Salary of prime min... David Cameron, 20...

- Fina... Corpora...
- Intern... strat... environ... **3**
- Cor... gr... **2**

SOURCE: DATA.GOV.UK, GRAPHIC: JENNY RIDLEY, COPY & RESEARCH: SIMON ROGERS

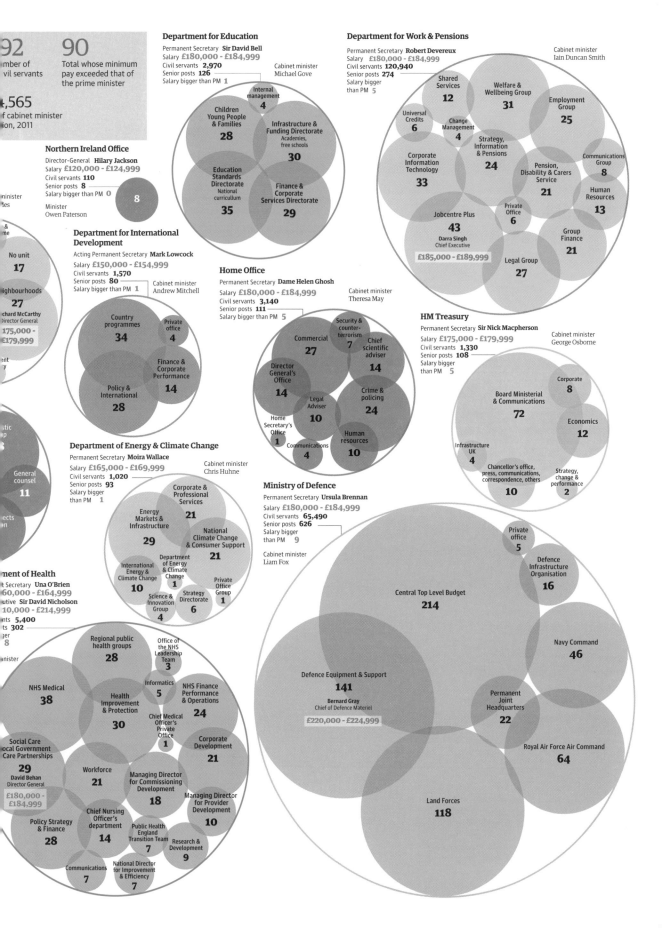

92
mber of
vil servants

90
Total whose minimum
pay exceeded that of
the prime minister

,565
f cabinet minister
ion, 2011

Department for Education
Permanent Secretary **Sir David Bell**
Salary **£180,000 - £184,999**
Civil servants **2,970**
Senior posts **126**
Salary bigger than PM **1**

Cabinet minister
Michael Gove

Internal management **4**
Children Young People & Families **28**
Infrastructure & Funding Directorate
Academies, free schools **30**
Education Standards Directorate
National curriculum **35**
Finance & Corporate Services Directorate **29**

Department for Work & Pensions
Permanent Secretary **Robert Devereux**
Salary **£180,000 - £184,999**
Civil servants **120,940**
Senior posts **274**
Salary bigger than PM **5**

Cabinet minister
Iain Duncan Smith

Shared Services **12**
Welfare & Wellbeing Group **31**
Employment Group **25**
Universal Credits **6**
Change Management **4**
Strategy, Information & Pensions **24**
Corporate Information Technology **33**
Pension, Disability & Carers Service **21**
Communications Group **8**
Human Resources **13**
Jobcentre Plus **43**
Darra Singh
Chief Executive
£185,000 - £189,999
Private Office **6**
Group Finance **21**
Legal Group **27**

Northern Ireland Office
Director-General **Hilary Jackson**
Salary **£120,000 - £124,999**
Civil servants **110**
Senior posts **8**
Salary bigger than PM **0**

Minister
Owen Paterson

8

minister
les

& me
No unit **17**

ighbourhoods **27**
chard McCarthy
irector General
175,000 -
£179,999

nt y

Department for International Development
Acting Permanent Secretary **Mark Lowcock**
Salary **£150,000 - £154,999**
Civil servants **1,570**
Senior posts **80**
Salary bigger than PM **1**

Cabinet minister
Andrew Mitchell

Country programmes **34**
Private office **4**
Finance & Corporate Performance **14**
Policy & International **28**

Home Office
Permanent Secretary **Dame Helen Ghosh**
Salary **£180,000 - £184,999**
Civil servants **3,140**
Senior posts **111**
Salary bigger than PM **5**

Cabinet minister
Theresa May

Commercial **27**
Security & counter-terrorism **7**
Chief scientific adviser **14**
Director General's Office **14**
Legal Adviser **10**
Crime & policing **24**
Home Secretary's Office **1**
Communications **4**
Human resources **10**

HM Treasury
Permanent Secretary **Sir Nick Macpherson**
Salary **£175,000 - £179,999**
Civil servants **1,330**
Senior posts **108**
Salary bigger than PM **5**

Cabinet minister
George Osborne

Board Ministerial & Communications **72**
Corporate **8**
Economics **12**
Infrastructure UK **4**
Chancellor's office, press, communications, correspondence, others **10**
Strategy, change & performance **2**

Department of Energy & Climate Change
Permanent Secretary **Moira Wallace**
Salary **£165,000 - £169,999**
Civil servants **1,020**
Senior posts **93**
Salary bigger than PM **1**

Cabinet minister
Chris Huhne

Corporate & Professional Services **21**
Energy Markets & Infrastructure **29**
National Climate Change & Consumer Support **21**
International Energy & Climate Change **10**
Department of Energy & Climate Change **1**
Private Office Group **1**
Science & Innovation Group **4**
Strategy Directorate **6**

stic
p

General counsel **11**

ects
n

Ministry of Defence
Permanent Secretary **Ursula Brennan**
Salary **£180,000 - £184,999**
Civil servants **65,490**
Senior posts **626**
Salary bigger than PM **9**

Cabinet minister
Liam Fox

Private office **5**
Defence Infrastructure Organisation **16**
Central Top Level Budget **214**
Defence Equipment & Support **141**
Bernard Gray
Chief of Defence Materiel
£220,000 - £224,999
Navy Command **46**
Permanent Joint Headquarters **22**
Royal Air Force Air Command **64**
Land Forces **118**

nent of Health
t Secretary **Una O'Brien**
60,000 - £164,999
utive **Sir David Nicholson**
10,000 - £214,999
nts **5,400**
ger **302**
8

inister

Regional public health groups **28**
Office of the NHS Leadership Team **3**
Informatics **5**
NHS Finance Performance & Operations **24**
NHS Medical **38**
Health Improvement & Protection **30**
Chief Medical Officer's Private Office **1**
Corporate Development **21**
Social Care ocal Government Care Partnerships **29**
David Behan
Director General
£180,000 - £184,999
Workforce **21**
Managing Director for Commissioning Development **18**
Managing Director for Provider Development **10**
Policy Strategy & Finance **28**
Chief Nursing Officer's department **14**
Public Health England Transition Team **7**
Research & Development **9**
Communications **7**
National Director for Improvement & Efficiency **7**

9

You don't have to be a programmer

You can become a top coder if you want. But the bigger task is to think about the data like a journalist, rather than an analyst. What's interesting about these numbers? What's new? What would happen if I mashed it up with something else? Answering those questions is more important than anything else.

This stuff works best when it's a combination of both. Our guide to Nato operations in Libya was dynamically fed from a spreadsheet, which updated from the Nato daily action briefing. It looked good because it had been well designed; it worked because it was easy to update every day.

Data journalism is not graphics and visualisations. It's about telling the story in the best way possible. Sometimes that will be a visualisation or a map. But sometimes it's a news story. Sometimes, just publishing the number is enough.

If data journalism is about anything, it's the flexibility to search for new ways of storytelling. And more and more reporters are realising that. Suddenly we have company – and competition. So being a data journalist is no longer unusual.

It's just journalism.

10

It's (still) all about the stories

Oxbridge entry
How a few schools dominate lists of entrants

Number of entrants, 2007-2009

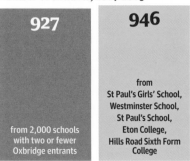

927
from 2,000 schools with two or fewer Oxbridge entrants

946
from
St Paul's Girls' School,
Westminster School,
St Paul's School,
Eton College,
Hills Road Sixth Form College

SOURCE: SUTTON TRUST

Britain's military
How war and cost-cutting have impacted the armed services

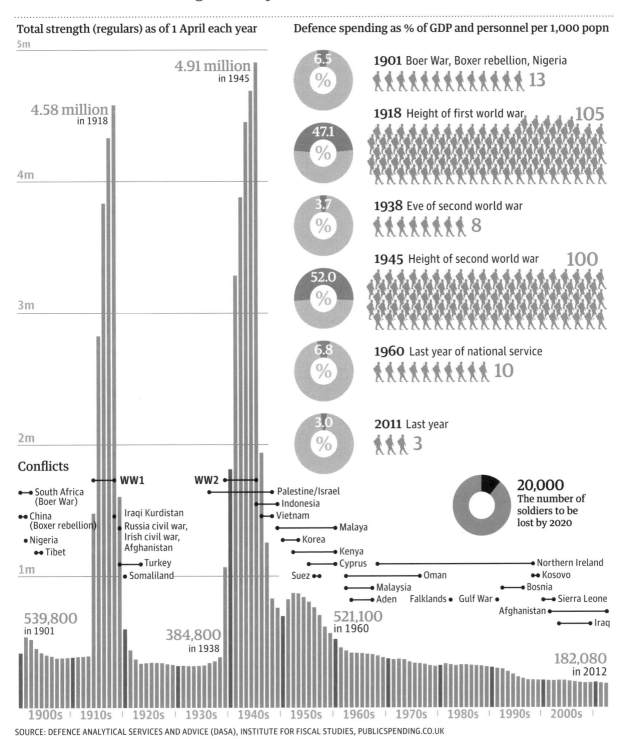

Total strength (regulars) as of 1 April each year

5m

4.91 million in 1945

4.58 million in 1918

4m

3m

2m

1m

Conflicts

- South Africa (Boer War)
- China (Boxer rebellion)
- Nigeria
- Tibet

WW1

Iraqi Kurdistan
Russia civil war, Irish civil war, Afghanistan
- Turkey
- Somaliland

WW2
- Palestine/Israel
- Indonesia
- Vietnam
- Malaya
- Korea
- Kenya
- Cyprus — Northern Ireland
Suez — Oman — Kosovo
- Malaysia — Bosnia
- Aden Falklands Gulf War — Sierra Leone
Afghanistan —
— Iraq

539,800 in 1901

384,800 in 1938

521,100 in 1960

182,080 in 2012

1900s | 1910s | 1920s | 1930s | 1940s | 1950s | 1960s | 1970s | 1980s | 1990s | 2000s |

Defence spending as % of GDP and personnel per 1,000 popn

6.5 % — **1901** Boer War, Boxer rebellion, Nigeria — 13

47.1 % — **1918** Height of first world war — 105

3.7 % — **1938** Eve of second world war — 8

52.0 % — **1945** Height of second world war — 100

6.8 % — **1960** Last year of national service — 10

3.0 % — **2011** Last year — 3

20,000 The number of soldiers to be lost by 2020

SOURCE: DEFENCE ANALYTICAL SERVICES AND ADVICE (DASA), INSTITUTE FOR FISCAL STUDIES, PUBLICSPENDING.CO.UK

How big is a billion?

Billions are everywhere. The US has a budget deficit of around $100bn a month; the UK's government spends nearly £700bn a year in budget deficits; the world now has over seven billion people in it. In terms of a lot of the stories we do, a billion is where a number really matters and has an impact.

Everyone knows that, right? You'd be surprised. For a number that is bandied around so readily, very few people really understand what it is.

It doesn't help that using the word "billion" depends on where you live. The US system, which is used by the government and the Bank of England in the UK, is shown here.

It basically goes up in thousands. A thousand times a thousand is a million, a thousand times a million is a billion and so on.

But if you're reading this from France or Germany, 1,000,000,000 is actually a "milliard" – a number that has not featured in a Guardian news story since 2004, except in the corrections column. The European billion is a million times a million – and this used to be called the British system. Confused yet? There's also the inexorable logic of inflation – a "trillion" is becoming common too. Then get your head around the fact that a US trillion is a European billion. And a European trillion? That's a "quintillion".

Mathematicians will tell you that the European system is more logical, but in a sense that is now academic. The nine-zero billion is in the ascendency.

Trillion

or 1×10^{12}. If you had a trilli pounds, you could buy 4.2 houses at the 2012 UK avera house price of £238,638; t total worth of all of Britair property in 2012 was £4.1 according to the ON

Quadrillion

or 1×10^{15}. The UK's most powerful computer, Blue Joule, based at the Science and Technology Facilities Council's Laboratory in Cheshire, can perform more than a quadrillion calculations a second. It was the 13th fastest computer in the world in 2012

,000,000,000,000,000

1,000,000,000,000

1,000,000,000

1,000,000

Billion

r 1x10^9. A billion pounds
would pay the £40,000 average
ousehold income in the UK to
5,000 families. Thirteen films have
rossed more than a billion dollars
worldwide to summer 2012,
ed by Avatar, which made
2.7bn following its release
n December 2009

1,000

Million

Thousand

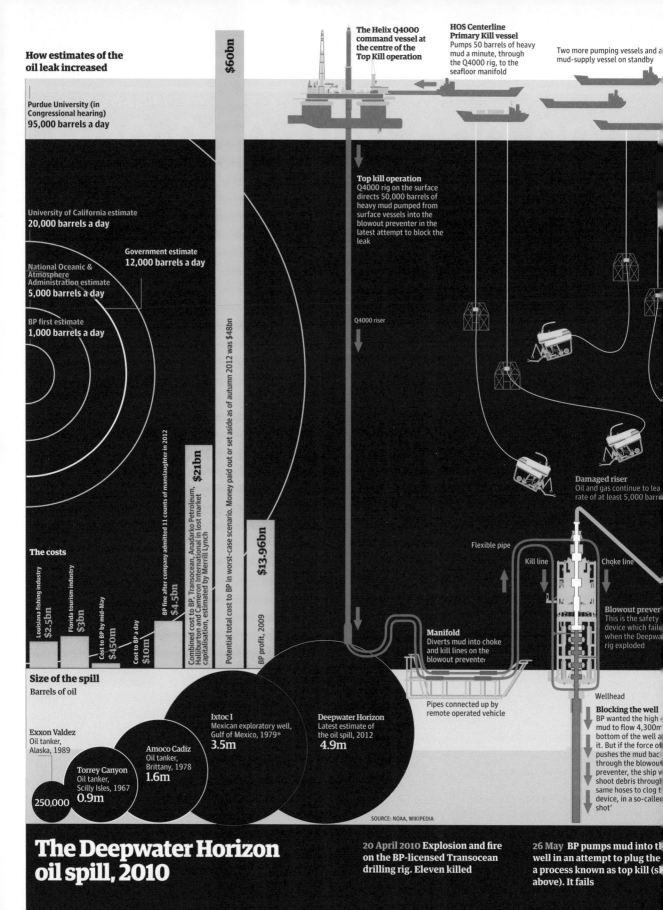

How estimates of the oil leak increased

Purdue University (in Congressional hearing)
95,000 barrels a day

$60bn

The Helix Q4000 command vessel at the centre of the Top Kill operation

HOS Centerline Primary Kill vessel
Pumps 50 barrels of heavy mud a minute, through the Q4000 rig, to the seafloor manifold

Two more pumping vessels and a mud-supply vessel on standby

Top kill operation
Q4000 rig on the surface directs 50,000 barrels of heavy mud pumped from surface vessels into the blowout preventer in the latest attempt to block the leak

University of California estimate
20,000 barrels a day

Government estimate
12,000 barrels a day

National Oceanic & Atmosphere Administration estimate
5,000 barrels a day

Q4000 riser

BP first estimate
1,000 barrels a day

Damaged riser
Oil and gas continue to lea rate of at least 5,000 barr

Flexible pipe

Kill line

Choke line

The costs

Louisiana fishing industry **$2.5bn**

Florida tourism industry **$3bn**

Cost to BP by mid-May **$450m**

Cost to BP a day **$10m**

Combined cost to BP, Transocean, Anadarko Petroleum, Halliburton and Cameron International in lost market capitalisation, estimated by Merrill Lynch **$4.5bn**

BP fine after company admitted 11 counts of manslaughter in 2012 **$21bn**

Potential total cost to BP in worst-case scenario. Money paid out or set aside as of autumn 2012 was $48bn

BP profit, 2009 **$13.96bn**

Blowout prever
This is the safety device which fail when the Deepwa rig exploded

Manifold
Diverts mud into choke and kill lines on the blowout preventer

Pipes connected up by remote operated vehicle

Wellhead

Blocking the well
BP wanted the high mud to flow 4,300m bottom of the well a it. But if the force of pushes the mud bac through the blowou preventer, the ship w shoot debris throug same hoses to clog t device, in a so-called shot'

Size of the spill
Barrels of oil

Exxon Valdez
Oil tanker, Alaska, 1989
250,000

Torrey Canyon
Oil tanker, Scilly Isles, 1967
0.9m

Amoco Cadiz
Oil tanker, Brittany, 1978
1.6m

Ixtoc I
Mexican exploratory well, Gulf of Mexico, 1979*
3.5m

Deepwater Horizon
Latest estimate of the oil spill, 2012
4.9m

SOURCE: NOAA, WIKIPEDIA

The Deepwater Horizon oil spill, 2010

20 April 2010 Explosion and fire on the BP-licensed Transocean drilling rig. Eleven killed

26 May BP pumps mud into th well in an attempt to plug the a process known as top kill (sl above). It fails

OV vessels
…work on the sea floor
…rried out by
…mote-operated
…hicles

Discoverer Enterprise
Oil recovery vessel
capable of pumping
2,000 barrels of oil a
day from the old
Deepwater Horizon riser
on the sea floor

Relief rigs
Two rigs drilling
new wells into the
bore hole used by
the Deepwater
Horizon

Floating booms
Boats laying booms to
corral biggest spills and
stop them from spreading.
Some of the oil was burned

**Biodegradable
detergents**
Aircraft spraying
thousands of gallons of
dispersant across the
slick

ROVs
Operate in pairs on a
wide range of jobs
including:
● Holding dispersant
injection boom into
oil plume
● Monitoring operations
● Fitting riser insertion
tool

…itoring the flow of oil
…eleased a short video of oil and gas gushing
…n the pipe – leading scientists to conclude
…the leak could be spewing out as much as
…00 barrels of oil a day

**Riser insertion
tube**
Installed on 16 May.
About 2,000 barrels
of oil raised per day
to the Discoverer
Enterprise oil
recovery vessel

Containment chamber
Failed as an oil capture and
recovery device after a
chemical reaction caused
ice crystals to form in the
top of the container.
The "top hat", a second
smaller device, also failed

**Deepwater
Horizon**
Destroyed oil rig
lying 457m from
the wellhead

Riser insertion tool

New drilling
To relieve the
pressure on the
Deepwater
Horizon, two rigs
are drilling
additional
wells at
converging
angles

MISSISSIPPI — Mobile — FLORIDA — Milton — Pensacola — Biloxi — Pascagoula — Gulfport — Bay St. Louis — Chandeleur Islands — GULF OF MEXICO — New Orleans — LOUISIANA — *Mississippi Delta* — Deepwater Horizon Rig — 25 MILES

Oil damage survey results, by end of May
— Heavy
— Moderate   ■ Extent of the slick
— Light   ■ Oyster beds
— Very light   □ Bird breeding grounds
— Tar balls   □ Nature reserve

Response in numbers

47,829 personnel deployed   **12,000** volunteers

9,700 vessels at peak of the operation

127 surveillance aircraft deployed   **9.7m** feet of soft boom deployed

1.4m barrels of liquid waste recovered

29,000 square miles of slick and sheen,
only slightly smaller than Scotland

1 …le killed in the
…nd explosion
…e Deepwater
…zon oil platform

87 Days it took for BP
to successfully cap
the oil leaks

1.8m Gallons of chemical
dispersant applied in
the Gulf

411 The estimated number
of in-situ oil burns to
get rid of surplus oil

A new containment cap
…uring half of the oil still
… However BP is still losing
… war; Obama angry at
…se

11 July BP use robots to remove a
leaking cap from the well, to allow
a replacement containment system
to be installed

15 July BP finally stops the flow
of oil, thanks to new more tightly
fitting containment cap

4 August BP announces that its
static kill operation – pumping
heavy drilling mud and cement
into the well – has succeeded

SOURCES: NOAA, BP, REUTERS. GRAPHIC: MICHAEL ROBINSON, JENNY RIDLEY, PAUL SCRUTON, IAN JEFFRIES

Chapter 2
Data everywhere

'Data journalism" or "computer-assisted reporting"? What is it? How do you describe it? Is it even real journalism? These are just two terms for the latest trend, a field combining spreadsheets, graphics, data analysis and the biggest news stories to dominate reporting in the last two years.

The WikiLeaks releases on Afghanistan, Iraq and the US embassy cables; the UK MPs' expenses scandal; the global recession; even the swine flu panic…reporting on all of those events was arguably only possible because of, and was irrevocably changed by, the existence of reporters who are not afraid of maths, know how to use a spreadsheet, work with the latest web visualisation tools and – crucially – know what questions to ask.

What is data journalism? It reflects the new transparency movement spreading across the globe, from Washington DC to Sydney, via California, London, Paris and Spain.

It's hard to know what came first: the data or the demand for it. Or maybe the two have grown symbiotically. But it seems there was a tipping point where a number of factors combined to form an unstoppable movement. I would argue they were:

- the widespread availability of data via the internet;
- easy-to-use spreadsheet packages on every home computer;
- a growing interest in visualising data, to make it easier to understand;
- some huge news stories that would not have existed without the statistics behind them.

A crucial early step was taken when President Barack Obama, as one of his first legislative acts, announced the US government would launch a new site: data.gov. This was not a million years ago – only 2009.

Data.gov would be a single portal for

378,529

Number of raw and geospatial datasets available on **data.gov** as of September 2012. The site, launched by President Barack Obama, also contains more than

1,400

apps using the data

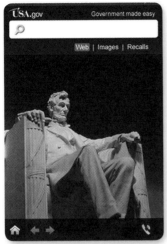

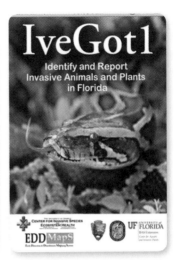

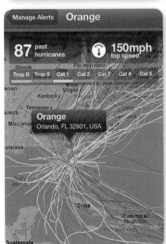

Top: The official app for usa.gov, which links tens of millions of web pages from federal, state, local, territorial, and tribal governments, and makes it easy to access thousands of records online.
Above: the Hurricane app, produced by the American Red Cross, uses weather data and records from the National Oceanic and Atmospheric Administration to track the paths of hurricanes, and advise people how best to escape and survive

Top: Nasa's Visualization Explorer, which uses data and photographs from the space agency's scientific reports, from pictures of the recent solar flares to satellite images showing changes in the Greenland ice sheet.
Above: The FBI app links to wanted pages, the Sex Offender Registry, crime statistics, and background checks

Top: An example of how the most local datasets can be used – this app uses mapping technology and data from the US National Parks Service, the University of Georgia and state conservation agencies to allow the public to report invasive species which could damage Florida's ecosystem.
Above: The America's Economy app accesses real-time updates for 16 key economic indicators released by the US Census Bureau, Bureau of Labor Statistics, and Bureau of Economic Analysis

government datasets, the spreadsheets hitherto published to deafening silence by individual government departments. Go to data.gov today and you will find thousands of datasets covering everything from crime rates through agricultural planning to the latest population estimates. Some of the stuff is esoterically weird – you can get live data for US river levels, for instance; and some of it is dramatically interesting – the FBI's homicide data gives a

12,996

Number of homicides in the US for 2010, according to the FBI, down 4% from 2009. Of these **8,775** were firearm killings. Some 67.52% of all murders were carried out with firearms. The number of deaths per 100,000 population on average was 2.84

The gun crime map of America
FBI Uniform Crime Report 2010

2010 figures for gun homicides across United States in 2010, does not include the District of Columbia

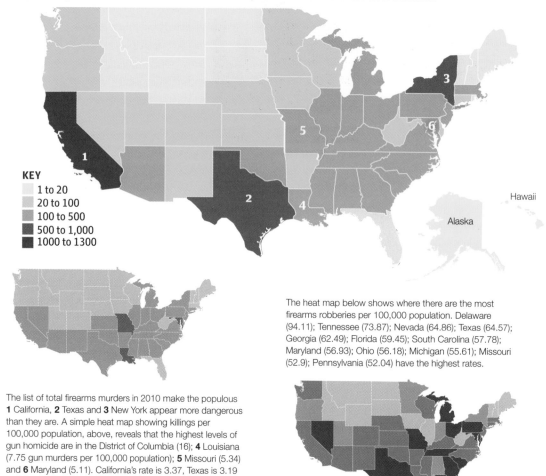

KEY
- 1 to 20
- 20 to 100
- 100 to 500
- 500 to 1,000
- 1000 to 1300

Hawaii

Alaska

The heat map below shows where there are the most firearms robberies per 100,000 population. Delaware (94.11); Tennessee (73.87); Nevada (64.86); Texas (64.57); Georgia (62.49); Florida (59.45); South Carolina (57.78); Maryland (56.93); Ohio (56.18); Michigan (55.61); Missouri (52.9); Pennsylvania (52.04) have the highest rates.

The list of total firearms murders in 2010 make the populous **1** California, **2** Texas and **3** New York appear more dangerous than they are. A simple heat map showing killings per 100,000 population, above, reveals that the highest levels of gun homicide are in the District of Columbia (16); **4** Louisiana (7.75 gun murders per 100,000 population); **5** Missouri (5.34) and **6** Maryland (5.11). California's rate is 3.37, Texas is 3.19 and New York is 2.64. Florida does not provide figures.

breakdown of firearm murders by each US state, with details of which kind of gun was responsible.

The US was followed by countries across the world: Australia, New Zealand and, in the UK, data.gov.uk, launched by inventor of the world wide web, Sir Tim Berners-Lee. At a more local level, cities and state governments joined the race too: London, Toronto, Vancouver, New York, San Francisco, as well as a good number of US states.

More recently, non-English language sites have been launched: more localised sites for Catalonia in Spain and for Paris in France, for instance. If you want to see more sites, you can check out our search engine of open data sites around the world: **guardian.co.uk/world-government-data.**

But you'd be wrong to think this process was entirely led by governments. There's the pioneering work of enthusiasts like Hans Rosling with his Gapminder project. Or the huge impression made by Al Gore's use of charts in his Inconvenient Truth lectures on climate change.

Then there are transparency campaigners like the Guardian's Free our Data movement, who have long called for governments to release the data they charge for. We have, after all, paid for it – why can't we have access to massive datasets such as postcode data and Ordnance Survey geography? Thanks to those campaigns, the UK's official mapmaker, Ordnance Survey, has been forced to release its data.

Locally, those big campaigns have translated to thousands of ultra-local journalists – reporters who might write about an area only a few miles wide.

These reporters either hunt down the data they need or demand their local governments give it to them through Freedom of Information legislation. This is the Open Data movement in action.

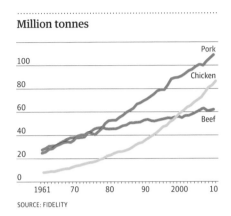

A world of meat-eaters
Global consumption

Million tonnes

SOURCE: FIDELITY

8,000+

Number of Australian suburbs you can compare on **suburbantrends.com.au**, which shows socio-economic standing, education levels, perceived safety levels and other indicators gleaned from government data. Created by Alejandro Metke and Michael Henderson, it won the 2009 Mashup Australia contest

Life expectancy at birth: In the UK...

Life expectancy at birth, all UK, years

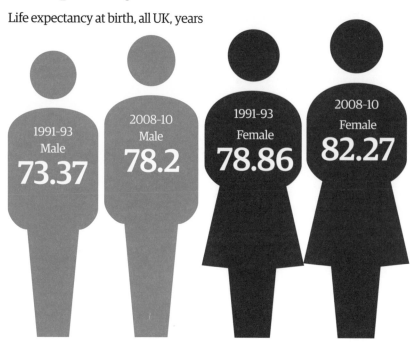

1991–93 Male **73.37**	2008–10 Male **78.2**
1991–93 Female **78.86**	2008–10 Female **82.27**

30%
of us were aged 50 and over in **1971**

42%
of us will be aged 50 or over by **2051** an estimated **32m** people in the UK

23%
average chance of a 20-year-old in 2011 to reach the age of 100 in the UK – the highest number ever

1841-2009

Life expectancy at birth, England and Wales

■ Female ■ Male

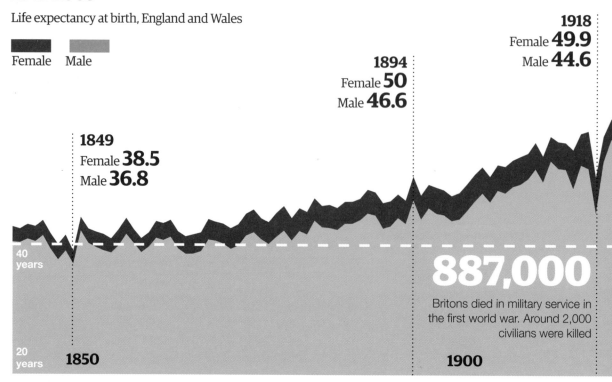

1849
Female **38.5**
Male **36.8**

1894
Female **50**
Male **46.6**

1918
Female **49.9**
Male **44.6**

40 years

887,000
Britons died in military service in the first world war. Around 2,000 civilians were killed

20 years

1850

1900

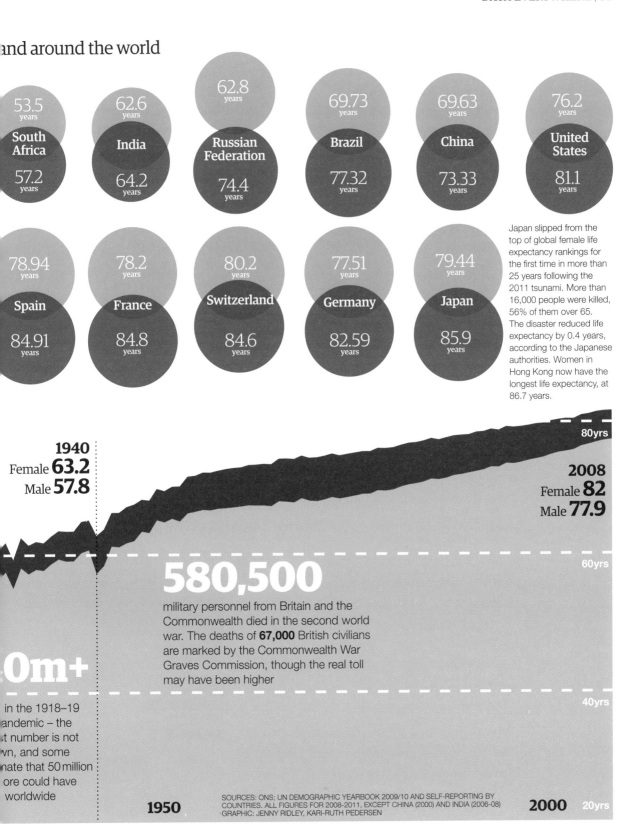

and around the world

53.5 years	**62.6** years	**62.8** years	**69.73** years	**69.63** years	**76.2** years
South Africa	**India**	**Russian Federation**	**Brazil**	**China**	**United States**
57.2 years	**64.2** years	**74.4** years	**77.32** years	**73.33** years	**81.1** years

78.94 years	**78.2** years	**80.2** years	**77.51** years	**79.44** years
Spain	**France**	**Switzerland**	**Germany**	**Japan**
84.91 years	**84.8** years	**84.6** years	**82.59** years	**85.9** years

Japan slipped from the top of global female life expectancy rankings for the first time in more than 25 years following the 2011 tsunami. More than 16,000 people were killed, 56% of them over 65. The disaster reduced life expectancy by 0.4 years, according to the Japanese authorities. Women in Hong Kong now have the longest life expectancy, at 86.7 years.

80yrs

1940
Female **63.2**
Male **57.8**

2008
Female **82**
Male **77.9**

60yrs

580,500
military personnel from Britain and the Commonwealth died in the second world war. The deaths of **67,000** British civilians are marked by the Commonwealth War Graves Commission, though the real toll may have been higher

40yrs

0m+

in the 1918–19
andemic – the
t number is not
wn, and some
nate that 50 million
ore could have
worldwide

1950

SOURCES: ONS; UN DEMOGRAPHIC YEARBOOK 2009/10 AND SELF-REPORTING BY COUNTRIES. ALL FIGURES FOR 2008-2011, EXCEPT CHINA (2000) AND INDIA (2006-08) GRAPHIC: JENNY RIDLEY, KARI-RUTH PEDERSEN

2000 20yrs

There are still some rules, of course: crucially, the data has to be available in a form you can manipulate – as an Excel spreadsheet or a CSV file. Why does that matter?

Well, traditionally, statistics were published in the least accessible format possible: books, and then later as Adobe PDF files. PDF files look like books, read like books and may as well be books; they're of absolutely no use to anyone wanting to analyse the data for themselves or to visualise that data. In the past, when we all relied on official bodies to tell us what we needed to know, it didn't matter if the data was aggregated and analysed for us. But now we trust governments very little, and traditional media outlets even less. We want to know the numbers behind the story for ourselves – to see if we're being told the truth and discover our own stories.

20m

The number of cultural items in Europe's digital library, Europeana, at **europeana.eu.** The collection of digitised books, paintings, photographs, recordings and films from over 2,200 contributing cultural heritage organisations is one of the largest ever releases of cultural data

If a dataset is published as a spreadsheet it's suddenly easier to use. If that data is properly formatted, i.e. country names have codes on them so you can tell the difference between 'Burma' and 'Myanmar', or Congo and Congo, Dem Rep – well, suddenly you can start mashing data together, combining poverty rates with carbon emissions or crime figures with economic growth, for instance.

Then you can start to create journalism which either works in words or even graphics – or both. Sometimes just reproducing a table tells you a story.

A lot of this isn't new – it's just now easier for us to all find.

In fact what governments have offered have been, for the most part, portals to collections of data they all offered anyway.

But there is new information out there too. In the UK, the coalition government elected in 2010 has committed itself to releasing a "tsunami

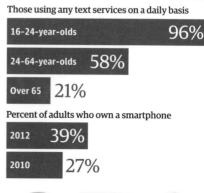

Communication change
The shift to texting, 2011

Those using any text services on a daily basis

16–24-year-olds	96%
24–64-year-olds	58%
Over 65	21%

Percent of adults who own a smartphone

2012	39%
2010	27%

150bn
texts sent in the UK in 2011

-5%
time spent talking on mobile

50
texts a week sent by average Briton

Adoption in decline
Fewer, earlier adoptions, England and Wales 1974–2011

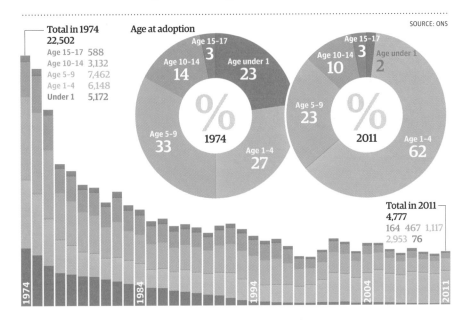

SOURCE: ONS

Total in 1974
22,502
Age 15-17 588
Age 10-14 3,132
Age 5-9 7,462
Age 1-4 6,148
Under 1 5,172

Age at adoption

Total in 2011
4,777
164 467 1,117
2,953 76

of data" as part of its transparency agenda. And we have seen huge data-sets released: every government item of spending over £25,000; salaries of senior civil servants; detailed Treasury spending records; street-by-street crime data and individual hospitals' performance on fighting superbugs like MRSA.

And in the UK, 2012 will see a whole new round of government transparency, with an epic dumping of government data onto the world: full court records in England and Wales, real-time transport data and detailed property data too.

Every local authority in England has been forced to publish every individual item of spending over £500 – albeit with variable results. But while some commentators worry about the end of local journalism with the closure of newspapers around the country, here is an endless source of stories just waiting to reward reporters hungry enough to find them.

Organisations are even starting to work out

71.6
The number of years a boy baby born in Glasgow can expect to live – the lowest in Britain. Life expectancy was highest in Kensington and Chelsea at 85.1/men and 89.8/women. The gap between the local areas with the highest and lowest life expectancies increased between 2004 and 2006 and 2008 and 2010

SOURCE: ONS

The North-South divide
Gross disposable income per person across the UK

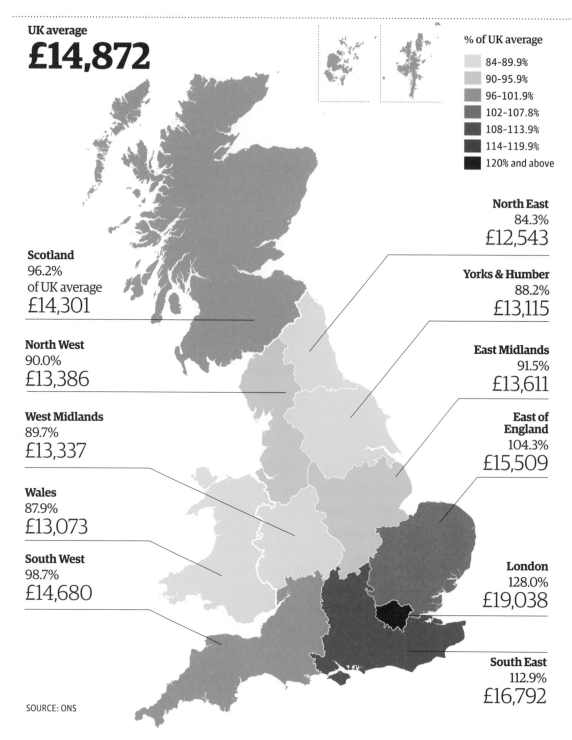

UK average
£14,872

% of UK average
- 84-89.9%
- 90-95.9%
- 96-101.9%
- 102-107.8%
- 108-113.9%
- 114-119.9%
- 120% and above

North East
84.3%
£12,543

Yorks & Humber
88.2%
£13,115

East Midlands
91.5%
£13,611

East of England
104.3%
£15,509

London
128.0%
£19,038

South East
112.9%
£16,792

Scotland
96.2%
of UK average
£14,301

North West
90.0%
£13,386

West Midlands
89.7%
£13,337

Wales
87.9%
£13,073

South West
98.7%
£14,680

SOURCE: ONS

how to make money out of this deluge of data, with bright developers building applications on the back of it. We're certainly not alone in jumping into this world.

If the Ordnance Survey, which makes money from data, is forced to publish, can Post Office postcode data be far behind? The government has created the Public Data Corporation – part of the purpose of which is to look for ways to make cash from data. But the big question will be what exactly is to be charged for? Will it be the data, or what you can do with it?

672

Libyans applied for asylum in the UK in 2011 – up from **65** the year before. Syrian applications rose in 2011 too – from 28 in in the 3Q of 2010 to **129** in the same period in 2011. In 2010, Iranians made the most asylum applications – **10%** of the **17,916** total; in 2009, Zimbabwean applications were abnormally high

SOURCE: HOME OFFICE

Either way, this new assumption that data must always be open has huge implications for business. Journalists now routinely use freedom of information legislation to obtain information from government – the logical extension of that is those requests being made about the deals between governments and business. As it is, when the government released details of all spending by departments over £25,000 last year, it shone a light on exactly how much each government contract is worth and to which companies. In that world, does commercial confidentiality even exist any more?

And that's the official data: the secret leaked data is another matter. The New York Times reported that the Bank of America had been forced to assemble a 20-person team because of the mere possibility of data leaks from its massive databases. The team was put in place, apparently, to create a damage-control plan in case a cache of secret documents said to be held by WikiLeaks was about the Bank. When you can store millions of items on a tiny flash stick, can anything remain secret for long?

In this new industry, all of that data has combined with a feeling, maybe even a hunch, that no-one trusts or likes their news source very much any more. At a time when established news organisations have to fight with bloggers and citizen journalists for their very existence, there has been a move towards explaining the news, to being open about the sources of our stories. One of the hits has been the independent website

The cost of bringing up baby

£218,024

This stacked bar chart reveals the average cost of raising a child from birth to the age of 21, assuming that child:

» attends a private nursery from six months to five years old, as parents return to work;

» attends state school, full time to the age of 18;

» takes an annual holiday from the age of one

» attends university for three years where tuition fees and living costs are paid in full by the parents.

FIGURES COMPILED BY LIVERPOOL VICTORIA (LV=), WHICH USED DATA FROM: ITS OWN SURVEY; ONS; NATIONAL UNION OF STUDENTS; THE DAYCARE TRUST; CHILD POVERTY ACTION GROUP; AA; NANNYTAX SURVEY. 2011-12

Childcare & babysitting
£62,099
▲57%

Education
£71,780
Difference from 2003
(year of first report)
▲120%

Per year
£10,400

Per month
£865

Per day
£28.44

PHOTOGRAPH: BERND VOGEL/CORBIS
GRAPHIC: KARI-RUTH PEDERSEN

Food
£18,667
▲25%

Clothing
£10,781
▼5%

Holidays
£15,532
▲36%

Pocket
money
£4,337
▲28%

Hobbies
& toys
£9,248
▲4%

Leisure &
recreation
£7,303
▲15%

Other*
£1,143
▲56%

Furniture
£3,373
▲62%

Personal
care
£1,143
▲36%

* INCLUDES
BIRTHDAY
PRESENTS,
CHRISTMAS
GIFTS, DRIVING
LESSONS,
FIRST CAR

Polar sea ice in peril
Arctic ice sheet at its lowest area yet, 2012

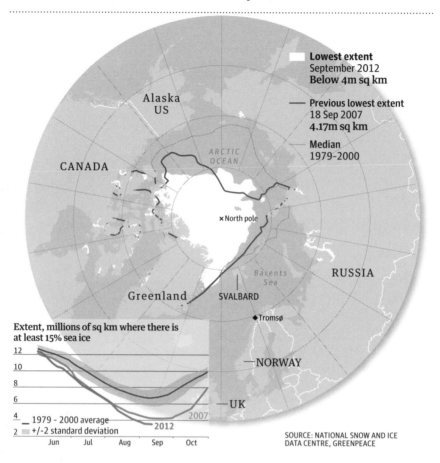

Lowest extent
September 2012
Below 4m sq km

Previous lowest extent
18 Sep 2007
4.17m sq km

Median
1979-2000

Alaska
US

ARCTIC
OCEAN

CANADA

×North pole

Barents
Sea

RUSSIA

Greenland   SVALBARD

◆Tromsø

NORWAY

UK

Extent, millions of sq km where there is
at least 15% sea ice

12
10
8
6
4 — 1979 - 2000 average
2 ▨ +/-2 standard deviation

2007
2012

Jun   Jul   Aug   Sep   Oct

SOURCE: NATIONAL SNOW AND ICE
DATA CENTRE, GREENPEACE

Where Does My Money Go? Its main purpose is simply to explain how the British government spends its money.

At the Guardian, we launched our first official foray into data journalism at the same time as we launched our Open Platform API. The Datablog (**guardian.co.uk/datablog**) – which I edit – was to be a small blog offering the full datasets behind our news stories. Now it consists of a front page (**guardian.co.uk/data**); searches of world government and global development data; data visualisations by Guardian graphic

11,057

Number of Google users the US government requested information on in the first six months of 2011 – almost equal to the number of requests made by **25** other developed countries, including the UK and Russia. Governments around the world requested private data on about **25,440** people

SOURCE: GOOGLE

artists and others; and tools for exploring public spending data.

As a news editor and journalist working with graphics, it was a logical extension of work I was already doing. Every day I was accumulating new datasets and wrangling with them to try to make sense of the news stories of the day. In turn, my professional life has been bookended by war. My first day on the paper's newsdesk was September 10, 2001. After the events of the following day, the results have been reverberating through the newspaper's pages ever since.

65.8%

Recycling in Rochford, Essex – the highest rate in England. The figures show that the average recycling rate for English councils was **41.2%** in the year from April 2010, up from **39.7%**. Recycling rates have risen annually for a decade but the rate of progress began to slow from 2008 onwards

SOURCE: DEFRA

Gradually, the Datablog's work reflected and added to the stories we faced. We crowdsourced 458,000 documents relating to MPs' expenses and we analysed the detailed data of which MPs had claimed what. We helped our users explore detailed Treasury spending databases and published the data behind the news.

But the game-changer for data journalism happened in spring 2010, with the WikiLeaks war logs.

That is just one set of stories, a single high-point in data journalism's road to acceptance. There are still reporters out there who don't know what all the fuss is about, who really don't want to know about maths or spreadsheets. But for others, this new wave represents a way to save journalism.

It represents a new role for journalists as a bridge and guide between those in power who have the data (and are rubbish at explaining it) and the public who desperately want to understand the data and access it but need help. We can be that bridge.

In future our role may even be in supplying data as trusted sources, as a "safe" location of quality information.

Sometimes people talk about the internet killing journalism. The WikiLeaks story was a combination of the two: traditional journalistic skills and the power of the technology, harnessed to tell an amazing story.

In future, data journalism may not seem amazing and new; for now it is. The world has changed and it is data that has changed it.

489,045

Number of burglaries in England and Wales recorded by the police in July 2011 to June 2012; 239,168 of these were in a dwelling. This was a burglary rate per 1,000 population of 9. For comparison, in April 2002 to March 2003, the rate per 1,000 population was 17. This represents a drop of 45% in burglaries in less than 10 years. In Scotland the crime of housebreaking has also dropped by 3% in the past year

72%

of all burglars break in through the door. 27% forced the lock, but in 15% of cases the door was not locked in the first place. 10% broke through a door panel. 7% pushed past a person who opened the the door. 5% had a key. 5% used false pretences to gain entry. In only 1% of cases was the door rammed or kicked in

26%

of all burglars break in through the window. 11% forced the window lock and 9% broke or cut the glass. In 6% of cases, the window was either open already or could be pushed open

Crime and perception

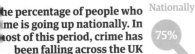

... assume crime is rising, even ... the statistics say otherwise.

... he percentage of people who ... me is going up nationally. In ... ost of this period, crime has been falling across the UK

% people who think crime is rising in their local area

Nationally
75% — 58% — 66% — 65% — 72% — 65% — 61% — 63% — 65% — 65% — 75% — 66% — 60%

My local area
55% — 46% — 50% — 51% — 54% — 48% — 42% — 42% — 41% — 39% — 36% — 31% — 28%

1996
1997
1998
1999
2000
2001/02
2002/03
2003/04
2004/05
2005/06
2006/07
2007/08
2008/09
2009/10
2010/11

66%
of burglaries happen during the week and 34% at the weekend (6pm Friday to 6am Monday). You're most likely to be burgled at night

62%
of burglaries happen from 6pm-6am; 30% from 6pm-midnight; 25% from midnight-6am; 8% at some point during the night

56%
people were at home when they were burgled, but only 27% saw the offender. 26% of people were not aware they were being burgled

86%
of offenders in burglaries are male. In 7% of cases they are female and in 7% there are offenders of both sexes

£2,040
is the average cost of each burglary in England and Wales in 2011-12. The most stolen items are purses/wallets and computer equipment - both 34% of cases. 30% of burglaries involved the loss of electrical equipment

SOURCES: ONS; HOME OFFICE; SCOTLAND.GOV.UK
PHOTOGRAPH: CHRISTOPHER THOMOND
FOR THE GUARDIAN

Data are or data is?

How do you say "data"?

I only ask because it's a contentious issue. Along with split infinitives, getting this one wrong offends and delights in equal measure. And, as we write about data every day, we're either getting it very wrong or very right.

The Wall Street Journal has recently moved away from data "are", saying: "Most style guides and dictionaries have come to accept the use of the noun data with either singular or plural verbs, and we hereby join the majority. As usage has evolved from the word's origin as the Latin plural of datum, singular verbs now are often used to refer to collections of information: Little data is available to support the conclusions. Otherwise, generally continue to use the plural: Data are still being collected."

We asked our readers what they thought, via Twitter – the results were much-polarised. People really care, and this is just a selection:

@jhugman

Data is plural. Unsure the correct "datum point" will catch on though. Referenda about latin declensions belong in musea.

@MKDDCC

No to datum. We need to relax about the data is/ are thing. It may not be good Latin, but we're not speaking Latin.

@DerekL

Of course data is plural. And what is wrong with datum for a single item of data?

@holizz

Singular data annoys the same people that find split infinitives objectionable – pedants with no understanding of linguistics.

Here's the root of the matter: strictly speaking, data is a plural term. If we're following the rules of grammar, we shouldn't write "the data is" or "the data shows" but instead "the data are" or "the data show".

The Oxford English Dictionary defines it like this: "In Latin, data is the plural of datum and, historically and in specialised scientific fields, it is also treated as a plural in English, taking a plural verb, as in 'the data were collected and classified'. In modern non-scientific use, however, despite the complaints of traditionalists, it is often not treated as a plural. Instead, it is treated as a mass noun, similar to a word like information, which cannot normally have a plural and which takes a singular verb. Sentences such as 'data was (as well as data were) collected over a number of years' are now widely accepted in standard English."

The Office for National Statistics endorses the traditional approach. The ONS style guide for those writing official statistics says: "The word data is a plural noun so write 'data are'. Datum is the singular."

Andrew Garratt of the Royal Statistical Society says the debate goes back to the 1920s. "We don't have an official view," he says. "Statisticians of a certain age and status refer to them as plural but people like me use it in the singular." National Geographic magazine has debated it too.

One user of the Datablog, Telescoper, commented that we're all correct: "It's not unusual for a noun to have two distinct forms. Think of "hair". This is a count noun when applied to individual strands, and a mass noun when compared to the stuff on someone's head. You can have many hairs or a lot of hair. Likewise you can have many data or a lot of data, depending on the situation."

For what it's worth, I can confidently say that this will probably be the only time I ever write the word "datum". Data as a plural term may be the proper usage but language evolves.

So, over to Guardian style guru David Marsh, who makes the rules in these parts about language use. He says: "It's like agenda – a Latin plural that is now almost universally used as a singular. Technically the singular is datum/agendum, but we feel it sounds increasingly hyper-correct, old-fashioned and pompous to say 'the data are.'"

11,438

People died in accidents in England in 2010, including 3,649 in falls, 1,523 accidental poisonings and 23 killed by animals. The figures show an 11% rise in dementia deaths between 2009 and 2010 – to 25,106. Alzheimer's and dementia are the third leading cause of death for women, after heart disease and stroke

SOURCE: ONS

The death penalty
Amnesty International's report on executions, 2011

676

executions were known
to have been carried out
in 2011, in **21** countries

1,923

people in **63** countries were known
to have been sentenced to death

Of the G8 group of major developed
nations, only the United States
carried out executions in 2011. Only
China, Iran, Iraq and Saudi Arabia
executed more people in that period

1,264

people were executed in the US
between the end of a moratorium
on the death penalty in 1976 and
2011. **474** of those – **37.5%** –
were in Texas. **12** of the overall total
were women

18,750

people worldwide remained on
death row at the end of 2011,
excluding those in China, which
does not provide figures

70%+

of the world's countries have
abolished the death penalty
in law or in practice

● Number of death sentences handed down in 2011
● Number of executions in 2011

US
43   78

St Lucia
①
Trinidad and Tobago
②

Guyana
③+

Morocco/
Western Sahara
⑤

Algeria
51+

Mauritania
⑧

Mali
②

Gambia
13   Guinea

Burkina Faso
③

Sierra Leone ②

16

Ghana
④

Niger
72

Liberia
①

These figures do not include the
thousands of people who are
thought to have been executed
in China. A plus sign (+) alone
indicates that death sentences
were passed or executions did
take place but that it was not
possible to specify a figure

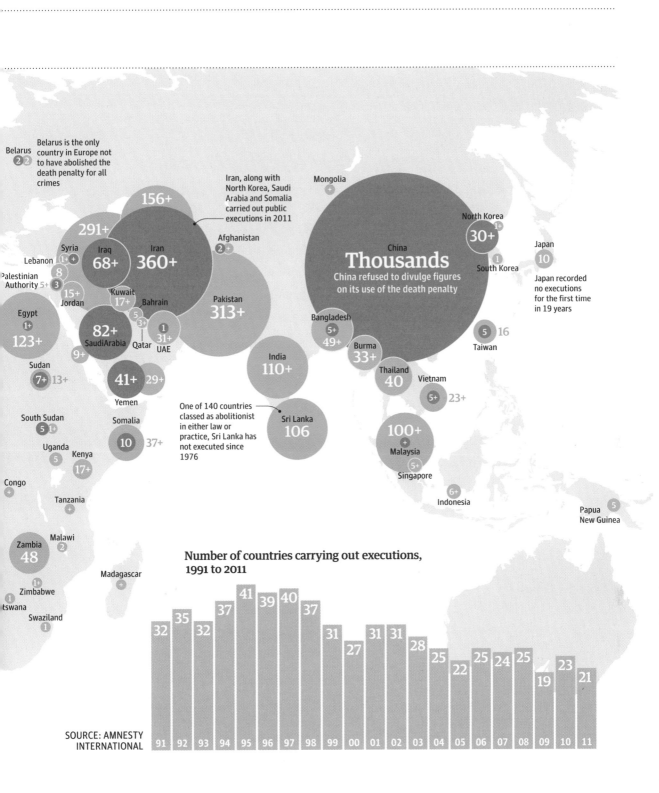

Belarus
2 2
Belarus is the only country in Europe not to have abolished the death penalty for all crimes

Iran, along with North Korea, Saudi Arabia and Somalia carried out public executions in 2011

Mongolia +

North Korea 1+
30+

Japan 10

Japan recorded no executions for the first time in 19 years

156+

291+

Syria 1+ +
Lebanon 8
Palestinian Authority 5+ 3

Iraq 68+

Iran 360+

Afghanistan 2 +

China
Thousands
China refused to divulge figures on its use of the death penalty

South Korea

Kuwait 17+
Bahrain 5

Pakistan 313+

Bangladesh 5+ 49+

Taiwan 5 16

Egypt 123+ 1+

Jordan 15+

Saudi Arabia 82+
Qatar 3+
UAE 1 31+

9+

India 110+

Burma 33+

Thailand 40

Vietnam 5+ 23+

Sudan 7+ 13+

41+ 29+
Yemen

One of 140 countries classed as abolitionist in either law or practice, Sri Lanka has not executed since 1976

Sri Lanka 106

100+
Malaysia
Singapore 5+

South Sudan 5 1+

Somalia 10 37+

Uganda 5
Kenya 17+

Indonesia 6+

Papua New Guinea 5

Congo +

Tanzania +

Zambia 48

Malawi 2

Madagascar +

Zimbabwe 1+
Botswana 1
Swaziland 1

Number of countries carrying out executions, 1991 to 2011

'91	'92	'93	'94	'95	'96	'97	'98	'99	'00	'01	'02	'03	'04	'05	'06	'07	'08	'09	'10	'11
32	35	32	37	41	39	40	37	31	27	31	31	28	25	22	25	24	25	19	23	21

SOURCE: AMNESTY INTERNATIONAL

How devolution is killing open government data

Are you British or Scottish? Do you live in the UK or England and Wales?

It matters because statistics – the way we actually have any idea about where we live – are increasingly not available for the UK as a nation.

And as it looks possible that devolution could become independence for Scotland, we could be seeing the end of the UK in data too. Love or loathe devolution, this matters – especially if you care for open data.

How does the UK split up? You'd think anyone who has studied geography here would know the answer, but there is still confusion. When we published our map of young adults who still live at home, based on information from the Office of National Statistics, one user commented:

"'Britain's' young adults? and the map shows Scotland, Wales and England. Not bothered about Northern Ireland, The isle of Man and the Channel Islands, then – or are they not part of Britain?"

For anyone not completely au fait with the geography, this is how the nation splits up. The United Kingdom is divided into England, Wales, Scotland and Northern Ireland. The Channel Islands, incidentally, are a British Crown dependency and not part of the UK. Britain is just England, Wales and Scotland – not Northern Ireland.

And the whole nation is divided up into what the Office for National Statistics (but not all of our users) calls local authorities, which manage local services in each area. If you want to see variations across the country, then that is the minimum local breakdown needed. Of course, many statistics are published at that local level and for the whole UK – unemployment, for instance. But often that is no longer the case.

Four separate statistics bodies operate in almost blissful independence of one another:

74%

of Scots voted for devolution in the 1997 referendum. There was a majority in favour of a devolved Scotland in every local authority. 64% also voted for the new Scottish parliament to have tax-varying powers. The Welsh devolution vote was closer: 50.3% in were in favour

SOURCE: SCOTLAND.GOV.UK; ASSEMBLYWALES.ORG

the Office for National Statistics, the Scottish Government, StatsWales and the Northern Ireland Statistics and Research Agency.

Take crime, for instance. Until recently the Home Office published something called the British Crime Survey, which surveyed thousands of people about their personal experiences of crime.

But in the late 1980s it stopped covering Scotland – where it was replaced by the Scottish Crime and Justice Survey. Now England and Wales has the Crime Survey for England and Wales and Northern Ireland has an irregular crime survey of its own.

The rationale is that because Scotland has its own criminal system, it's not comparable. Yet the UN manages to compare a variety of crimes from completely different countries for its annual crime survey and there are more differences between entirely separate nations in crime, say, than in a devolved single nation.

And the result? We rarely see studies comparing crime in London, say, with Glasgow.

The census is another example: it is split into England and Wales, Scotland and Northern Ireland. Recorded every ten years, this is arguably the UK's most important dataset, yet published at different times and for different regional breakdowns.

But even for less controversial data, each week brings separate releases from separate places. In September 2012, the National Statistics gateway shows 98 government releases are available for the UK as a whole. But how many of those are broken down? Most are the big figures such as GDP; if you want a breakdown even at country level (i.e. England and Wales, Scotland, etc.), then there are 12 releases. And only another seven are available at local authority and county level – which is the minimum breakdown you need for any kind of regional rigour. Only one was valuable at the really granular "super output area": the child tax credit statistics for 2010 from the HMRC.

That's one dataset which is two years old.

If we look at the releases for a 30-day period in September–October 2012, Northern Ireland has seen releases on population and women; Scotland has published child immunisation statistics and reconviction rates

Scotland

5.2m

population, 2008

Wales

2.9m

population, 2008

Health
£11.55bn

Finance and
sustainable
growth £3.27bn

Devolved
spending
2008-09

£33bn
+6.26%

Local
government
& social
justice £4.4bn

£1.88bn

Education £2.82bn

Children &
education

NHS & teachers'
pensions £2.55bn

Economy &
transport
£1.19bn

Justice £1.71bn

Rural affairs,
environment
£0.48bn

Wales has put out exam results and health statistics. Meanwhile, England has published school admission appeals, drug treatment figures and museum activity.

The argument is beyond devolution of power or different statistical fiefdoms. After all, not everything is national – but when you are publishing equivalent figures for different parts of the UK, why not coordinate them? Why not publish the same census details on the same day – instead of different figures at different times?

The answer is probably resources – and a gradual parting of the statistical ways as different organisations produce the statistics wanted at the devolved government level.

In fact, it is often easier to get across statistics from European countries

Northern Ireland

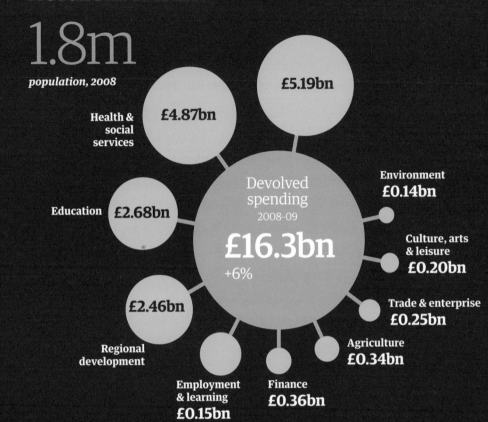

1.8m
population, 2008

Health &
social
services

£4.87bn

£5.19bn

Education £2.68bn

Devolved
spending
2008-09

£16.3bn
+6%

Environment
£0.14bn

Culture, arts
& leisure
£0.20bn

Trade & enterprise
£0.25bn

£2.46bn

Agriculture
£0.34bn

Regional
development

Employment
& learning
£0.15bn

Finance
£0.36bn

bn

Health &
social
services

Devolved
spending
2008-09

£15bn
.27%

Rural
affairs
£0.15bn

ironment
.76bn

SOURCES: REGIONAL GOVERNMENTS; HM TREASURY PESA

via Eurostat now than it is to get figures for the whole of the UK at a local level. That is because Eurostat has a single operation to combine data from across the European Union into single accessible datasets by coordinating all the national statistics agencies. The UK, with increasingly disparate data sources, needs that now. And it's kind of what we expect from the Office for National Statistics. The title says it all.

Yes, it would cost money. But if things carry on as they are now, the long-term effect is that England is compared only to England; Scotland to Scotland; Wales to Wales; and Northern Ireland to Northern Ireland.

Maybe, in a devolved nation, that's what we want. But it raises a bigger question, which is pretty fundamental for all of us: if the UK gradually ceases to exist as a statistical entity, then does it still exist as a country?

How the BBC spends your money

Television £2,334.9 m (-1.7% on 2011)

BBC1 £1,337.6m
-4.7%

B B C
one

BBC3 £112.9m
+2.5%

BBC2 £537.1m
+1.7%

CBBC
£107.3m
+8.1%

BBC4
£67.8m
+1.0%

BBC News
Channel
£57.5m
-5.9%

CBeebies
£42.4m
+6.8%

BBC Red
button
£37.2m
-5.8%

BBC Parliament
£9.3m +16.3%

Other TV
£25.8m

T

£3,161.8m Total BBC spend as regulated by service licence, 2012

£5.09bn BBC revenu in the year March 201

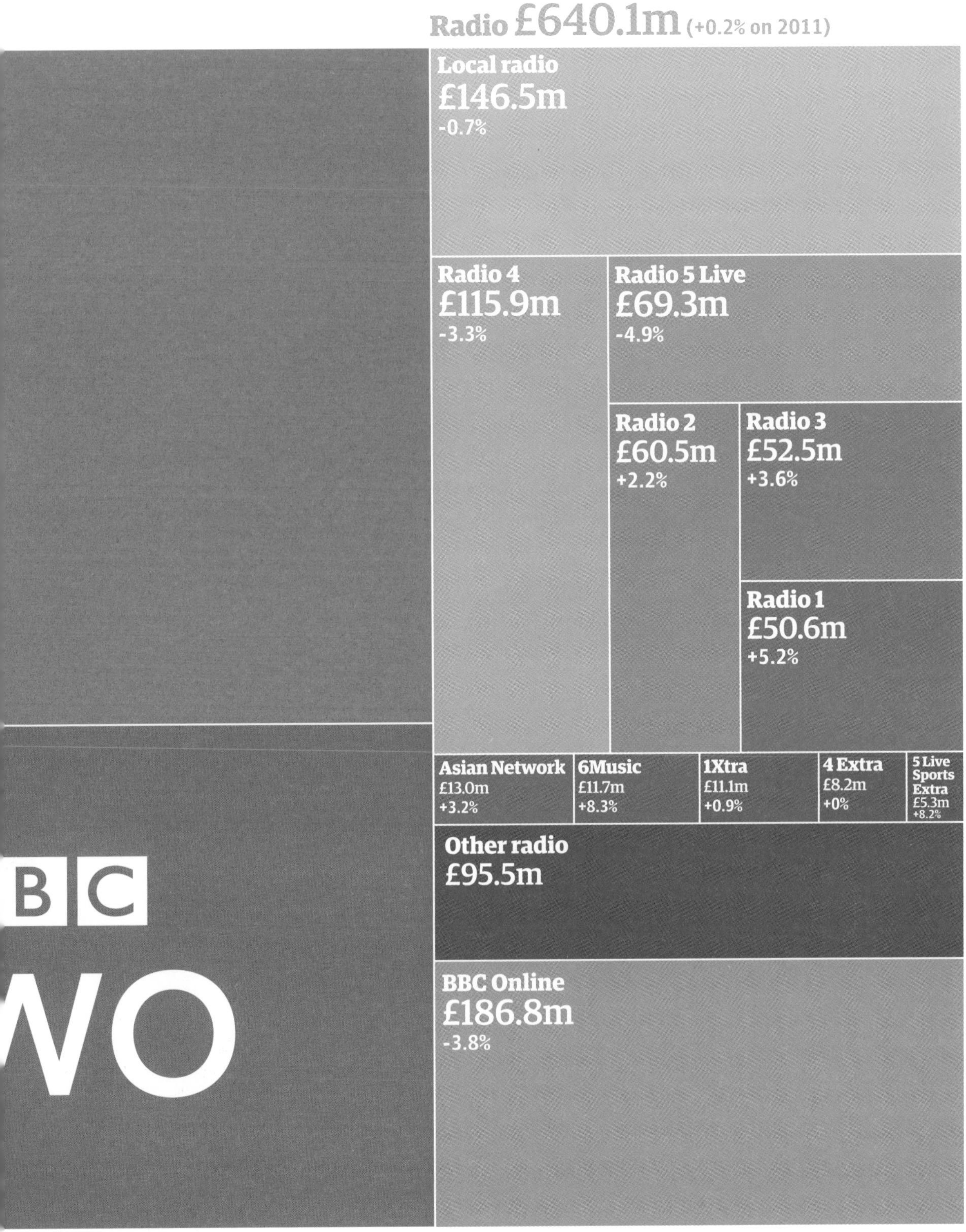

Local radio
£146.5m
-0.7%

Radio 4
£115.9m
-3.3%

Radio 5 Live
£69.3m
-4.9%

Radio 2
£60.5m
+2.2%

Radio 3
£52.5m
+3.6%

Radio 1
£50.6m
+5.2%

Asian Network
£13.0m
+3.2%

6Music
£11.7m
+8.3%

1Xtra
£11.1m
+0.9%

4 Extra
£8.2m
+0%

5 Live Sports Extra
£5.3m
+8.2%

Other radio
£95.5m

BBC Online
£186.8m
-3.8%

BBC

WO

£15.7m Paid out to stars earning £500,000+ a year

25.7m The number of households paying for a TV licence

SOURCE: BBC

The world in chocolate
importers, exporters and eaters, 2011

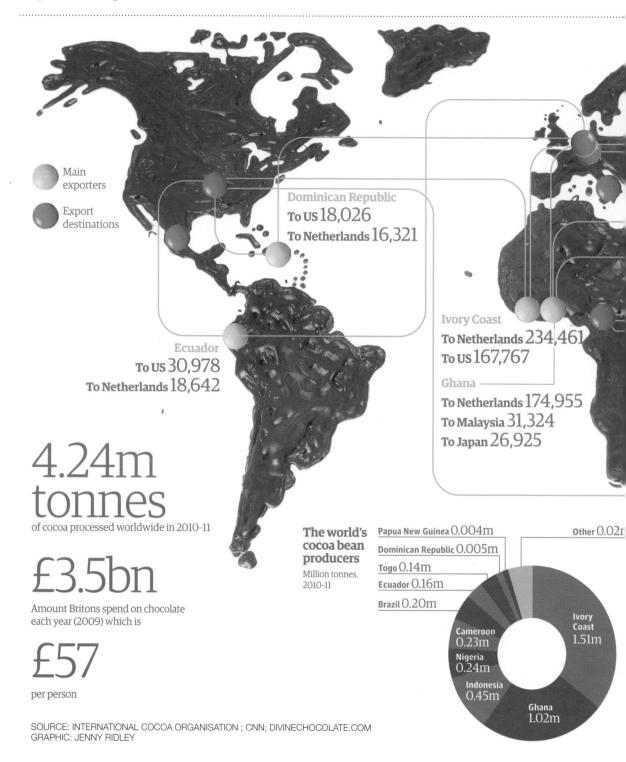

Main exporters

Export destinations

Dominican Republic
To US 18,026
To Netherlands 16,321

Ecuador
To US 30,978
To Netherlands 18,642

Ivory Coast
To Netherlands 234,461
To US 167,767

Ghana
To Netherlands 174,955
To Malaysia 31,324
To Japan 26,925

4.24m tonnes
of cocoa processed worldwide in 2010-11

£3.5bn
Amount Britons spend on chocolate each year (2009) which is

£57
per person

The world's cocoa bean producers
Million tonnes, 2010-11

Papua New Guinea 0.004m
Dominican Republic 0.005m
Togo 0.14m
Ecuador 0.16m
Brazil 0.20m
Cameroon 0.23m
Nigeria 0.24m
Indonesia 0.45m
Ghana 1.02m
Ivory Coast 1.51m
Other 0.02m

SOURCE: INTERNATIONAL COCOA ORGANISATION ; CNN; DIVINECHOCOLATE.COM
GRAPHIC: JENNY RIDLEY

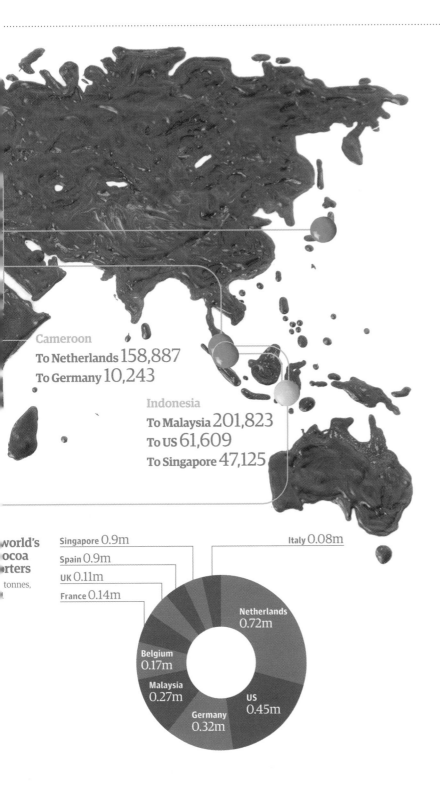

Cameroon
To Netherlands 158,887
To Germany 10,243

Indonesia
To Malaysia 201,823
To US 61,609
To Singapore 47,125

world's
ocoa
rters

tonnes,

Singapore 0.9m
Spain 0.9m
UK 0.11m
France 0.14m

Italy 0.08m

Netherlands
0.72m

Belgium
0.17m

Malaysia
0.27m

Germany
0.32m

US
0.45m

The prices of cocoa beans
US cents per lb

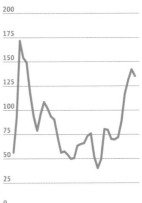

49.3%
of world consumption of
cocoa is in Europe

24.2%
is in North America, 20.19% of
it in the United States alone.
In the US, 58m lbs of chocolate
is sold in the week of Valentine's
day alone

14.5%
is in Asia and Oceania. Chocolate
consumption in China alone was
expected to rise 19% in 2012

8.68%
is in South America

3.28%
is in Africa, the continent which
produces more than 70% of
the world's cocoa

Chapter 3
In the beginning...

What you'll find out in this chapter:
» Leaked data was always with us » Why Florence Nightingale is as important to the history of statistics as she is to the history of medicine » Who invented the pie chart

May 5, 1821.

Data journalism is not new: the very first Guardian – or Manchester Guardian as it then was – in May 1821 contained a table of data. For the first time, we've extracted that table so you can see it for yourselves.

The numbers would seem uncontroversial today: a list of schools in Manchester and Salford, with how many pupils attended each one and average annual spending. It told us, for the first time, how many pupils received free education – and how many poor children there were in the city.

In today's world of Ofsted reports and education department school rankings, this list would not seem unusual. In 1821, it caused a sensation. Leaked to the Guardian by a credible source only identified as "NH", it showed how official estimates of only 8,000 children receiving free education were inaccurate – in fact the total was nearer 25,000.

In 1821 the official statistics for the city were collected by just four clergymen: an impossible task and one which resulted in inaccurate and faulty data.

The list that the Guardian printed gave a true picture for the first time. Some of the schools still exist today: the Blue Coat School in Oldham dates back to 1810.

17,000

The discrepancy between the official estimated number of children receiving free education (8,000) and the list leaked by "NH" to the Guardian in 1821, which showed it was closer to 25,000 children

3,212

Scottish witch court cases from the early 1500s to the mid 1700s. The most famous was the North Berwick witch hunt in which women were tried for the crime of attempting to sink a ship with Queen Anne on board and "troubling King James after he went to get her in Denmark". 387 of the cases involved male suspects

SOURCE: EDINBURGH UNIVERSITY

Much education at the time was provided by Sunday schools, as many children had to work during the week. In fact, education was not compulsory until 1880. St Clements & St Luke's, of Bennett Street, was "perhaps, the largest school in the kingdom" with 1,906 pupils. This movement was the forerunner of the state education system, teaching 1.25m children in Britain by 1831. It was a huge political and religious movement, far removed from the Sunday schools of today.

The start of Guardian data journalism
Manchester and Salford schools, 1821

The table is also a product of its time: the "establishment" referred to in the table is the Church of England. All other denominations were "dissenters", including Catholicism (anti-Catholic legislation was not liberalised until 1829). The data also refers to offertory money – church collections, in other words.

NH's reasons for supplying the data were clear:

"At all times such information it contains is valuable; because without knowing ... the best opinions which can be formed of the condition and future progress of society must be necessarily incorrect."

In other words, without knowing the state of society, how can things ever get any better? This was using data to help fight for a decent education system.

The tools we have to analyse the data may have changed; that motivation has stayed exactly the same.

William Playfair's innovations
One of the first bar charts, showing Scottish trade, 1780-81

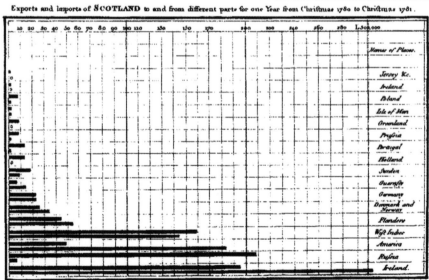

This chart, from William Playfair's book, The Commercial and Political Atlas, published in 1786, is thought to contain the first bar chart. The book pioneered the use of graphics to explain economic data

Florence Nightingale
Nurse, campaigner
... data journalist?

A visual argument
A comparison of mortality rates for soldiers and civilians

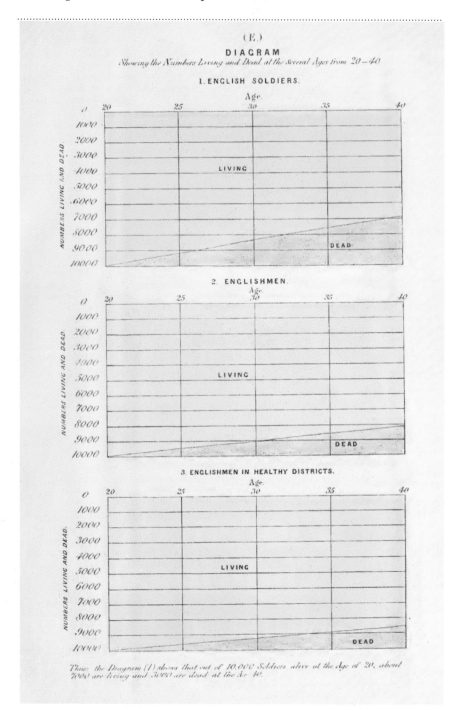

F lorence Nightingale and statistics – it turns out the two are intimately connected. Graphics are terribly trendy at the moment, but sometimes it's good to know that they are not entirely new.

We all have an image of Nightingale – who died over 100 years ago – as a nurse, lady with the lamp, medical reformer and campaigner for soldiers' health. But she was also a data journalist.

After the disasters of the Crimean War, Florence Nightingale returned to become a passionate campaigner for improvements in the health of the British army.

She improved and popularised the visual presentation of information, including the pie chart, first developed by William Playfair in 1801. Nightingale also used statistical graphics

16,000

Estimated number of British soldiers killed by sickness and poor care of wounds during the Crimean War of 1853–56. Only **2,600** were killed in battle

SOURCE: SCIENCEMUSEUM.ORG

Marshalling the statistics
Nightingale's calculations of death rates

TABLE D.

NUMBER of DEATHS of NON-COMMISSIONED OFFICERS and MEN, showing also the Number of Deaths that would have occurred if the Mortality were 9·2 per 1,000, such as it was among Men of the Soldier's Ages in England and Wales, in the Years 1849–53.

YEARS.	Deaths that would have occurred in England and Wales among Males of the Soldiers' Ages.	Deaths of Non-commissioned Officers and Men.	Excess of Deaths among Non-commissioned Officers and Men.
1839	910	2,914	2,004
1840	989	3,300	2,311
1841	1,022	4,167	3,145
1842	1,060	5,052	3,992
1843	1,091	5,270	4,179
1844	1,098	3,867	2,769
1845	1,086	4,587	3,501
1846	1,110	5,125	4,015
1847	1,171	4,232	3,061
1848	1,177	3,213	2,036
1849	1,138	4,052	2,914
1850	1,096	3,119	2,023
1851	1,075	2,729	1,654
1852	1,091	3,120	2,029
1853	1,097	3,392	2,295
Total ..	16,211	58,139	41,928

This Table may read thus:—In the year 1839 the number of deaths among non-commissioned officers and men was 2,914 out of the Strength (98,912—see preceding Table); whereas the deaths among the *same number of men*, of the same *ages*, living in England and Wales, would have been only 910! Consequently the excess of deaths in the Army amounted to 2,004.

B 2

The bat's wing
Florence Nightingale's first charts on the Crimean War (1854-56)

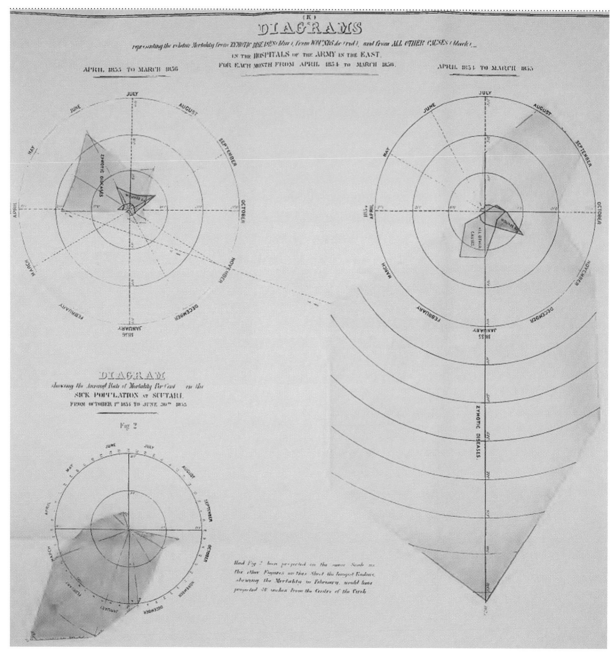

The "bat's wing" graphic shows, on the right, mortality rates before the arrival of the Sanitary Commission and, on the left, how the death rate plummeted after the implementation of cleanliness regimens and better nutrition. This diagram was seen as misleading because it implies that the shaded area represents the mortality rate, when the lengths of the radials are the key indicators. Nightingale's next effort would be more successful

The coxcomb, or rose diagram
Nightingale's most famous chart

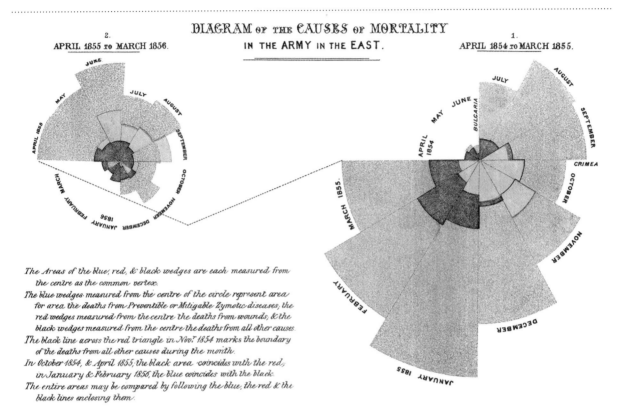

DIAGRAM of the CAUSES of MORTALITY
IN THE ARMY IN THE EAST.

2.
APRIL 1855 to MARCH 1856.

1.
APRIL 1854 to MARCH 1855.

The Areas of the blue, red, & black wedges are each measured from
the centre as the common vertex.

The blue wedges measured from the centre of the circle represent area
for area the deaths from Preventible or Mitigable Zymotic diseases; the
red wedges measured from the centre the deaths from wounds, & the
black wedges measured from the centre the deaths from all other causes.

The black line across the red triangle in Nov.r 1854 marks the boundary
of the deaths from all other causes during the month.

In October 1854, & April 1855, the black area coincides with the red;
in January & February 1856, the blue coincides with the black.

The entire areas may be compared by following the blue, the red & the
black lines enclosing them.

in reports to Parliament, realising this was the most effective way of bringing data to life.

The key report is Mortality of the British Army, published in 1858. It was packed with diagrams and tables of data. The most famous is her "Coxcomb", a spiral of sections, each one representing deaths per month – and that the vast majority of deaths were from preventable diseases rather than bullets and shells. We still use this device today.

She produced two versions of this. There's a great paper on it by Hugh Small where he explains how Nightingale formulated and refined the diagram.

"The circle on the right has twelve sectors going clockwise representing the first twelve months of the war. The circle on the left is the second twelve months," he writes. "The superimposed dark shapes show the monthly death rates. The diagram illustrates how the Sanitary Commission, sent out in the middle of the war, dramatically reduced the death rate. The length of the radial line in each month is proportional to the death rate, but both the text and the appearance imply that it is the shaded area that is proportional to the death rate, rather than the length of the radial lines. Florence recognised this error and inserted an erratum slip, but then replaced this diagram in later documents with what I will call the 'wedges' diagram."

Jil Matheson of the Office for National Statistics recognises Nightingale's influence. She says she was inspired by Nightingale to get involved in statistics: "Florence is an inspirational figure for many women in particular. The 'lady with the lamp' was also a lady with powerful ideas, with the commitment and passion to put them into practice. As a consequence, she made a lasting and important impact in the fields of both medicine and statistics."

Nightingale's bar charts
Mortality of Foot Guards v civilian population

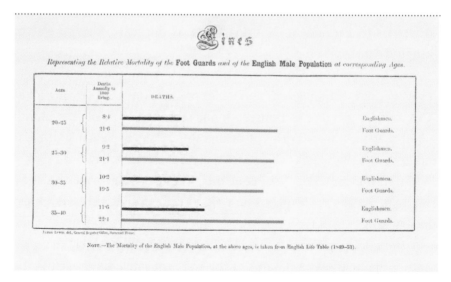

Case study
WikiLeaks

A BRITISH SOLDIER ON PATROL NEAR BASRA, IRAQ. PHOTOGRAPH: SEAN SMITH FOR THE GUARDIAN

A civilian close to the frontline in Ubaydi, Iraq, during Operation Steel Curtain in November 2005. US marines and the new Iraqi Army battled insurgents for control of Anbar province. Photograph: Sean Smith for the Guardian

I t began with one of the investigative reporting team asking: "You're good with spreadsheets, aren't you?"

And this was one hell of a spreadsheet: 92,201 rows of data, each one containing a detailed breakdown of a military event in Afghanistan. This was the WikiLeaks war logs. Part one, that is. There were to be two more episodes to follow: Iraq and the cables. The official term was SIGACTS: the US military significant actions database.

An article in the New York Times explained how US soldiers were drowning under the weight of detailed datasets. SIGACTS was one of these. Recorded by soldiers in the field, this was war as it was fought, complete with military jargon and incredible detail.

The task we faced was probably not for any reporter who thinks data is not for them, that numbers are boring and spreadsheets are for accountants. It's only boring if you're not interested in journalism.

The WikiLeaks logs
The size of the datasets

Afghan war logs

92,201

rows of data from the US military significant actions database, covering military action in Afghanistan from 2004 to early 2010

Iraq war logs

391,000

incidents from the US military significant actions database, covering operations in Iraq between 1 January 2004 and 31 December 2009 (with the exception of May 2004 and March 2009)

US embassy cables

251,287

cables sent by embassies on SIPRNet, the worldwide US military internet system, up to February 2010. Some 56,813 documents were from 2009 alone, the first year of the Obama administration

We'd had to handle major datasets before. The release of the UK treasury's huge spending database (COINS) was bigger and scarier. The last government had refused to release it – the coalition published it within weeks of taking power. It had every item of public spending, by every department, since 2005. Millions of items, intrinsically complicated and difficult to manipulate.

But that complicated dataset gave us real news. Our developers built the COINS explorer, which allowed Guardian reporters and users to search for stories. They unearthed great tales.

With the WikiLeaks files we had the same criteria of success: help our journalists access the information, break down and analyse the data – and make it available for our users.

The WikiLeaks Afghanistan war logs – shared with the New York Times and Der Spiegel – showed data journalism in action. What we wanted to do was enable our team of specialist reporters to get great human stories from the information – and we wanted to analyse it to get the big picture, to show how the war really is going.

It was central to what we would do quite early on that we would not publish the full database. WikiLeaks was already going to do that and we wanted to make sure that we didn't reveal the names of informants or unnecessarily endanger Nato troops. At the same time, we needed to make the data easier to use for our team of investigative reporters led by David Leigh and Nick Davies (who had negotiated releasing the data with Julian Assange, the founder of WikiLeaks). We also wanted to make it simpler to access key information, out there in the real world – as clear and open as we could make it.

The data came to us as a huge Excel file – over 92,201 rows of data, some with nothing in at all or poorly formatted. Anything over 60,000 rows or so brought our version of Excel down in dramatic fashion and saving took a painfully long time (tip number one: turn automatic saving off in preferences…). It didn't help reporters trying to trawl through the data for stories and was too big to run meaningful reports on.

After COINS, huge datasets held no fear for us. Our team built a simple internal database. Reporters could now search stories for key words or events. Suddenly the dataset became accessible and generating stories became easier.

The Afghan war logs
Spreadsheet from
the database

This screenshot shows the spreadsheet of incidents recorded in the war logs for Afghanistan. These are open and searchable for all readers at guardian.co.uk/data »

	A ENTRIES IN BLUE HAVE BEEN ADDED BY THE GUARDIAN reportkey ▼	B Guardian incident url ▼
59	5564D1A3-EF0A-4C22-96F2-91BE3724B77A	http://www.guardian.co.uk/world/ afghanistan/warlogs/5564D1A3-EF0A-4C22-96F2-91BE3724B77A
60	B0CD129D-1BB9-4B9A-8075-E9762FA8F4E3	http://www.guardian.co.uk/world/ afghanistan/warlogs/B0CD129D-1BB9-4B9A-8075-E9762FA8F4E3
61	30405E00-6F3E-4554-A97E-B739DA6EEEE1	http://www.guardian.co.uk/world/ afghanistan/warlogs/30405E00-6F3E-4554-A97E-B739DA6EEEE1
62	C481DE0E-F2D1-49C0-BBC6-ABA60677AB11	http://www.guardian.co.uk/world/ afghanistan/warlogs/C481DE0E-F2D1-49C0-BBC6-ABA60677AB11
	2C6983DB-E948-4922-A2F5-7C4B-1DA94E5C	http://www.guardian.co.uk/world/ afghanistan/warlogs/2C6983DB-E948-4922-A2F5-7C4B1DA94E5C

> The overview data doesn't convey the enormity of the thousands of explosions. The three days in the run-up to the presidential election saw more than 100 IEDs explode

The data was well structured: each event had the following key data: time, date, a description, casualty figures and – crucially – detailed latitude and longitude.

We also started filtering the data to help us tell one of the key stories of the war: the rise in IED (Improvised Explosive Device) attacks – home-made roadside bombs which are unpredictable and difficult to fight. This dataset was still massive, but easier to manage. There were around 7,500 IED explosions or ambushes (an ambush is where the attack is combined with, for example, small arms fire or rocket grenades) between 2004 and 2009. There were another 8,000 IEDs which were found and cleared. We wanted to see how they changed over time

	D	E	F	G	H	I	J
	long.	Guardian headline	date occurred	type	category	Guardian edited category	Title
42166	69.20159149	Police shoot out window of soldiers' vehicle	22/12/2006 11:30:00	Friendly Fire	GREEN-GREEN	Afghan friendly fire	FRIENDLY FIRE Kabul
466988	65.85738373	Civilian shot dead on Kandahar road	27/12/2006 05:55:00	Other	Planned Event	Other	OTHER CIV KAF 1 CIV KIA
133041	70.22242737	Border patrol shell Pakistani helicopter	11/01/2007 07:30:00	Friendly Fire	GREEN-GREEN	Afghan friendly fire	FRIENDLY FIRE
5213013	66.88878632	Automatic fire from convoy wounds driver	11/01/2007 09:10:00	Enemy Action	Other (Hostile Action)	Other	ENG - OTHER CIV Qalat 1 CIV WIA
16704178	63.42435074	Border patrol storm police post in corruption row	30/01/2007 16:43:00	Friendly Fire	GREEN-GREEN	Afghan friendly fire	FRIENDLY FIRE ANP 2ANP WIA

Six years of IED attacks located

This map shows the location of every Improvised Explosive Device attack logged by the database. It includes IED explosions and ambushes (where an explosion includes Taliban small arms fire and RPG attacks, for instance). It excludes hoaxes and suicide bombers

UZBEKISTAN

Mazar-e Sharif

TURKMENISTAN

Meymaneh

AFGHANISTAN

Kabul The capital has been rocked by a series of daring Taliban attacks on five-star hotels, shopping centres, UN guesthouses and government ministries

A01

Herat

A01

Highway One (A01) Key 1,375-mile road ringing the country. The busiest stretch, from Kabul to Kandahar, is a life-threatening journey for all but the most heavily protected vehicles

Highway One (A01)

Last recorded IED attack of 2009 Sangin, 31 December: A dismounted patrol of The Rifles hit by an IED which killed one soldier and wounded two more

A01

A01

Kandahar

IRAN

See enlarged detail

HELMAND   KANDAHAR

Quetta

100 miles

IEDs exploded and cleared

Explosion/ambush
■ Total 7,553

Found/cleared
■ Total 8,582

400

300

1 Jan 2006 - British troops move into southern Afghanistan as part of Nato International Security Assistance Force (ISAF)

9 Sep 2008 - Extra 4,500 US troops to Afghanistan - the "quiet surge"

20 Aug 2009 Presidential election
537
454

200

9 Oct 2004 - Hamid Karzai wins presidential elections with 55% of vote

100

1 Dec 2009 - Obama boosts US troop numbers by 30,000, bringing total to 100,000

0

2004   2005   2006   2007   2008   2009

Where the IEDs exploded

West
364

Total*
7,553

East
2,9

South
3,701

*Unknown 10

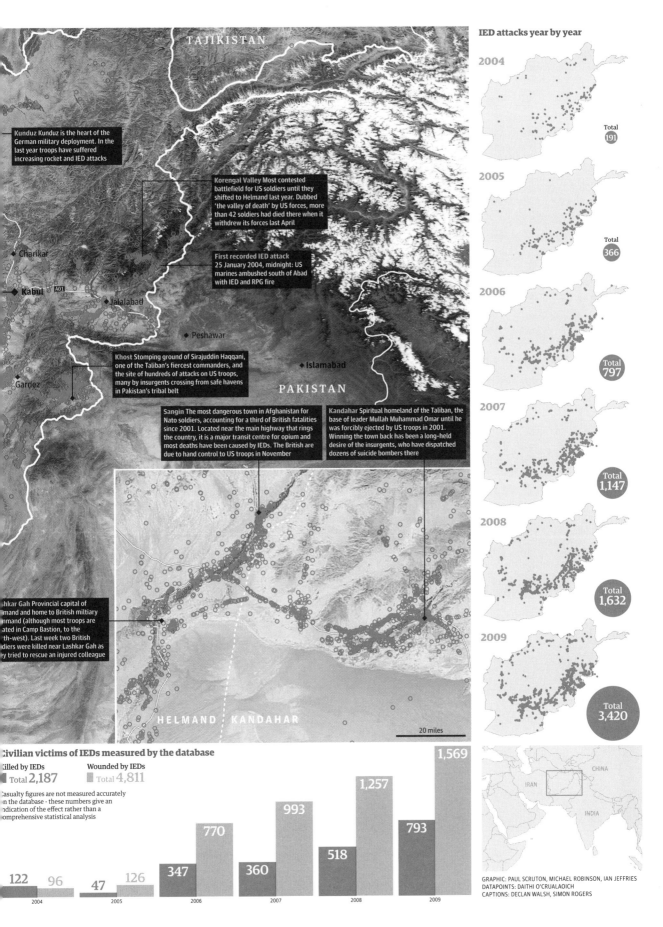

IED attacks year by year

Kunduz Kunduz is the heart of the German military deployment. In the last year troops have suffered increasing rocket and IED attacks

Korengal Valley Most contested battlefield for US soldiers until they shifted to Helmand last year. Dubbed 'the valley of death' by US forces, more than 42 soldiers had died there when it withdrew its forces last April

First recorded IED attack 25 January 2004, midnight: US marines ambushed south of Abad with IED and RPG fire

Charikar

Kabul A01

Jalalabad

Peshawar

Islamabad

PAKISTAN

Khost Stomping ground of Sirajuddin Haqqani, one of the Taliban's fiercest commanders, and the site of hundreds of attacks on US troops, many by insurgents crossing from safe havens in Pakistan's tribal belt

Gardez

Sangin The most dangerous town in Afghanistan for Nato soldiers, accounting for a third of British fatalities since 2001. Located near the main highway that rings the country, it is a major transit centre for opium and most deaths have been caused by IEDs. The British are due to hand control to US troops in November

Kandahar Spiritual homeland of the Taliban, the base of leader Mullah Muhammad Omar until he was forcibly ejected by US troops in 2001. Winning the town back has been a long-held desire of the insurgents, who have dispatched dozens of suicide bombers there

shkar Gah Provincial capital of mand and home to British miltiary nmand (although most troops are ated in Camp Bastion, to the th-west). Last week two British diers were killed near Lashkar Gah as y tried to rescue an injured colleague

HELMAND   KANDAHAR

20 miles

TAJIKISTAN

2004 Total 191

2005 Total 366

2006 Total 797

2007 Total 1,147

2008 Total 1,632

2009 Total 3,420

Civilian victims of IEDs measured by the database

Killed by IEDs Total 2,187   Wounded by IEDs Total 4,811

Casualty figures are not measured accurately in the database - these numbers give an indication of the effect rather than a comprehensive statistical analysis

	2004	2005	2006	2007	2008	2009
Killed	122	47	347	360	518	793
Wounded	96	126	770	993	1,257	1,569

CHINA

IRAN

INDIA

GRAPHIC: PAUL SCRUTON, MICHAEL ROBINSON, IAN JEFFRIES
DATAPOINTS: DAITHI O'CRUALAOICH
CAPTIONS: DECLAN WALSH, SIMON ROGERS

The emerging form of disclosure through the internet, pioneered ... by WikiLeaks deserves our praise and needs to be defended against the reactionary forces that seek to avoid exposure

Roy Greenslade

– and how they compared. This data allowed us to see that the south, where British and Canadian troops were based then, was the worst-hit area – which backed up what our reporters who had covered the war knew.

The casualties data brought its own challenges, repeated again when we dealt with the Iraq data. It was often inaccurately compiled and incomplete – we compared Nato-recorded casualties too, to test the veracity of the data, and the results varied.

But the overview data doesn't convey the enormity of the thousands of explosions. One particular period – the three days in the run-up to the presidential election in September 2010 – saw more than 100 IEDs explode. Imagine living with that every time you set off in a truck down the road.

It's inevitably the case that the work that helps shape a story is less interesting than the story itself. But in the future, as more and more of these datasets are released, these are skills that journalists will have to grapple with. As UK media commentator Roy Greenslade wrote at the time: "The emerging form of disclosure through the internet, pioneered so successfully in the past couple of years by WikiLeaks, deserves our praise and needs to be defended against the reactionary forces that seek to avoid exposure."

24,498
Deaths in Afghanistan recorded by the WikiLeaks database – over 4,000 of them civilians caught up in the conflict

The IED interactive
Mapping incidents reveals concentration of attacks in south and east

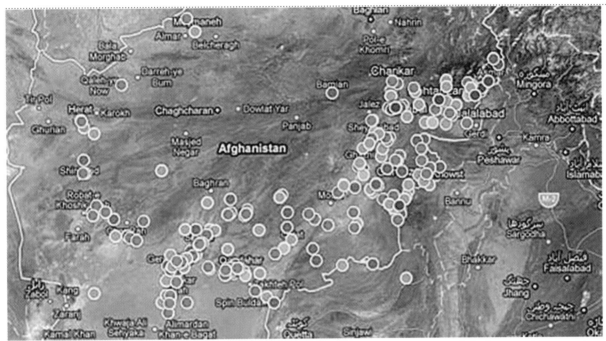

The logs listed all IED incidents recorded by allied forces. Plotted over time these reveal the insurgents' increasing reliance on IEDs. Watch the visualisation created by the Guardian interactive team at **guardian.co.uk/afghanistan »**

Afghan civilians killed
2007-2011, UN figures

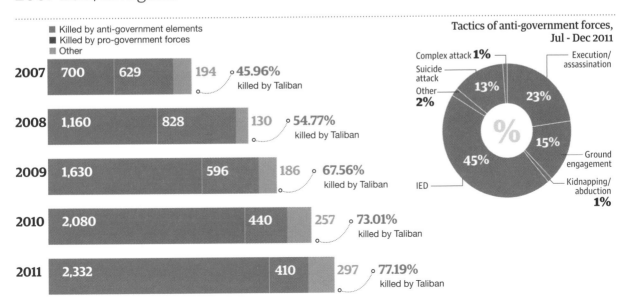

■ Killed by anti-government elements
■ Killed by pro-government forces
■ Other

Year	Killed by anti-government elements	Killed by pro-government forces	Other	% killed by Taliban
2007	700	629	194	45.96% killed by Taliban
2008	1,160	828	130	54.77% killed by Taliban
2009	1,630	596	186	67.56% killed by Taliban
2010	2,080	440	257	73.01% killed by Taliban
2011	2,332	410	297	77.19% killed by Taliban

Tactics of anti-government forces,
Jul - Dec 2011

Complex attack **1%**
Suicide attack
Other **2%**
13%
Execution/assassination 23%
15% Ground engagement
45% IED
Kidnapping/abduction **1%**

The war logs part II: Iraq

The Iraq war logs release in October 2010 dumped another 391,000 records from the war in Iraq into the public arena.

This was in a different league to the Afghanistan leak – there's a good case for saying this made the war the most documented in history. Every minor detail was now there for us to analyse and break down. But one factor stands out: the sheer volume of deaths, most of which are civilians. Overleaf are some key numbers which show the process we went through

As with Afghanistan, the Guardian decided not to republish the entire database, largely because we couldn't be sure the summary field didn't contain confidential details of informants and so on. But we did allow our users to download a spreadsheet containing the records of every incident where somebody died, nearly 60,000 in all. We removed the summary field so it was just the basic data: the military heading, numbers of deaths and the geographic breakdown.

We also took all these incidents where someone had died and put it on a map, to show the patterns of destruction which had ravaged Iraq.

But the release raised questions over the quality of the data. Academics have been able to analyse the SIGACTS database for some time. One who worked with parts of the database gave us a fascinating insight into how it was collated. The database was so huge that by only selecting deaths for our map we could be missing an even bigger picture, said Jacob Shapiro, Assistant Professor of Politics and International Affairs at Princeton University. He pointed out three major issues with the SIGACTS:

This is not "every death" or anything close to it. This is every death recorded by Multi-National Forces Iraq. There is underreporting in these data for a number of reasons including: (1) there was no Coalition or Iraqi unit around to record the death; (2) the Coalition and Iraqi units in the area were engaged in such high levels of combat that they did not have time to track down every casualty on all sides; or (3) the outcome of the incident was ambiguous.

One needs to understand how the data was created. This is critical for understanding the likely biases and weaknesses in the data. In particular, the reporting standards for Significant Actions (SIGACT) changed dramatically over time and the reporting procedure varied across units. There were also big changes in how reports from Iraqi units entered the data. In general, the data is likely to be more complete later in the war, when reporting standards were more uniform and the integration of information from Iraqi units was better.

Only reviewing incidents that resulted in casualties may result in a heavily skewed view of the war. Whether a violent incident causes casualties, especially civilian ones, has a large random component and so we should be careful in the inferences we can draw from this reduced dataset.

So, although the data painted a grim picture, the facts are likely to be much, much worse, because of underreporting.

The death toll
UK and US soldiers killed in Iraq, 2003–11

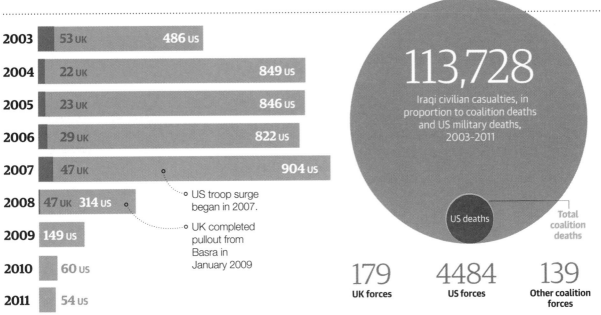

2003	53 UK — 486 US
2004	22 UK — 849 US
2005	23 UK — 846 US
2006	29 UK — 822 US
2007	47 UK — 904 US
2008	47 UK — 314 US
2009	149 US
2010	60 US
2011	54 US

US troop surge began in 2007.

UK completed pullout from Basra in January 2009

113,728
Iraqi civilian casualties, in proportion to coalition deaths and US military deaths, 2003–2011

US deaths

Total coalition deaths

179
UK forces

4484
US forces

139
Other coalition forces

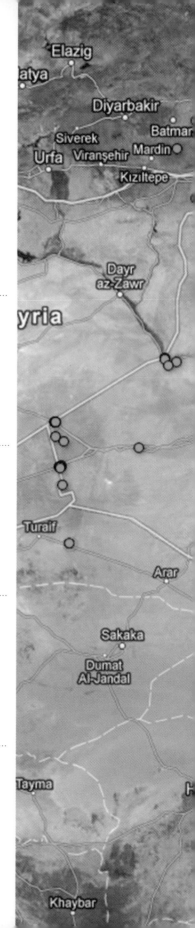

Some key facts showing the process we went through

109,032

deaths in total recorded in the WikiLeaks database

66,081
civilians

15,196
Iraqi security forces

23,984
insurgents

45,497

people were killed in Baghdad, the worst place for deaths. It was followed by MND north (the region that goes from Baghdad to Kurdistan) where another 34,210 died. The quietest place was the north-east, with only 328 deaths

34,814

people were recorded as murdered in 24,840 incidents. The deadliest month was December 2006 – 2,566 people were murdered. The deadliest year was 2006, when 16,870 people were murdered

12,578

escalation of force incidents were recorded in the database. Escalation of force incidents include events such as someone getting shot for driving too fast at a checkpoint. These resulted in 778 recorded deaths

65,439

IED explosions over the period covered by the database, and of the deaths recorded 31,780 were from IEDs alone. 44,620 IEDs were found and cleared. The worst month for IED explosions was May 2007 with 2,080

A visualisation, generated with Google Fusion Tables, maps incidents from the SIGACTS database and shows the intensity of the battles with insurgents

One day in Iraq
The Guardian interactive team examines a deadly day in 2006

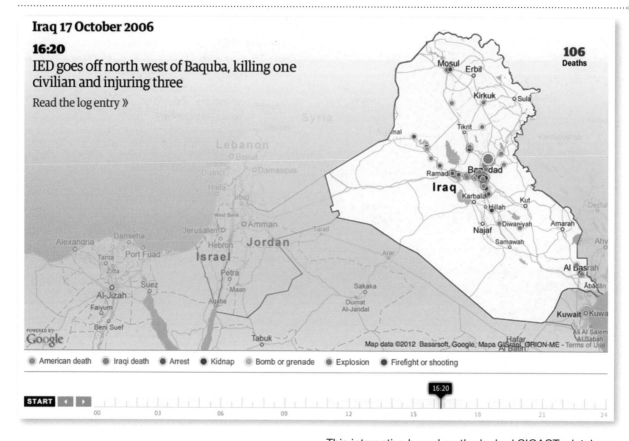

Iraq 17 October 2006

16:20

IED goes off north west of Baquba, killing one civilian and injuring three

Read the log entry »

106
Deaths

● American death   ● Iraqi death   ● Arrest   ● Kidnap   ● Bomb or grenade   ● Explosion   ● Firefight or shooting

START ◄ ►

00   03   06   09   12   15   16:20   18   21   24

This interactive based on the leaked SIGACTs database took a different approach, slicing through the data to look at just one day during one of the most violent post-invasion periods. 17 October 2006 – three and a half years after the invasion and just three since George Bush declared "mission accomplished" – was picked as typical. The logs recorded 146 deaths and 24 hours of car bombs and mortars, of tortured corpses being found in every major city, of snipers, kidnaps and death squads. Each of the logs was plotted on a map, which was turned into an animated timeline to accompany the story of the day, written by Guardian and Observer correspondent James Meek. Readers could halt the timeline to click into the log entry for each incident. The logs are packed with military abbreviations, so there is also a glossary to help readers make sense of the shorthand. You can view the Guardian interactive team's work at **guardian.co.uk/world/iraq-war-logs** »

Key	46B76C70-ADD6-4342-93B0-1C4A31FF22B7
Date	2006-10-17 17:10:00
Type	Criminal Event
Category	Kidnapping
Tracking no.	2006-290-202513-0591
Title	ATT MURDER/KIDNAPPING ON CIV IN AL MAMMON (ZONE 37 S); 1 CIV INJ, 0 CF INJ/DAMAG
Summary	AT 17 1610C OCT06: IN AL MAMMON (ZONE 37 S) IVO 38SMB 36660 82660 TAC/B/4-23 IVO MB 3666 8266 RPTS 4 WHITE TOYOTA LAND CRUISERS SHOT A LN WITHIN VISUAL RANGE OF HIM. THEY ARE FLEEING THE SCENE AND B6 IS ATTEMPTING TO REGAIN CONTACT. FIRST 2 VEHICLES HAD POLICE LIGHTS ON TOP. 1LN MALE WIA. 1 NP POSS KIDNAPPED.
	1612: AWT REQUESTED
	1624: B6 RPTS THAT HE HAS RETURNED TO THE SCENE AND PICKED UP THE BROTHER OF THE KIDNAP VICTIM. THE BROTHER IS LEADING THEM TO A LIKELY KILL/DUMP SITE WHERE HE BELIEVES HIS BROTHER WILL BE KILLED. BROTHER LED THEM TO BLDG LOC MB 37147 81587.
	1710 CLEARED BLDG FOUND NP UNIFORMS GOING TO CHECK NP STATIONS IN AO FOR 4 VICTORS.
	1732: A6 CHECKED 2/7/2 COMPOUND, NO PID.
	1734: TAC/B MOVING TO AL YARMOOK HOSPITAL TO CHECK ON WIA. APPARENTLY, THE WIA WAS INITIALLY KIDNAPPED, THEN HE TRIED TO ESCAPE OUT OF THE CAR AND WAVE DOWN CF, THE AIF SHOT HIM.
	SUMMARY:
	1 X ATTEMPTED MURDER 1 X LN KIDNAPPED
	CLOSED

The United States embassy cables and beyond

December 2010 saw the release of the cables. This was in another league altogether, a huge dataset of official documents: 251,287 dispatches, from more than 250 worldwide US embassies and consulates. It's a unique picture of US diplomatic language – including over 50,000 documents covering the current Obama administration. But what did the data include?

The cables themselves came via the huge Secret Internet Protocol Router Network, or SIPRNet. SIPRNet is the worldwide US military internet system, kept separate from the ordinary civilian internet and run by the Department of Defense in Washington. Since the attacks of September 2001, there has been a move in the US to link up archives of government information, in the hope that key intelligence no longer gets trapped in information silos or "stovepipes". An increasing number of US embassies have become linked to SIPRNet over the past decade, so that military and diplomatic information can be shared. By 2002, 125 embassies were on SIPRNet: by 2005, the number had risen to 180, and by now the vast majority of US missions worldwide are linked to the system – which is why the bulk of these cables are from 2008 and 2009. As David Leigh wrote:

> "An embassy dispatch marked SIPDIS is automatically downloaded onto its embassy classified website. From there, it can be accessed not only by anyone in the state department, but also by anyone in the US military who has a security clearance up to the 'Secret' level, a password, and a computer connected to SIPRNet"

…which astonishingly covers over 3m people. There are several layers of data in here – ranging up to the "SECRET NOFORN" level, which means that they are designed never be shown to non-US citizens. Instead, they are supposed to be read by officials in Washington up to the level of Secretary of State Hillary Clinton. The cables are normally drafted by the local ambassador or subordinates. The "Top Secret" and above foreign

Diplomatic concerns
The most frequently used words in the embassy cables

intelligence documents cannot be accessed from SIPRNet.

Unlike the previous releases, this was predominantly text, not quantified or with identical data. This is what was included:

● A source, i.e. the embassy or body which sent it

● A list of recipients – normally cables were sent to a number of other embassies and bodies

● A subject field – basically a summary of the cable

● Tags – each cable was tagged with a number of keyword abbreviations

● Body text – the cable itself. We opted not to publish these in full, for obvious security reasons

The 251,287 dispatches included:

● The US state department sent the most cables in this set, followed by Ankara in Turkey, then Baghdad and Tokyo

● 97,070 of the documents were classified as 'Confidential'

● 28,760 of them were given the tag 'PTER', which stands for prevention of terrorism

The earliest of the cables is from 1966, with most, 56,813, from 2009. Analysis of the cables is a huge task which may never be entirely finished.

Where are the Wikileaks cables from?

The Wikileaks data covers a specific chunk of leaked cables - it's not all cables sent over the period, but rather a selection. These are the top locations the cables were sent from

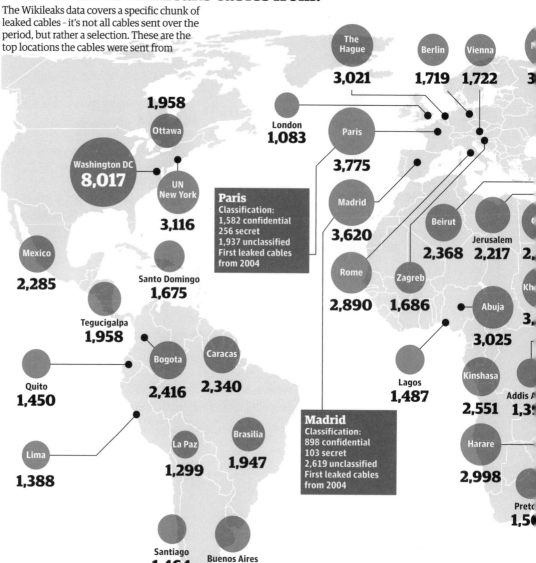

1,958
Ottawa

The Hague 3,021

Berlin 1,719

Vienna 1,722

London **1,083**

Paris **3,775**

Washington DC **8,017**

UN New York **3,116**

Paris
Classification:
1,582 confidential
256 secret
1,937 unclassified
First leaked cables
from 2004

Madrid **3,620**

Beirut 2,368

Jerusalem **2,217**

Rome **2,890**

Zagreb **1,686**

Abuja **3,025**

Mexico **2,285**

Santo Domingo **1,675**

Tegucigalpa **1,958**

Lagos **1,487**

Kinshasa **2,551**

Addis A **1,3**

Quito **1,450**

Bogota **2,416**

Caracas **2,340**

Harare **2,998**

Lima **1,388**

La Paz **1,299**

Brasilia **1,947**

Madrid
Classification:
898 confidential
103 secret
2,619 unclassified
First leaked cables
from 2004

Preto **1,5**

Santiago **1,464**

Buenos Aires **2,233**

When were the Wikileaks cables sent?

The selection of cables covers a period from the 1960s onwards - but the bulk are from the last ten years

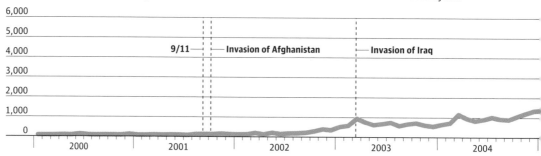

| | 6,000 |
| 5,000 |
| 4,000 | 9/11 | Invasion of Afghanistan | Invasion of Iraq |
| 3,000 |
| 2,000 |
| 1,000 |
| 0 |

2000   2001   2002   2003   2004

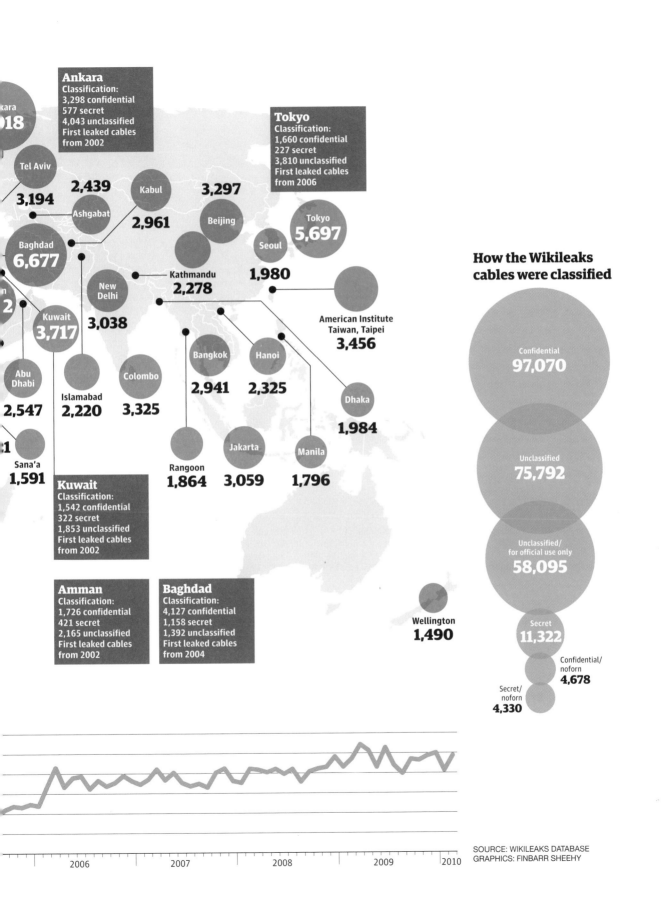

Ankara
Classification:
3,298 confidential
577 secret
4,043 unclassified
First leaked cables from 2002

Tokyo
Classification:
1,660 confidential
227 secret
3,810 unclassified
First leaked cables from 2006

kara
018

Tel Aviv
3,194

2,439

Kabul
2,961

Ashgabat

3,297

Beijing

Tokyo
5,697

Baghdad
6,677

Seoul
1,980

Kathmandu
2,278

New Delhi
3,038

2

Kuwait
3,717

American Institute Taiwan, Taipei
3,456

Colombo
3,325

Bangkok
2,941

Hanoi
2,325

Abu Dhabi
2,547

Islamabad
2,220

Dhaka
1,984

1

Sana'a
1,591

Rangoon
1,864

Jakarta
3,059

Manila
1,796

Kuwait
Classification:
1,542 confidential
322 secret
1,853 unclassified
First leaked cables from 2002

Amman
Classification:
1,726 confidential
421 secret
2,165 unclassified
First leaked cables from 2002

Baghdad
Classification:
4,127 confidential
1,158 secret
1,392 unclassified
First leaked cables from 2004

Wellington
1,490

How the Wikileaks cables were classified

Confidential
97,070

Unclassified
75,792

Unclassified/ for official use only
58,095

Secret
11,322

Confidential/ noforn
4,678

Secret/ noforn
4,330

2006   2007   2008   2009   2010

SOURCE: WIKILEAKS DATABASE
GRAPHICS: FINBARR SHEEHY

Drone wars

12 of the most frequently used unmanned aerial surveillance vehicles

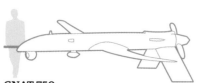

GNAT 750
Reconnaissance UAV, introduced in 1989

Length **16ft 5in**	Maximum speed **120mph**
Wingspan **35ft 4in**	Endurance **48 hours**
	Service ceiling **25,000ft**

MQ-1B Predator
Remoted piloted UAV, introduced in 1995

Length **27ft**	Armament
Wingspan **48ft 8in**	2 × 114 Hellfire air-to-
Max speed **135mph**	ground missiles
Range **675 miles**	4 × 92 Stinger missiles
Endurance **24 hours**	6 × Griffin air-to-
Service ceiling **25,000ft**	surface missiles

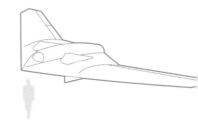

RQ-4 Global Hawk
Surveillance UAV, introduced in 1998
Unit cost **$104m**

Length **44ft 5in**	Cruise speed **404mp**
Wingspan **116ft 2in**	Range **15,525 mile**
Height **15ft 2in**	Endurance **36 hour**
Max speed **497mph**	Service ceiling **65,0**

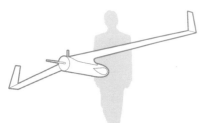

Boeing ScanEagle
Small UAV, introduced in 2005

Wingspan **10ft**
Maximum speed **86mph**
Cruise speed **69mph**
Endurance record **22 hours**

Wasp Block III
Small lightweight RC UAV, introduced in 2007

Length **15in**	Armament
Wingspan **2ft 4.5in**	High resolution, day/
Loaded weight **14.4lbs**	night cameras with
Cruise speed **25-40mph**	digital image
Range **3 miles**	stabilisation

RQ-170 Sentinel
Stealth UAV, introduced in 2007

Length **14ft 9in**
Wingspan **39ft 4in** estimated
Height **6ft** est.
Service ceiling **50,000 ft** est.

56

different kinds of drones are in operation all over the world, according to data collected by the International Institute for Strategic Studies

807

Drones are known to be in service, operated by 11 different countries. However, this number is almost certainly a large underestimate because information about the programmes run by Russia, China and Turkey is not available

678

Number of verified drones in operation by the United States, which is the country which is most open about its drone stocks. According to IISS data, by 2012 they were operating at least 18 different types

MQ-9 Reaper
Remote or auto UAV, introduced in 2007

Length **36ft 1in**
Wingspan **65ft 7in**
Maximum speed **555mph**
Range **1,150 miles**
Service ceiling **50,000ft**

Armament
Up to 14 AGM-114 Hellfire air-to-ground missiles or four Hellfire missiles and two 500lb laser-guided bombs

Nano Hummingbird
Hand-held hover flight, introduced in 2011

Wingspan **6.3in**
Total weight **0.67oz**
Endurance **11 mins**

Switchblade
Anti-personnel UAV weapon, introduced in 2012

Wingspan **2ft**
Length **2ft**
Weight **5.5lbs**
Maximum speed **98mph**
Usual altitude of flight **500ft**

MQ-8B Fire Scout
UAV helicopter, introduced in 2002
Developed into the Sikorsky S-434

Length **23ft 11.5in**
Rotor dia. **27ft 6in**
Height **9ft 8.5in**
Max speed **132mph**

Cruise speed **124mph**
Endurance **8 hours**
Service ceiling **20,000ft**

RQ-7 Shadow
Reconnaissance UAV, introduced in 2002

Cost **$15.5m** per system
Length **11ft 2in**
Wingspan **14ft**
Height **3ft 3.4in**

Maximum speed **127mph**
Range **68 miles**
Endurance **6 hours**
Service ceiling **15,000ft**

RQ-11B Raven B
Remote-controlled UAV, introduced in 2003

Wing Span **4ft 7in**
Length **3ft**
Cruising speed approx. **35mph**
Range **6.2 miles**
Endurance approx. **60–90 min**

10

The RAF's stocks of the MQ-9 Reaper heavy drone (above). It is not known how many stocks of the Hermes 450 and Watchkeeper drones the army continues to operate. Surveillance drones are also used by civilian authorities The MoD is reported to have spent £2bn on developing drones

349

The number of drone attacks in Pakistan recorded in the Bureau of Investigative Journalists database as of October 2012. These are largely in the tribal areas of Waziristan, which border Afghanistan. Up to nine attacks in Somalia and 35-45 attacks in Yemen have been documented by the BIJ

850

Number of civilians killed in drone attacks in Pakistan, according to the BIJ, out of a total death toll of 3,300+ across Pakistan, Yemen and Somalia. This is almost certainly an underestimate. Data is reliant on reports from the ground, so accurate figures are near-impossible

Deadly milestone
Number of British dead in Afghanistan passes 400, March 2012

The deaths of six soldiers in a massive IED blast in Helmand on 6 March 2012 took the British death toll in Afghanistan over 400. The Ministry of Defence's data releases reveal who the soldiers were and where they come from, and also the most dangerous parts of Afghanistan

17.3

Death rate for British troops serving in Afghanistan during 2009, per 1,000 personnel hours. The figure for US troops in the same period was half that: **8.4**. The death rate is higher than for British forces serving in the Korean War

SOURCE: MEDICAL RESEARCH COUNCIL

Home towns of UK troops killed in Afghanistan since the start of the war

- ● Australia
- ◉◉◉◉◉◉ Fiji
- ● Jamaica
- ◉◉◉◉◉◉◉ Nepal
- ● New Zealand
- ◉◉◉◉◉◉ South Africa
- ● US
- ● Zimbabwe
- ◉● Not released

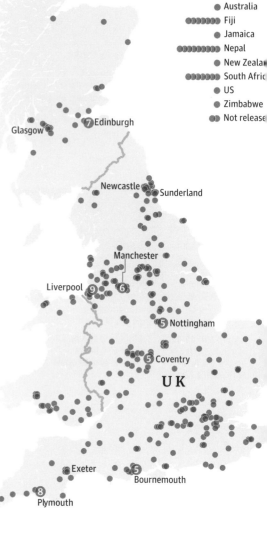

Glasgow · Edinburgh ⑦ · Newcastle · Sunderland · Manchester · Liverpool ⑨ ⑥ · Nottingham ⑤ · Coventry ⑤ · U K · Exeter · Bournemouth ⑤ · Plymouth ⑧

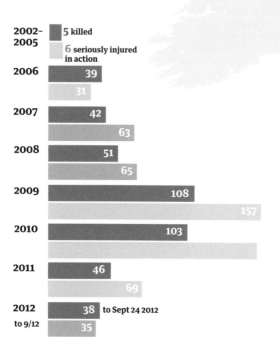

2002–2005	
■ 5 killed	
□ 6 seriously injured in action	

2006	39
	31
2007	42
	63
2008	51
	65
2009	108
	157
2010	103
2011	46
	69
2012 to 9/12	38 to Sept 24 2012
	35

144
of the 404 soldiers killed by March 2012 were aged 21–25; 70 were under 20 and 107 were 26 to 30 years old

12
of the soldiers were aged over

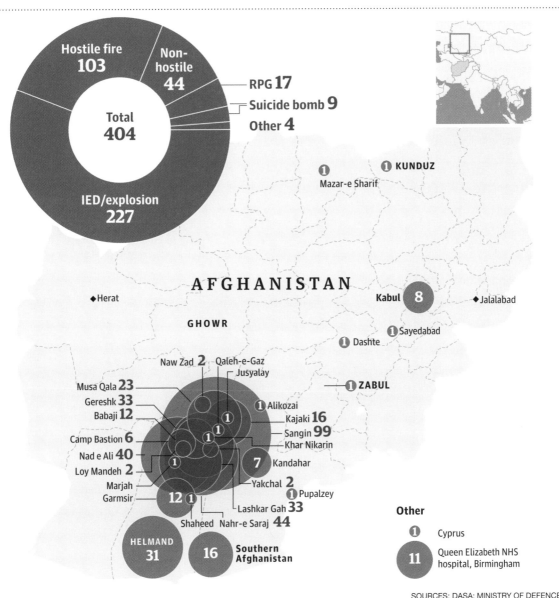

Hostile fire
103

Non-hostile
44

RPG **17**

Suicide bomb **9**

Other **4**

Total
404

IED/explosion
227

AFGHANISTAN

◆Herat

◆Jalalabad

GHOWR

❶ Mazar-e Sharif

❶ **KUNDUZ**

Kabul ❽

❶ Sayedabad

❶ Dashte

❶ **ZABUL**

Naw Zad **2** Qaleh-e-Gaz
Jusyalay

Musa Qala **23**

Gereshk **33**

Babaji **12**

Camp Bastion **6**

Nad e Ali **40**

Loy Mandeh **2**

Marjah

Garmsir

❶ Alikozai

Kajaki **16**

Sangin **99**

Khar Nikarin

❼ Kandahar

Yakchal **2**

❶ Pupalzey

Lashkar Gah **33**

12 ❶

Shaheed Nahr-e Saraj **44**

HELMAND
31

16 **Southern Afghanistan**

Other

❶ Cyprus

11 Queen Elizabeth NHS hospital, Birmingham

SOURCES: DASA; MINISTRY OF DEFENCE
GRAPHIC: JENNY RIDLEY

37
of those killed were officers and 178 were privates or equivalent

189
were non-commissioned officers

53
of those killed were members of the Rifles, the worst-hit regiment

48
of the 404 killed were Royal Marines

32
were from the Parachute Regiment

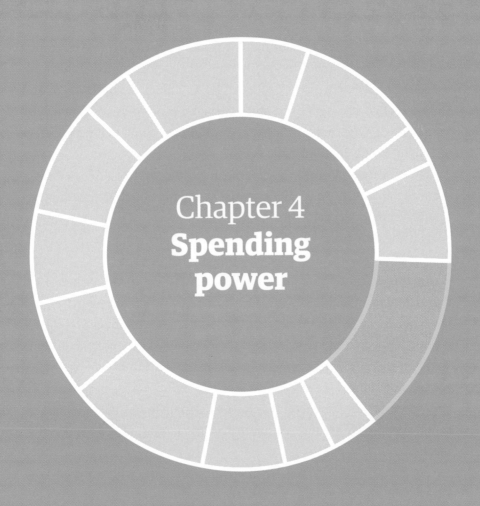

Chapter 4
Spending power

What you'll find out in this chapter:
» The price of the first UK austerity measures » How the government spends your money each year » 99% vs 1% vs 47% – just how unequal is society in the United States?

'We want an army of armchair auditors scrutinising the public accounts to see whether government is providing value for money." So said the Conservatives' transparency manifesto published before the 2010 election.

So why have they made it so hard? It's an object lesson in where the ambition of government to be more open and produce more data meets the reality of Whitehall intransigence – and it's a game that gets played out again and again around the world.

Every year we publish our signature piece: a complete guide to public spending, in which we break down the key items of public spending by UK government departments.

It is the only place where you can meaningfully compare the cost of Libya operations with the price of setting up free schools.

In this world of cuts and austerity, signing up to the principle of retrenchment in general terms is easy. Politicians become much more coy when it gets to the specific question of exactly what they would cut. It's not limited to the Conservatives and Liberal Democrats and their coalition government. Before the last election, Gordon Brown promised to cut four things: "costs", "inefficiencies", "unnecessary programmes" and "lower priority budgets". We could all sign up to that shopping list of savagery, but only because we haven't got the faintest idea what it really means.

So if you were charged with wielding the axe, where would you strike? Our atlas of public expenditure (overleaf) shows you how tough the decision would be.

The big grey blob of at the centre is the total number the politicians say they want to reduce. Unlike them, however, we break this great grey mass into coloured blocks – each to scale – for all the different departments. And then we break them down further into individual programmes spent within each programme.

We can see how that spending fits together – and how anything less than a billion is really not that much in government terms, particularly compared to a budget deficit of £121bn for 2011–12.

£3.77bn

Cost of British military operations in Afghanistan in 2010/11 – more than was spent on the entire British rail system in the same year. The British government spent **£691.67bn** in total

The recession bites
Personal bankruptcy in the economic downturn, 2009

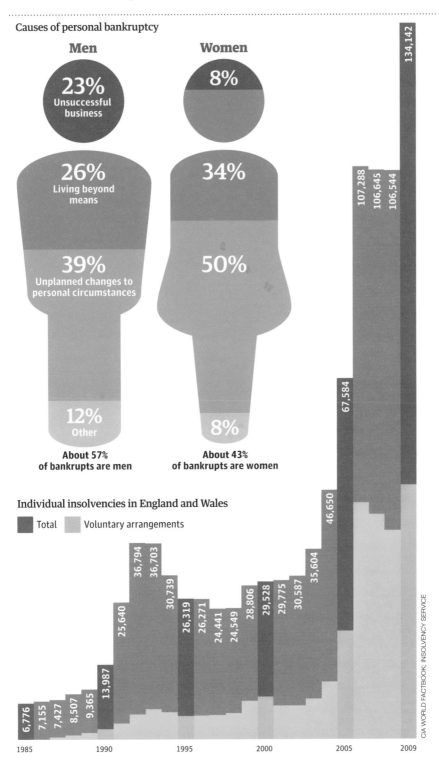

Causes of personal bankruptcy

Men

23% Unsuccessful business

26% Living beyond means

39% Unplanned changes to personal circumstances

12% Other

About 57% of bankrupts are men

Women

8%

34%

50%

8%

About 43% of bankrupts are women

Individual insolvencies in England and Wales

■ Total   ■ Voluntary arrangements

6,776
7,155
7,427
8,507
9,365
13,987
25,640
36,794
36,703
30,739
26,319
26,271
24,441
24,549
28,806
29,528
29,775
30,587
35,604
46,650
67,584
107,288
106,645
106,544
134,142

1985   1990   1995   2000   2005   2009

CIA WORLD FACTBOOK; INSOLVENCY SERVICE

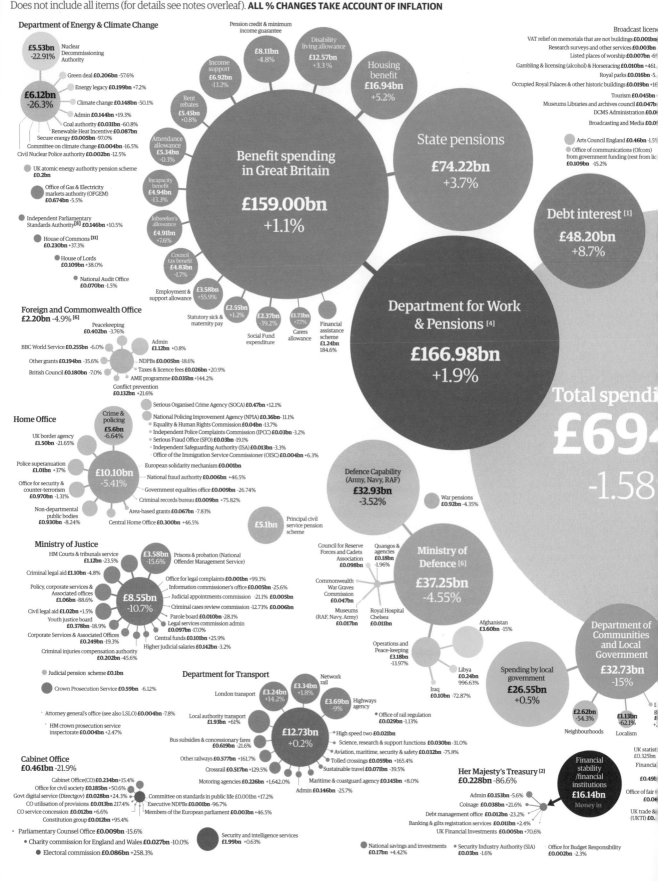

Public spending by UK central government departments, 2011-12

Does not include all items (for details see notes overleaf). **ALL % CHANGES TAKE ACCOUNT OF INFLATION**

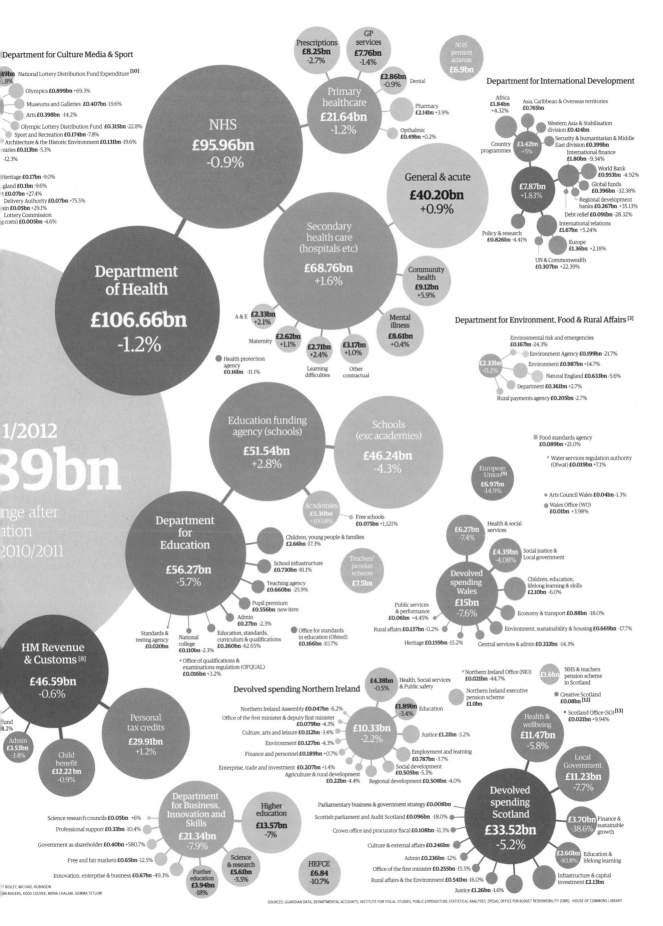

Department for Culture Media & Sport

.49bn National Lottery Distribution Fund Expenditure [10]
.8%
Olympics **£0.899bn** +69.3%
Museums and Galleries **£0.407bn** -19.6%
Arts **£0.398bn** -14.2%
Olympic Lottery Distribution Fund **£0.315bn** -22.8%
Sport and Recreation **£0.174bn** -7.8%
Architecture & the Historic Environment **£0.131bn** -19.6%
raries **£0.113bn** -5.3%
-12.3%

Heritage **£0.17bn** -9.0%
gland **£0.1bn** -9.6%
t **£0.07bn** +27.4%
Delivery Authority **£0.07bn** +75.5%
ain **£0.05bn** +29.1%
Lottery Commission
g costs) **£0.005bn** -4.6%

Prescriptions **£8.25bn** -2.7%
GP services **£7.76bn** -1.4%
Dental **£2.86bn** -0.9%
Pharmacy **£2.14bn** +3.9%
Opthalmic **£0.49bn** +0.2%

Primary healthcare **£21.64bn** -1.2%

NHS pension scheme **£6.9bn**

Department for International Development

Africa **£1.84bn** +4.32%
Asia, Caribbean & Overseas territories **£0.765bn**
Western Asia & Stabilisation division **£0.414bn**
Security & humanitarian & Middle East division **£0.399bn**
Country programmes **£3.42bn** +5%
International finance **£1.80bn** -9.34%
World Bank **£0.953bn** -4.92%
Global funds **£0.396bn** -32.38%
£7.87bn +1.83%
Regional development banks **£0.267bn** +35.13%
Debt relief **£0.091bn** -28.32%
International relations **£1.67bn** +5.24%
Policy & research **£0.826bn** -4.41%
Europe **£1.36bn** +2.18%
UN & Commonwealth **£0.307bn** +22.39%

NHS £95.96bn -0.9%

General & acute **£40.20bn +0.9%**

Department of Health £106.66bn -1.2%

Secondary health care (hospitals etc) **£68.76bn +1.6%**

Community health **£9.12bn** +5.9%

Department for Environment, Food & Rural Affairs [3]

Environmental risk and emergencies **£0.167bn** -24.3%
Environment Agency **£0.199bn** -21.7%
Environment **£0.987bn** +14.7%
£2.33bn -0.2%
Natural England **£0.633bn** -5.6%
Department **£0.361bn** +2.7%
Rural payments agency **£0.205bn** -2.7%

A & E **£2.33bn** +2.1%
Maternity **£2.62bn** +1.1%
Learning difficulties **£2.71bn** +2.4%
Other contractual **£3.17bn** +1.0%
Mental illness **£8.61bn** +0.4%

Health protection agency **£0.16bn** -11.1%

Food standards agency **£0.089bn** +21.0%
Water services regulation authority (Ofwat) **£0.019bn** +7.1%
Arts Council Wales **£0.04bn** -1.3%
Wales Office (WO) **£0.01bn** +3.98%

European Union [9] **£6.97bn** -14.9%

1/2012

39bn

nge after
ation

2010/2011

Education funding agency (schools) **£51.54bn +2.8%**

Schools (exc academies) **£46.24bn -4.3%**

Academies **£5.30bn** +190.8%
Free schools **£0.075bn** +1,121%

Children, young people & families **£2.66bn** -17.3%
School infrastructure **£0.730bn** -81.1%
Teaching agency **£0.660bn** -25.9%
Pupil premium **£0.556bn** new item
Admin **£0.27bn** -2.3%

Department for Education £56.27bn -5.7%

Teachers' pension scheme **£7.5bn**

Health & social services **£6.27bn** -7.4%
Social justice & Local government **£4.39bn** -4.08%
Children, education, lifelong learning & skills **£2.10bn** -6.0%

Devolved spending Wales £15bn -7.6%

Standards & testing agency **£0.020bn**
National college **£0.110bn** -2.3%
Education, standards, curriculum & qualifications **£0.260bn** -62.65%
Office for standards in education (Ofsted) **£0.166bn** -10.7%

Office of qualifications & examinations regulation (OFQUAL) **£0.016bn** +3.2%

Public services & performance **£0.06bn** +4.45%
Rural affairs **£0.137bn** -0.2%
Heritage **£0.159bn** -15.2%
Economy & transport **£0.88bn** -18.0%
Environment, sustainability & housing **£0.669bn** -17.7%
Central services & admin **£0.332bn** -14.3%

HM Revenue & Customs [8] £46.59bn -0.6%

fund
.2%
Admin **£3.53bn** -3.4%
Child benefit **£12.22 bn** -0.9%

Personal tax credits **£29.91bn +1.2%**

Health, Social services & Public safety **£4.38bn** -0.5%
Northern Ireland Office (NIO) **£0.021bn** -44.7%
Northern Ireland executive pension scheme **£1.0bn**
NHS & teachers pension scheme in Scotland **£1.6bn**
Creative Scotland **£0.08bn** [12]
Scotland Office (SO) [13] **£0.021bn** +9.94%

Devolved spending Northern Ireland

Northern Ireland Assembly **£0.047bn** -6.2%
Office of the first minister & deputy first minister **£0.079bn** -4.3%
Culture, arts and leisure **£0.112bn** -3.4%
Environment **£0.127bn** -4.3%
Finance and personnel **£0.189bn** +0.7%
Enterprise, trade and investment **£0.207bn** +1.4%
Agriculture & rural development **£0.22bn** -4.4%

Education **£1.89bn** -3.4%
£10.33bn -2.2%
Justice **£1.21bn** -3.2%
Employment and learning **£0.787bn** -3.7%
Social development **£0.505bn** -5.3%
Regional development **£0.508bn** -4.0%

Health & wellbeing **£11.47bn** -5.8%

Local Government **£11.23bn** -7.7%

Devolved spending Scotland £33.52bn -5.2%

Parliamentary business & government strategy **£0.008bn**
Scottish parliament and Audit Scotland **£0.096bn** -18.0%
Crown office and procurator fiscal **£0.108bn** -11.3%
Culture & external affairs **£0.246bn**
Admin **£0.236bn** -12%
Office of the first minister **£0.255bn** -15.5%
Rural affairs & the Environment **£0.541bn** -16.0%
Justice **£1.26bn** -1.6%

Finance & sustainable growth **£3.70bn** -38.6%
Education & lifelong learning **£2.60bn** -10.8%
Infrastructure & capital investment **£2.13bn**

Department for Business, Innovation and Skills £21.34bn -7.9%

Science research councils **£0.05bn** +6%
Professional support **£0.33bn** -10.4%
Government as shareholder **£0.40bn** +580.7%
Free and fair markets **£0.65bn** -12.5%
Innovation, enterprise & business **£0.67bn** -49.3%

Higher education **£13.57bn -7%**

Further education **£3.94bn** -18%
Science & research **£5.61bn** -5.5%

HEFCE **£6.84** -10.7%

RIDLEY, MICHAEL ROBINSON
N ROGERS, KOOS COUVEE, MONA CHALABI, GEMMA TETLOW

SOURCES: GUARDIAN DATA, DEPARTMENTAL ACCOUNTS, INSTITUTE FOR FISCAL STUDIES, PUBLIC EXPENDITURE STATISTICAL ANALYSES (PESA), OFFICE FOR BUDGET RESPONSIBILITY (OBR), HOUSE OF COMMONS LIBRARY

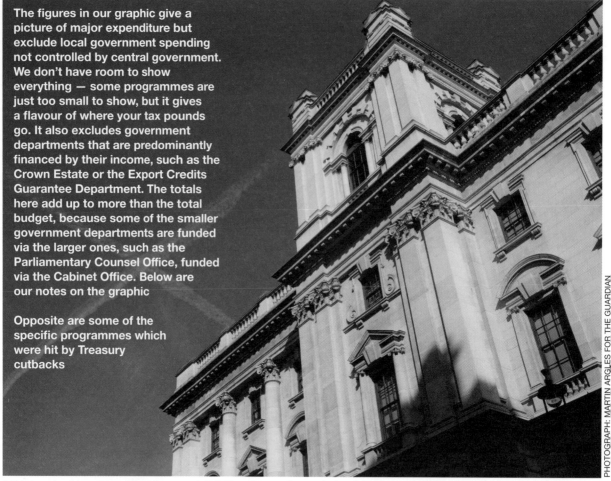

The figures in our graphic give a picture of major expenditure but exclude local government spending not controlled by central government. We don't have room to show everything — some programmes are just too small to show, but it gives a flavour of where your tax pounds go. It also excludes government departments that are predominantly financed by their income, such as the Crown Estate or the Export Credits Guarantee Department. The totals here add up to more than the total budget, because some of the smaller government departments are funded via the larger ones, such as the Parliamentary Counsel Office, funded via the Cabinet Office. Below are our notes on the graphic

Opposite are some of the specific programmes which were hit by Treasury cutbacks

PHOTOGRAPH: MARTIN ARGLES FOR THE GUARDIAN

[1] Interest paid on the public debt.

[2] Treasury spending in 2008-09 and 2009-10 was dominated by the impact of interventions in the financial sector — the figure shown here is gross spending. In fact, in 2010-11 the net effect of financial stability activities was to yield income to the Treasury. Loans to financial institutions were repaid to the Treasury in 2010-11 and there was no further purchase of shares and other assets in the year — so we have shown the core department spending separately. The increase is due to the provision for Equitable Life.

[3] The Rural Payments Agency distributes CAP payments — covered by transfers from EU so do not show up as net spending here.

[4] Benefit spending excludes child benefit, guardians' allowance, widows' pensions, statutory paternity pay, statutory adoption pay — these paid by HMRC, MoD, BIS respectively.

[5] Excludes spending on family health services. GP running costs include salaries, hospitality budgets, home and overseas accommodation costs.

[6] Data from Treasury COINS database. Operations spending in Libya, Iraq and Afghanistan paid for separately out of Treasury Special Reserve. Details from House of Commons Library.

[7] The amount of government funding from BIS and DCMS, rest from licence fees from broadcasters and media organisations.

[8] MPs' expenses now administered by the Independent Parliamentary Standards Authority (IPSA).

[9] Overall contribution, includes the effects of the UK's rebate, without which the 2011-12 contribution would be £15.6bn.

[10] This cash is distributed to 'good causes'. This financial year £135m went to the Olympics and Paralympics - on top of over £750m in April 2012.

[11] Increase due to the 2010 election: the absence of MPs during the campaign reducing costs substantially.

[12] Took over from Arts Council of Scotland this year.

[12] Includes non-voted costs of elections in Scotland, without which spending was £7.1m.

Main pension schemes are forecasts for 2011-12

Police

−6.64%

£5.6bn budget

Home Office

Bus subsidies

−21.6%

£0.619bn

Dept of Transport

Neighbourhoods

−54.3%

£2.62bn

Dept for Communities and Local Government

Children & families

−17.3%

£2.66bn

Dept for Education

The Green Deal

−57.6%

£0.206bn

Dept for Energy and Climate Change

Climate change

−50.1%

£0.148bn

Dept for Environment, Food and Rural Affairs

Roads

−9%

£3.69bn

Dept for Transport

Further Education

−18%

£3.94bn

Dept for Education

Sport

−7.8%

£0.174bn

Dept for Culture, Media and Sport

Aviation, maritime security & safety

−75.8%

£0.032bn

Dept for Transport

BBC World Service

−8.69%

£2.955bn

Dept for Culture, Media and Sport

Arts Council England

−1.5%

£0.46bn

Dept for Culture, Media and Sport

Museums & galleries

−19.6%

£0.407

Dept for Culture, Media and Sport

Prisons

−15.6%

£3.58bn

Ministry of Justice

Average spending cut

17.4%

We have identified 45 departments or non-departmental public bodies undergoing cuts in spending – those groups have suffered £72bn cuts in real terms in a single year, equivalent to around 10% of annual spending

A quick glance reveals why it is that the politicians are so much keener to discuss the black hole in general rather than specific terms. The biggest blobs are for health, pensions and family benefits (DWP and Inland Revenue) and education. These three big areas have been growing as a share of the total near-continuously since the second world war, and are the toughest to trim.

By contrast, those few things which politicians are most keen to talk about cutting explicitly are tiny. Quangos are a favourite target – the dots for the Electoral Commission and the Postal Services Commission, for example, are barely visible.

So what does the latest data show?

Public spending in 2011–12 was £694.89bn – compared to £689.63bn in 2010–11. That may look like an increase but once inflation is taken into account, it is a real-terms cut of 1.58%, or £10.8bn.

However, that £10.8bn cut masks big drops in spending in over 40 government departments and quangos, including "protected" areas such as health and education. We have identified 45 departments or non-departmental public bodies with cuts in spending – those groups have suffered £72bn cuts in real terms in a single year, equivalent to around 10% of annual spending.

In particular, education is down by 5.7% in real terms. The government had pledged to protect this budget from the cuts and had added the pupil premium to help poorer children. However, the annual reports clearly show DfE spending going from £58.28bn to £56.27bn – a cut even before inflation is taken into account. Within the education budget, there have been big cuts to schools infrastructure (-81%, largely as a result of scrapping the Building Schools for the Future programme) and children, young people and families (-17%, with big cuts to Sure Start). Meanwhile, the Department of Health – another protected area – faces a -1.2% change in its budget after inflation is taken into account.

The Department of Health says this apparent drop in total spending is actually due to the transfer of personal social services from its budget to the Department for Communities and Local Government in 2011–12.

37.1

The number of children per primary school class in China – the highest in the OECD. The UK has a rate of 24.5. Finland, Japan and Portugal have the highest graduation rates of upper secondary school students. The UK has a rate of 92% whereas the US has a rate of 76%

SOURCE: OECD

Spared the axe
The projects given greater funding despite austerity measures

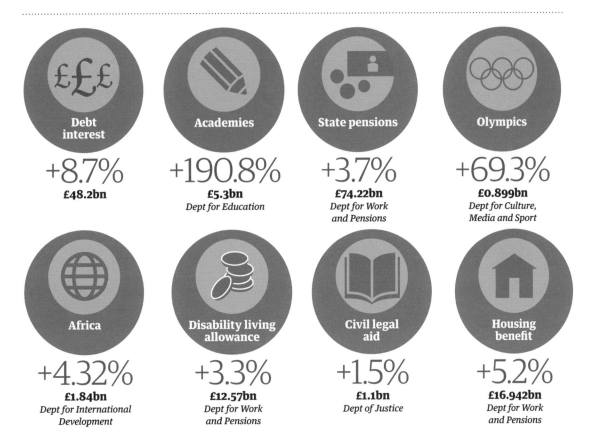

Debt interest
+8.7%
£48.2bn

Academies
+190.8%
£5.3bn
Dept for Education

State pensions
+3.7%
£74.22bn
Dept for Work and Pensions

Olympics
+69.3%
£0.899bn
Dept for Culture, Media and Sport

Africa
+4.32%
£1.84bn
Dept for International Development

Disability living allowance
+3.3%
£12.57bn
Dept for Work and Pensions

Civil legal aid
+1.5%
£1.1bn
Dept of Justice

Housing benefit
+5.2%
£16.942bn
Dept for Work and Pensions

Not everything is down: the Department for Work and Pensions, Britain's biggest department, spent £166.98bn in 2011–12 – an inflation increase of nearly 2% on the year before. Benefits spending was up by 1.11%. And there's the public sector debt: interest payments stood at £48.2bn, a rise of 8.73% including inflation.

If you are any kind of armchair auditor, this is the most basic of information on the way government works. So getting hold of it should be easy, right?

In fact, public spending by government departments is a mystery. It shouldn't be:

£379,999

Maximum salary for the Nuclear Decommissioning Authority's chief executive, Tony Fountain – Britain's best-paid civil servant or quango chief. The government has published the salaries of all public servants, including quango chiefs, who earn £150,000 or more

SOURCE: CABINET OFFICE

Where UK exports go
UK exports to top 20 trading partners, 2009

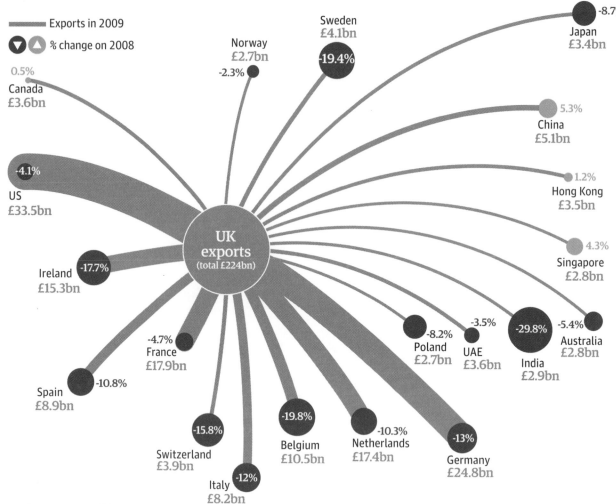

Exports in 2009
▼ ▲ % change on 2008

Canada £3.6bn — 0.5%

Norway £2.7bn — -2.3%

Sweden £4.1bn — -19.4%

Japan £3.4bn — -8.7%

China £5.1bn — 5.3%

US £33.5bn — -4.1%

Hong Kong £3.5bn — 1.2%

Singapore £2.8bn — 4.3%

Ireland £15.3bn — -17.7%

UK exports (total £224bn)

Poland £2.7bn — -8.2%

UAE £3.6bn — -3.5%

India £2.9bn — -29.8%

Australia £2.8bn — -5.4%

France £17.9bn — -4.7%

Spain £8.9bn — -10.8%

Switzerland £3.9bn — -15.8%

Italy £8.2bn — -12%

Belgium £10.5bn — -19.8%

Netherlands £17.4bn — -10.3%

Germany £24.8bn — -13%

What we sell

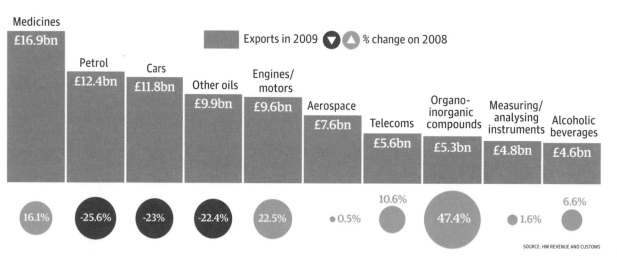

Exports in 2009 ▼ ▲ % change on 2008

Medicines £16.9bn	Petrol £12.4bn	Cars £11.8bn	Other oils £9.9bn	Engines/ motors £9.6bn	Aerospace £7.6bn	Telecoms £5.6bn	Organo-inorganic compounds £5.3bn	Measuring/ analysing instruments £4.8bn	Alcoholic beverages £4.6bn
16.1%	-25.6%	-23%	-22.4%	22.5%	0.5%	10.6%	47.4%	1.6%	6.6%

SOURCE: HM REVENUE AND CUSTOMS

Where UK imports come from
UK imports from top 20 trading partners, 2009

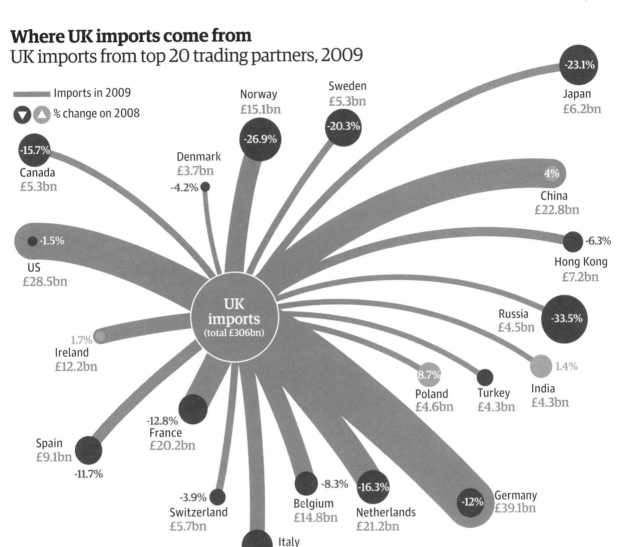

Imports in 2009
% change on 2008

Norway £15.1bn — -26.9%
Sweden £5.3bn — -20.3%
Japan £6.2bn — -23.1%
Denmark £3.7bn — -4.2%
Canada £5.3bn — -15.7%
China £22.8bn — 4%
US £28.5bn — -1.5%
Hong Kong £7.2bn — -6.3%
UK imports (total £306bn)
Russia £4.5bn — -33.5%
Ireland £12.2bn — 1.7%
Poland £4.6bn — 8.7%
Turkey £4.3bn
India £4.3bn — 1.4%
France £20.2bn — -12.8%
Spain £9.1bn — -11.7%
Switzerland £5.7bn — -3.9%
Belgium £14.8bn — -8.3%
Netherlands £21.2bn — -16.3%
Germany £39.1bn — -12%
Italy £12.0bn — -14.8%

What we buy

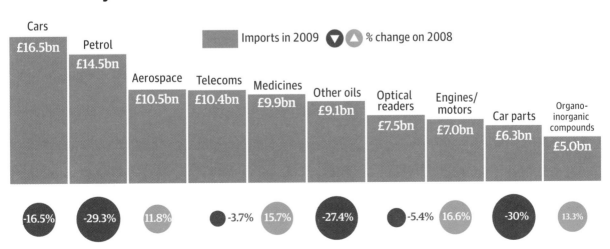

Imports in 2009   % change on 2008

Cars	Petrol	Aerospace	Telecoms	Medicines	Other oils	Optical readers	Engines/ motors	Car parts	Organo-inorganic compounds
£16.5bn	£14.5bn	£10.5bn	£10.4bn	£9.9bn	£9.1bn	£7.5bn	£7.0bn	£6.3bn	£5.0bn
-16.5%	-29.3%	11.8%	-3.7%	15.7%	-27.4%	-5.4%	16.6%	-30%	13.3%

Class facts
Education spending, pupil numbers and types of school

2.73m

Secondary school pupils forecast in the UK by 2014, down **5%** from 2009

9.5

Pupils per teacher in independent schools

26.2

Pupils per teacher in state primary schools, England & Wales, 2008

20.9

Pupils per teacher in state secondary schools, England & Wales, 2008

23.2

Pupils per teacher in state primary schools, Scotland, 2008. No secondary figures

16.7

Pupils per teacher across all state schools, Northern Ireland, 2009

Education spending
As a percentage of GDP, 1987-2009

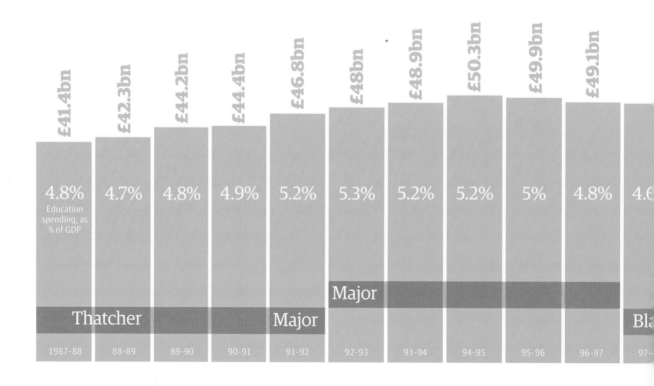

£41.4bn	£42.3bn	£44.2bn	£44.4bn	£46.8bn	£48bn	£48.9bn	£50.3bn	£49.9bn	£49.1bn
4.8% Education spending, as % of GDP	4.7%	4.8%	4.9%	5.2%	5.3%	5.2%	5.2%	5%	4.8%	4.6
		Thatcher			Major	Major				Bla
1987-88	88-89	89-90	90-91	91-92	92-93	93-94	94-95	95-96	96-97	97-

68%

of state-maintained faith schools are Church of England schools

30%

of state-maintained faith schools are Catholic

54

state-maintained faith schools are non-Christian as of 2010: **38** Jewish; **11** Muslim; **4** Sikh; **1** Hindu

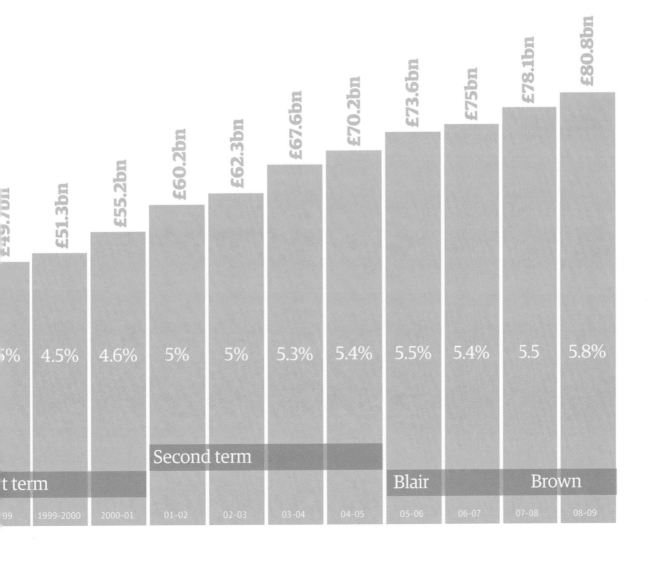

£49.7bn £51.3bn £55.2bn £60.2bn £62.3bn £67.6bn £70.2bn £73.6bn £75bn £78.1bn £80.8bn

5% 4.5% 4.6% 5% 5% 5.3% 5.4% 5.5% 5.4% 5.5 5.8%

First term | Second term | Blair | Brown

99 | 1999-2000 | 2000-01 | 01-02 | 02-03 | 03-04 | 04-05 | 05-06 | 06-07 | 07-08 | 08-09

HM Treasury publishes a guide to public spending every year. But if the number of phone calls we have to make to government press officers is any indication, getting hold of this data is becoming increasingly difficult. While the Treasury's reports are useful, what they don't give us is the granular breakdown of exactly where the money goes.

7.5%
of pupils taking computing A-level are girls. Physics, the second most male-dominated subject, has a **20.2%** female intake
SOURCE: DEPARTMENT FOR EDUCATION

It shouldn't be so hard. Each department publishes an annual report and accounts which break down its spending by type. Recently, those reports changed, with the new government abandoning old-style annual reports (regarded as PR jobs) in favour of new "resource accounts". The idea is that every government entity, from a Whitehall department down to an NHS trust, would produce a report in an identical format, using well-worn accounting standards. These would be bolstered with new business plans, which would list each department's achievements.

Said the manifesto: "We will scrap Labour's failed target regime and instead require every department to publish a business plan, with senior management accountable to more rigorous departmental boards for their performance."

Downturn or depression
How this recession compares

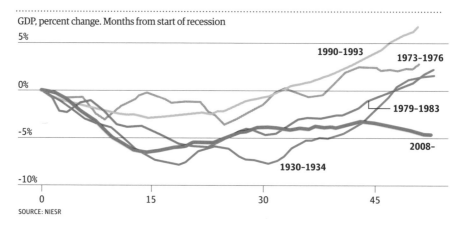

GDP, percent change. Months from start of recession

SOURCE: NIESR

It's part of the government's approach to something called the Whole Government

Accounts – the WGA. By being consistent across departments, the government claims to be making things simpler. In its guidelines, the Treasury says: "WGA is requiring bodies within the public sector to prepare data on a consistent basis. It is thereby improving the comparability of financial data."

It's a simple idea and it makes sense, at first glance. But it leads to the question: who are these reports actually for? If they are for the nation's accountants, then job done. If they are for the rest of us to find out the most crucial aspects of what each department actually spends its money (or should that be our money) on, then they are a colossal failure.

Here's why.

1. PDFs

Every single department publishes its annual resource account as a PDF. Those PDFs are full of tables, but not one department publishes these as a spreadsheet or any accessible format. This really matters because we then have to spend a long time extracting the data from each report. We don't want to do this by hand because we do not want to make mistakes. Presumably the departments themselves don't particularly care if we make a mistake or not; we do.

1,738

drugs-related deaths in 2008, the latest year for which figures are available. 374 were women. In 763 cases, an accidental overdose was the principal cause of death. 439 of them were aged 29 or under. Drug deaths have increased by 19% over the past decade – equivalent to an extra 281 deaths each year

18%

Increase in energy use by UK households in the last 40 years. Despite greener homes, and campaigns on insulation and energy use, domestic energy use is up from 37m tonnes of oil equivalent (mtoe) in 1970 to 44 mtoe in 2009, up 18%. We prefer our homes hotter now, up from an average of 14°C in 1971 to 17°C in 2008

2. Being consistent

Within each department's report is a set of core tables, including total departmental spending. These are really vital, not least because to work out how much each department spends on what, you have to add together capital and resource spending across what are called Departmental Expenditure Limits (DEL) and Annually Managed Expenditure

Budget 2012
George Osborne's tax and spending plans visualised

Borrowing

A jump in spending and collapse in tax receipts during the recession left the UK with shockingly high debts. The annual rise is moderating, but is likely to remain high for years to come, with each year's total adding inexorably to the national debt

£91br

Business rates
Business groups say a steep rise in rates after a freeze in 2010 has been made worse by a bureaucratic appeals system. Receipts are expected to hit £25bn in 2011/12 before moving to £26bn in 2012/13

VAT
The third biggest tax in terms of receipts after income tax and national insurance at around £100bn. A rise to 20% in January 2011 is expected to bring in an extra £13.4bn

Corporation tax
Only worth about 9% of total tax receipts, revenue from corporation tax is due to decline further after the chancellor said the rate will fall to 22% by 2014/15, at a cost of £1bn in that year compared to keeping it at the 28% rate the government inherited

Excise duties
Expected to raise £46bn in 2011/12, duties on beer and cigarettes have already gone up under this government. More rises are expected

National insurance
An emergency rise in national insurance in 2011, raising an extra £3bn a year, is not likely to be repeated after intense pressure from employers, despite rising unemployment restricting receipts to £101bn

Council tax
There is much talk of reforming the only tax on property, possibly creating new top tiers to capture million-pound homes. A freeze last year cost £630m, limiting receipts to £26bn

Income tax
The biggest element of government tax receipts, income tax has been hit by the steep rise in unemployment to 8.4%. A rise in income tax personal allowances will reduce receipts

Other – including stamp duty, vehicle excise duty
Stamp duty receipts from share trades and house-buying are expected to jump. A rise in petrol prices could still force the government to abandon a fuel duty increase planned for the autumn

26 Business rates

102 VAT

45 Corporation tax

48 Excise duties

106 National insurance

26 Council tax

155 Income tax

84 Other

In
£592b
Total receipts
2012/13

TEXT: PHILLIP INMAN
GRAPHIC: JENNY RIDLEY, SOURCE: IFS
Figures rounded

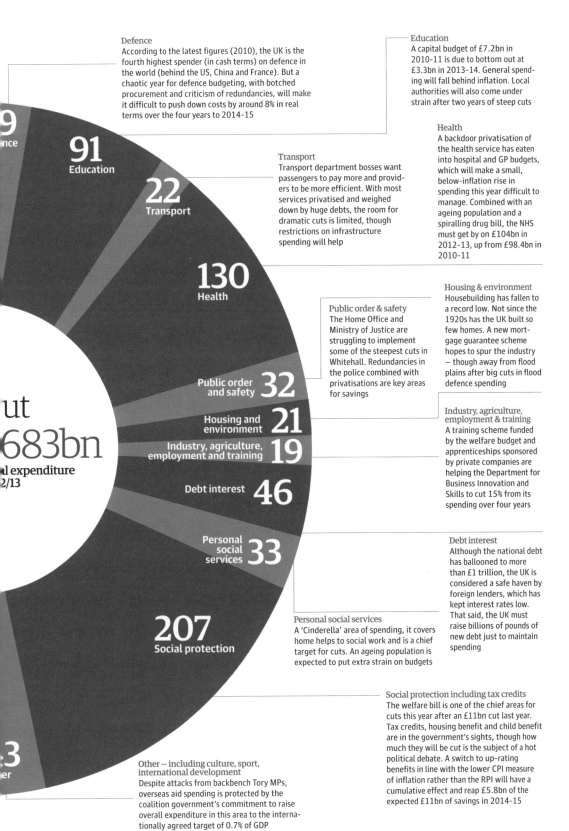

Defence
According to the latest figures (2010), the UK is the fourth highest spender (in cash terms) on defence in the world (behind the US, China and France). But a chaotic year for defence budgeting, with botched procurement and criticism of redundancies, will make it difficult to push down costs by around 8% in real terms over the four years to 2014-15

Education
A capital budget of £7.2bn in 2010-11 is due to bottom out at £3.3bn in 2013-14. General spending will fall behind inflation. Local authorities will also come under strain after two years of steep cuts

Health
A backdoor privatisation of the health service has eaten into hospital and GP budgets, which will make a small, below-inflation rise in spending this year difficult to manage. Combined with an ageing population and a spiralling drug bill, the NHS must get by on £104bn in 2012-13, up from £98.4bn in 2010-11

Transport
Transport department bosses want passengers to pay more and providers to be more efficient. With most services privatised and weighed down by huge debts, the room for dramatic cuts is limited, though restrictions on infrastructure spending will help

Public order & safety
The Home Office and Ministry of Justice are struggling to implement some of the steepest cuts in Whitehall. Redundancies in the police combined with privatisations are key areas for savings

Housing & environment
Housebuilding has fallen to a record low. Not since the 1920s has the UK built so few homes. A new mortgage guarantee scheme hopes to spur the industry — though away from flood plains after big cuts in flood defence spending

Industry, agriculture, employment & training
A training scheme funded by the welfare budget and apprenticeships sponsored by private companies are helping the Department for Business Innovation and Skills to cut 15% from its spending over four years

Debt interest
Although the national debt has ballooned to more than £1 trillion, the UK is considered a safe haven by foreign lenders, which has kept interest rates low. That said, the UK must raise billions of pounds of new debt just to maintain spending

Personal social services
A 'Cinderella' area of spending, it covers home helps to social work and is a chief target for cuts. An ageing population is expected to put extra strain on budgets

Social protection including tax credits
The welfare bill is one of the chief areas for cuts this year after an £11bn cut last year. Tax credits, housing benefit and child benefit are in the government's sights, though how much they will be cut is the subject of a hot political debate. A switch to up-rating benefits in line with the lower CPI measure of inflation rather than the RPI will have a cumulative effect and reap £5.8bn of the expected £11bn of savings in 2014-15

Other — including culture, sport, international development
Despite attacks from backbench Tory MPs, overseas aid spending is protected by the coalition government's commitment to raise overall expenditure in this area to the internationally agreed target of 0.7% of GDP

91 Education
9 [Defence]
22 Transport
130 Health
32 Public order and safety
21 Housing and environment
19 Industry, agriculture, employment and training
46 Debt interest
33 Personal social services
207 Social protection

ut
683bn
expenditure
2/13

3 [Other]

Austerity hits flood preparations
How spending cuts halted projects in 2012

Changes in flood defence funding by Regional Flood and Coastal Committee and projects deferred or cut

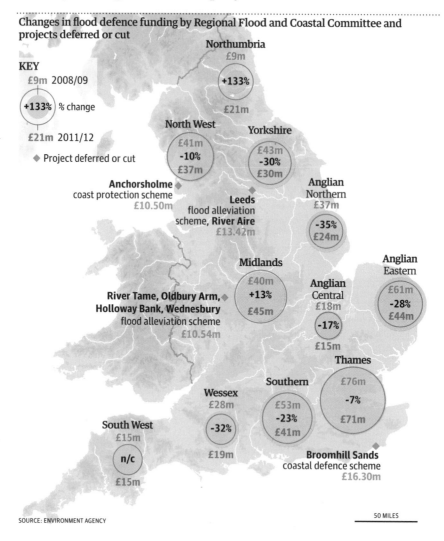

KEY

£9m 2008/09

+133% % change

£21m 2011/12

◆ Project deferred or cut

Northumbria
£9m
+133%
£21m

North West
£41m
-10%
£37m

Yorkshire
£43m
-30%
£30m

Anglian Northern
£37m
-35%
£24m

Anglian Eastern
£61m
-28%
£44m

Midlands
£40m
+13%
£45m

Anglian Central
£18m
-17%
£15m

Thames
£76m
-7%
£71m

Wessex
£28m
-32%
£19m

Southern
£53m
-23%
£41m

South West
£15m
n/c
£15m

Anchorsholme ◆
coast protection scheme
£10.50m

Leeds
flood alleviation
scheme, **River Aire**
£13.42m

River Tame, Oldbury Arm, ◆
Holloway Bank, Wednesbury
flood alleviation scheme
£10.54m

Broomhill Sands ◆
coastal defence scheme
£16.30m

SOURCE: ENVIRONMENT AGENCY

50 MILES

The Environment Agency publish data on flood prevention projects. But unfortunately for people who like to use data, the Environment Agency do not provide enough information to answer questions such as how this funding has changed over time. The Guardian Environment team collated all the information released and helped produce this graphic. They were assisted by a question asked in the House of Commons which revealed that 137 flood and coastal erosion schemes in the planning stage had yet to be awarded. Of these, 38 schemes have either not yet started or will no longer proceed, and one scheme was reclassified as primarily delivering navigation benefits.

(AME). Nominally, these are the "Total Departmental Spending" tables, but in fact, these are barely even given the same labels from one report to another, so finding these in the mass of the report takes time and has to be done by hand. When we do find these, to get the real specifics we often have to look elsewhere within a report – but not always: it changes from document to document.

67.4

The number of pregnant teenagers per 1,000 15–17-year-olds in Blackpool – the highest rate in England and Wales. The lowest is in Windsor & Maidenhead at 11.4. In fact, the teen pregnancy rate for 2009 (of 38,259 girls aged 18 or younger in England and Wales) was at its lowest since the early 1980s

SOURCE: ONS

3. Beyond compare

You cannot compare one year's report with another (as anyone who has one or more of our spending wallcharts will have spotted). This is because pretty much every year, each department shifts its spending around and changes the way it counts things. This is why we always just show the latest financial year and use the figures for the previous year given in the same report, but this also means…

4. Measuring different things

…each year we have to show different things for each department, because each year's report is completely different. Often the reports' specifics have been replaced with general aims which are so broad as to mean nothing.

5. They don't match other government data

This government has certainly not been shy in producing huge amounts of spending data: COINS, spending over £25,000 and so on. But try and use that data to cross-reference with these numbers and it quickly becomes apparent that the two are entirely incomparable. How departments get from one to the other remains a mystery, possibly to the departments themselves.

Who knows how much public money was spent

4,971

Britons needing consular assistance in Spain in the year to March 2011, out of 19,228 calls for help received by the UK Foreign & Commonwealth Office. Total arrests abroad in the same period reached 5,700 – a reduction from 6,439 in 2009/10. Arrests of Britons for drugs offences overseas were 799 – almost 20% down on 2009–10

SOURCE: FCO

Teachers' pay

How selected OECD
countries pay their
teachers, 2009

$x Starting salary for a newly qualified
secondary school teacher

$x Per capita GDP
of country, 2009

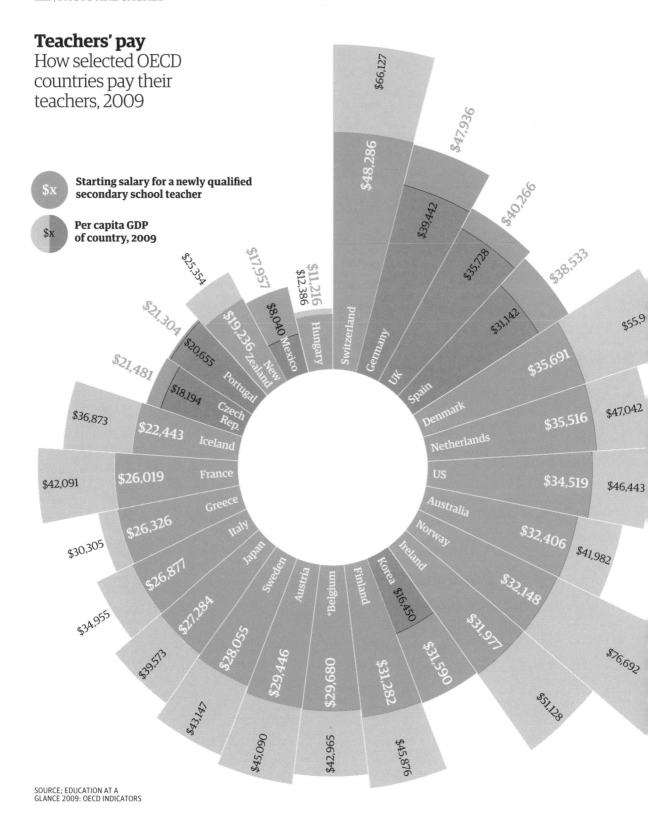

Switzerland $66,127 / $48,286
Germany $47,936 / $39,442
UK $40,266 / $35,728
Spain $38,533 / $31,142
Denmark $55,9... / $35,691
Netherlands $47,042 / $35,516
US $46,443 / $34,519
Australia $41,982 / $32,406
Norway $51,128 / $32,148
Ireland $76,692 / $31,977
Korea $45,876 / $31,590
Finland $31,282 / $42,965
Belgium $29,089 / $45,060
Austria $29,446 / $43,147
Sweden $28,055 / $39,573
Japan $26,877 / $34,955
Italy $26,326 / $30,305
Greece $26,019 / $42,091
France $22,443 / $36,873
Iceland $18,194 / $21,481
Czech Rep. $20,655 / $21,304
Portugal $19,236 / $25,354
New Zealand $8,040 / $17,957
Mexico $11,216 / $12,386
Hungary $16,450

SOURCE; EDUCATION AT A
GLANCE 2009: OECD INDICATORS

Private education
How the UK compares to
other OECD nations in private
involvement in education, 2009

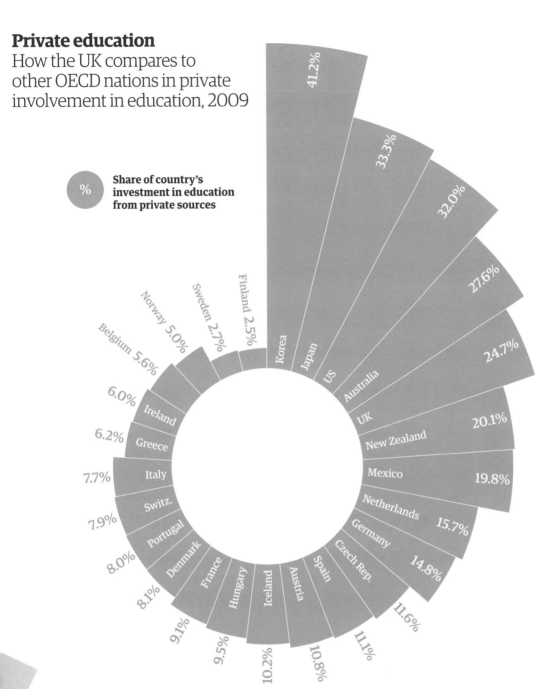

% **Share of country's
investment in education
from private sources**

Korea 41.2%
Japan 33.3%
US 32.0%
Australia 27.6%
UK 24.7%
New Zealand 20.1%
Mexico 19.8%
Netherlands 15.7%
Germany 14.8%
Czech Rep. 11.6%
Spain 11.1%
Austria 10.8%
Iceland 10.2%
Hungary 9.5%
France 9.1%
Denmark 8.1%
Portugal 8.0%
Switz. 7.9%
Italy 7.7%
Greece 6.2%
Ireland 6.0%
Belgium 5.6%
Norway 5.0%
Sweden 2.7%
Finland 2.5%

The wage gap
How CEO pay compares to workers' pay

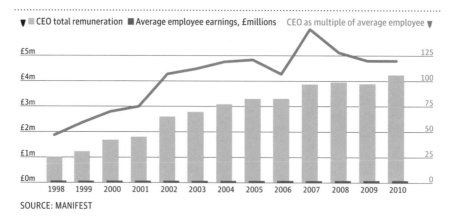

▼ ■ CEO total remuneration ■ Average employee earnings, £millions   CEO as multiple of average employee ▼

| | 1998 | 1999 | 2000 | 2001 | 2002 | 2003 | 2004 | 2005 | 2006 | 2007 | 2008 | 2009 | 2010 |

SOURCE: MANIFEST

finding out the key numbers for us – data that should have been published anyway?

And what are these reports for? They garner no publicity; very few people actually look at them. Are they just to allow departments to say they've hit their targets and published what they're supposed to publish each year?

"Because sunlight is the best disinfectant, we will bring the operation of government out into the open so that everyone can see whether we are delivering good value for money," said the Conservatives' transparency manifesto.

Yet finding out about the most basic operation of government is more difficult than ever. And there seems to be no incentive for this most basic operation to improve. Effectively, they can publish ever more obscure accounts every year for ever more – without any repercussions.

Maybe we need some more disinfectant.

20%
Gap in university achievement for babies born in August. They are 20% less likely than those born 11 months earlier, in September, to end up going to Russell Group universities – the top flight that includes Oxford and Cambridge. They were more likely to study vocational courses instead

SOURCE: IFS

How you can find out UK public spending

Fancy doing this for yourself? This is how we put it together. The first thing to do is to find each department's annual resource accounts, which come out in July each year. They give you the figures you want, just not in the format you need. Government departmental spending is split into four parts:

Departmental Expenditure Limits (DEL) – capital
Departmental Expenditure Limits (DEL) – resource
Annually Managed Expenditure (AME) – capital
Annually Managed Expenditure (AME) - resource

Add those four together and you get the department's total spending – in most of the resource accounts, this is table 1 of the core tables, always labelled Total Departmental Spending. Most of them now sum up the department's totals but not the totals for individual projects. So, you need to add together those four numbers, the resource and capital DEL and AME figures for each project.

The new departmental resource accounts, which are designed to be read by accountants, as opposed to the general public, have made this process harder.

When you get the two figures, you may want to work out the %-change including inflation – which makes small increases effectively a cut in spending. Thanks to Gemma Tetlow of the Institute for Fiscal Studies, here's how to do it:

Inflation-adjusted changes are calculated by deflating the cash spending figures by the change in the GDP deflator, which is

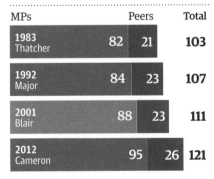

Growing government
Number of paid government posts

	MPs	Peers	Total
1983 Thatcher	82	21	**103**
1992 Major	84	23	**107**
2001 Blair	88	23	**111**
2012 Cameron	95	26	**121**

SOURCE: DEMOCRATIC AUDIT & HOUSE OF COMMONS

The real cost of PFI
Public-private finance initiative repayments

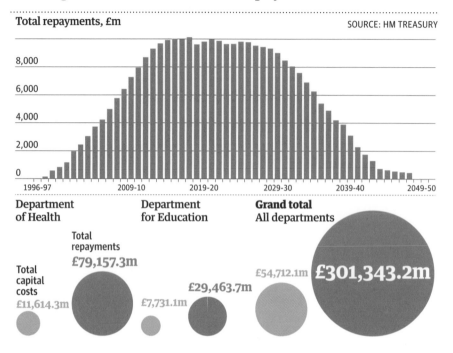

Total repayments, £m

SOURCE: HM TREASURY

8,000

6,000

4,000

2,000

0

1996-97   2009-10   2019-20   2029-30   2039-40   2049-50

Department of Health

Total repayments
£79,157.3m

Total capital costs
£11,614.3m

Department for Education

£29,463.7m

£7,731.1m

Grand total
All departments

£54,712.1m **£301,343.2m**

---

available from HM Treasury. Inflation between 2010–11 and 2011–12 was 2.38%. So:

Total spending figures (Total Managed Expenditure, in nominal terms) were as follows:

2010–11 = £689.634bn

2011–12 = £694.888bn

Real change in total spending was -1.58%, calculated as:

2011–12 spending, in 2010–11 prices = 694.888/(1+2.38/100) = £678.734bn

[where 2.38% is economy-wide inflation between 2010–11 and 2011–12]

% real growth in total spending = 100*(678.734/689.634-1) = -1.58%

433

Murder victims under the age of 20 in London between 2006 and 2011. The UK has around **600** murders a year, and the capital annually accounts for 100–150 of those. The worst two boroughs for murders are also two of London's poorest: Lambeth in the south and Newham in the east

SOURCE: METROPOLITAN POLICE

Data in the news: UK court records

More than a million detailed individuals' court records released by the Ministry of Justice are an unprecedented exercise in open data – especially for a courts system long criticised for operating a Victorian method of closed information.

The database itself comprises 1.2m cases sentenced in 322 magistrates' and Crown courts in England and Wales. The defendant's name is not included but details such as age, ethnicity, type of offence and sentence are. Having access to those details allows anyone with a computer to find out how those sentences break down – you can see how many white people are sentenced to jail for driving offences, and how old they are, for instance.

"Open justice is a long-standing and fundamental principle of our legal system. Justice must be done and must be seen to be done if it is to command public confidence," the then-justice secretary Kenneth Clarke said. "Modern technology allows us to be more open. This government has ambitious plans to increase transparency at every stage to allow everyone to see what is happening better and how the system works."

We spend a considerable amount of money on courts and yet they are in danger of becoming an elitist enclave, out of touch ... unless the results of what happens in them are shared openly

Heather Brooke, campaigner

Details of every offence and every defendant have long been recorded by every court in the country – their analysis is how the Ministry of Justice manages to publish figures showing length of sentences or what happens to cases. Traditionally court reporters have had access to individual records, but printed on paper as court listings for the day. Names, ages and even addresses of defendants amount to public information under the law, except in youth cases where their identity is protected.

The Guardian's Reading the Riots study is based on magistrates' court

Defendants and the courts, 2011
How millions enter the criminal justice system each year, England and Wales

More than two million people were sentenced in the courts of England and Wales in 2011. A huge Ministry of Justice data release in June 2012 showed what happened to them. The figures include those sentenced for the August 2011 riots

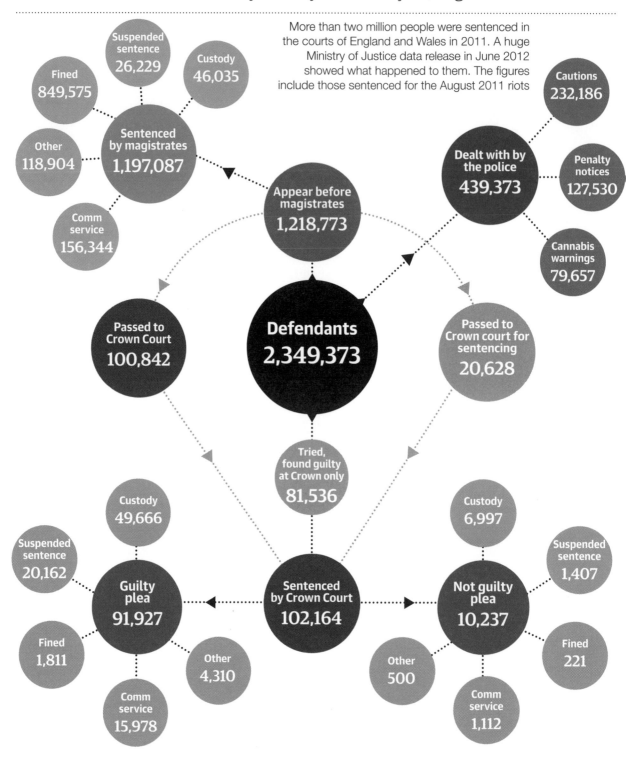

Fined 849,575

Suspended sentence 26,229

Custody 46,035

Cautions 232,186

Other 118,904

Sentenced by magistrates 1,197,087

Dealt with by the police 439,373

Penalty notices 127,530

Comm service 156,344

Appear before magistrates 1,218,773

Cannabis warnings 79,657

Passed to Crown Court 100,842

Defendants 2,349,373

Passed to Crown court for sentencing 20,628

Tried, found guilty at Crown only 81,536

Custody 49,666

Custody 6,997

Suspended sentence 20,162

Guilty plea 91,927

Sentenced by Crown Court 102,164

Not guilty plea 10,237

Suspended sentence 1,407

Fined 1,811

Other 4,310

Other 500

Fined 221

Comm service 15,978

Comm service 1,112

data. The courts initially refused to release this public information until directed to do so by the MoJ. It now forms the basis of a major report with the London School of Economics.

The transparency campaigner William Perrin, who advises the MoJ on opening up its data, says the release was a big step: "Publishing the details of each sentence handed down in each court is a great leap forward for transparency in the UK for which MoJ should be warmly praised. Courts have to be accountable to the local populations they serve."

The Freedom of Information writer and journalist Heather Brooke agrees: "We spend a considerable amount of money on courts and yet they are in danger of becoming an elitist enclave, out of touch with the general public unless the results of what happens in them are shared openly with the public. Until now, court results were kept secret for no good reason. This is a good first step but there is a long way to go to make the courts relevant to society again."

But Perrin, like some campaigners, believes the MoJ should go further, releasing the names of defendants too. "The data published is anonymised, flying in the face of hundreds of years of tradition of open courts and 'public justice,'" he says. "The MoJ need to have an open and public debate about the conflict between the central role in our society of open public courts where you can hear the name and details of offenders read out in public and crude misapplication of data protection."

Administering justice
Ethnicity and gender of judges, England & Wales

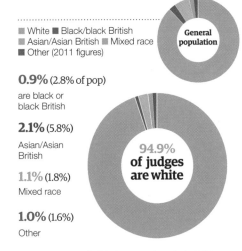

■ White ■ Black/black British
■ Asian/Asian British ■ Mixed race
■ Other (2011 figures)

General population

0.9% (2.8% of pop)
are black or black British

2.1% (5.8%)
Asian/Asian British

1.1% (1.8%)
Mixed race

1.0% (1.6%)
Other

94.9%
of judges are white

22.3% of all judges are female but this proportion falls at a senior level

Appeal court judges (37)   33   4

Supreme court judges (12)   11   1

SOURCE: LORDS CONSTITUTION COMMITTEE

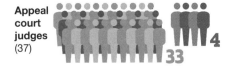

2,056,358

people were fined or tried with crimes in the 12 months to June 2011 – twice the population of Birmingham, and 1 in 31 people in the UK. A quarter of them were dealt with by police through fixed penalty notices and cannabis fines. Magistrates' courts tried the vast majority

SOURCE: MINISTRY OF JUSTICE.

Data in the news:
Is it really 99% vs 1%?

17

of the 50 states in the US experienced rises in the number and percentage of people in poverty between 2010 and 2011. For 10 of those states it was the third consecutive annual rise. Median household income declined in 18 states and rose in just one, Vermont

SOURCE: US CENSUS BUREAU

"99% vs 1%". It became the rallying cry of the Occupy Wall Street movement and the Occupy protests around the world. It's a really good example of how a bit of data enters the popular imagination, becoming part of the debate. Protesters from Wall Street to St Paul's have carried banners declaring this to be true. But is it?

The data does show that some people have done better out of America's economic booms of the last 20 years than others, as a report from the Congressional Budget Office shows. It looked at US incomes between 1979 and 2007, a period covering the America of Ronald Reagan, both Bushes and Bill Clinton. It found that over that time income grew by 275% for the top 1% of households and 18% for the bottom fifth. It also found that the share of in-

The wealth divide by race
Assets of middle-income families, 1984-2007

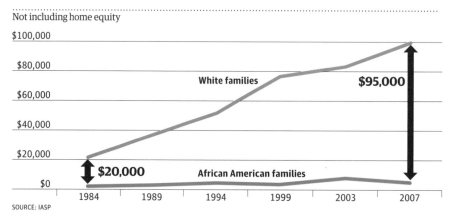

Not including home equity

A study by Brandeis University found that even high-income African-American families were less likely to accumulate assets than white families because tax deductions on inheritances, mortgages, and retirement and college savings disproportionately benefited white families. Black families were much more likely to be offered high-cost mortgage deals, which meant the home foreclosure crisis of the past five years hit them hardest   SOURCE: IASP

Occupy around the world
From Wall Street demo to lasting protest, autumn 2011

Estimated number of protesters still in cities

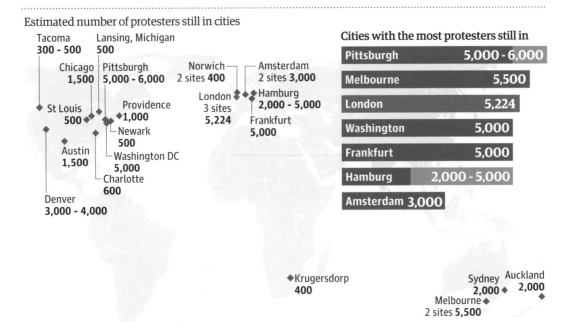

Tacoma	Lansing, Michigan
300 - 500	**500**

Chicago **1,500**

Pittsburgh **5,000 - 6,000**

Norwich 2 sites **400**

Amsterdam 2 sites **3,000**

London 3 sites **5,224**

Hamburg **2,000 - 5,000**

St Louis **500**

Providence **1,000**

Frankfurt **5,000**

Newark **500**

Austin **1,500**

Washington DC **5,000**

Charlotte **600**

Denver **3,000 - 4,000**

Krugersdorp **400**

Sydney **2,000**

Auckland **2,000**

Melbourne 2 sites **5,500**

Cities with the most protesters still in

Pittsburgh	5,000 - 6,000
Melbourne	5,500
London	5,224
Washington	5,000
Frankfurt	5,000
Hamburg	2,000 - 5,000
Amsterdam	3,000

come going to higher-income households rose, while the share going to lower-income households fell.

But when Americans are asked how US wealth is distributed, they think the very richest fifth own up to 40% of the national wealth – that includes 90% of Republicans surveyed.

In fact, that richest group owns 85% of the nation's wealth. Those surveyed also thought the bottom 120 million people own around 10% of the national wealth. The reality: 0.3%.

The super-rich – the top 0.01% of the population – own more of the national wealth now than at any time since 1928, just before the Great Depression. And the richest 1% of the US population? They own a third of US net worth.

In Bill Clinton's boom of 1993–2000, average incomes went up, just as they did during George W. Bush's boom at the beginning of his presidency. But if you were rich, you gained even

951

Number of Occupy protests in 82 countries on one day in October 2011. The protests began with Occupy Wall Street in New York City, on 17 September 2011. The protest movement continued well into 2012 despite evictions

SOURCE: OCCUPY MOVEMENT

Land of the free
The key facts about inequality in the United States

−1.3%

The fall in median household income in the US between 2010 and 2011, from $51,144 to $50,502, according to the American Community Survey. This figure disguises large regional variations: 27 states have a lower figure than the average, the lowest being $36,919 in Mississippi

46.2m

The number of Americans living below the poverty line in 2010 – **one in seven** of the population. Of every **17** Americans, at least one will be earning below the minimum wage of **$7.25** per hour

14.5%

The percentage of Americans households are defined as "food insecure". That means for every seven households, one will have trouble putting enough food on the table

20.5m

This represents the **6.7%** of the US population which makes up the poorest poor, defined as those at 50% or less of the official poverty level. In 2010 the poorest poor had an income of **$5,570** or less for an individual, and **$11,157** for a family of four. That 6.7% share is the highest in the 35 years that the Census Bureau has maintained such records

SOURCES: US CENSUS BUREAU; FORBES; IRS

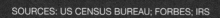

3.1m

Number of millionaires in America as of 2010, up from 2.86m the previous year and above the pre-crash levels of 3m. Around 40,000 of these are worth more than $30m. **63%** of North American millionaires are men, and **37%** are women

34.6%

The share of the US net worth which is owned by the richest 1% of the population. The richest 20% of the population control **85%** of the US's wealth. The bottom 40% own just **0.2%** of the vast wealth of the US...

400

billionaires in the US. In the Forbes survey of the world's richest people, 11 of the top 20 are American. At no2 is Bill Gates of Microsoft, whose wealth increased $2bn to **$61bn** between 2010 and March 2012. Third is investor Warren Buffett, now worth **$44bn**, up $5bn in two years. In sixth place is Larry Ellison of Oracle, worth **$33bn** (up $3bn in two years)

$19.6bn

Taxes paid by the wealthiest 400 households in America in 2008. This represents **1.9%** of all the income tax collected by the IRS. Americans earning between $100,000 and $200,000 pay an effective tax rate of **25%** before payroll taxes. The 400 richest tax returns surveyed by the IRS in 2008 paid an effective tax rate of **18.1%** in 2008

-4%

Drop in the income of the wealthiest 400 households between 2006 and 2008

-10%

Drop in average income for the 24 million least wealthy households in America, from **$12,276** in 2006 to **$11,034** in 2010

The assets of the 1% vs middle-class America
Why the housing crash hit ordinary Americans so hard

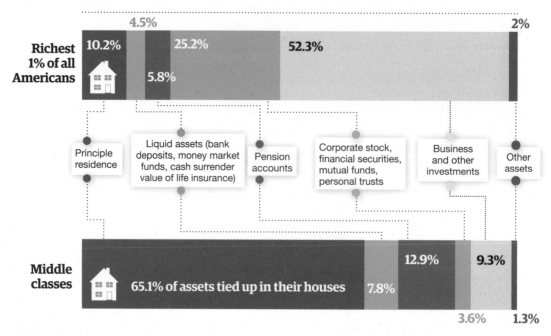

more: nearly half of all the growth in the Clinton boom years. Under George W. Bush it was 65%.

There are now over 3.1m millionaires in the US, and over 400 billionaires – more than any other country in the world. Who's at the top of that pile? Bill Gates, with a net worth of $59bn, Warren Buffett ($39bn), Lawrence Ellison ($33bn). That's just over the combined budget shortfall of every state in the US for 2011.

In 2010, the average American earned $26,487 – down over $2,000 in real terms on 2006. That's a drop of 5.27%, including inflation. If you were poor it's been an even bigger drop – the 24 million least wealthy households in America saw their average income go down by 10%, from $12,276 in 2006 to $11,034 in 2010.

21%

of children in the United States were in poverty in 2008, according to the OECD – higher than the OECD average and 7m children under 18 years old were without health insurance in 2011. Obama's healthcare reforms will reduce this number

SOURCE: STANFORD UNIVERSITY;
US CENSUS BUREAU; OECD

Rising inequality
Who gets rich when the good times roll?

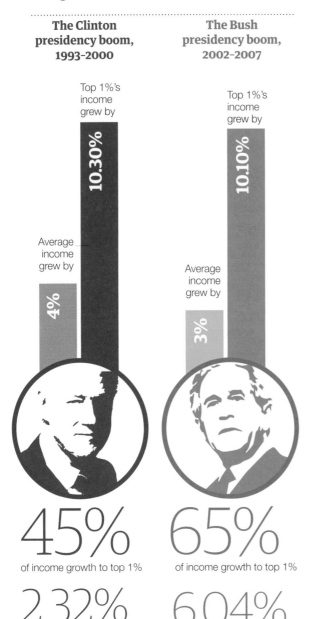

The Clinton presidency boom, 1993-2000

Top 1%'s income grew by

10.30%

Average income grew by

4%

The Bush presidency boom, 2002-2007

Top 1%'s income grew by

10.10%

Average income grew by

3%

45%
of income growth to top 1%

2.32%
Income share of the top 0.01% in 1993. It was 5.07% by the time Clinton left office

65%
of income growth to top 1%

6.04%
Income share of top 0.01% at the time of the 2007 financial crisis. Figure includes capital gains

SOURCES: SOURCE: PIKETTY AND SAEZ (2003); EMMANUEL SAEZ

If you were super rich it went down too. The 400 wealthiest American households lost around 4%, including inflation. Between 2006 and 2008 – the latest year we have the data – the richest 400's household income went down by 4% if you include inflation. That's to an average of $270.5m per household. Nearly 5,400 times the average household income in the United States.

Part of the reason average Americans have been hit so hard is where their wealth comes from. Before the crash, middle-class Americans had 65% of their wealth tied up in their house. But the richest 1% of the population kept most of their wealth in stocks and shares and business. So when house prices went south, many Americans found their wealth disappearing too.

Now, one in every seven Americans lives below the poverty line – that's a record 46.2 million people (although it might actually be higher):

● One in six Americans has no health insurance – 50 million people, a population twice the size of Texas (27m people).

● Of every 17 Americans, at least one will be earning below the minimum wage of $7.25 per hour.

● 14.5% of Americans households are defined as "food insecure". That means for every seven households, one will have trouble putting enough food on the table. Meanwhile, a Washington Post investigation found that: "Since the 1970s, median pay for executives at the nation's largest companies has more than quadrupled, even after adjusting for inflation, according to researchers. Over the same period, pay for a typical non-supervisory worker has dropped more than 10%"

What about taxes? The 400 wealthiest households paid $19.6bn in taxes in 2008, the latest year for which we have data. That's 1.9% of all the income tax the IRS collects. If you are in the top tax bracket, your tax rate is 35%. But it doesn't quite work like that. Imagine you are a billionaire and your income comes mostly from investments. Imagine you are Warren Buffett. You would end up paying a tax rate of under 20%. In fact, Buffett paid 17.4% tax last year. This is the "effective" tax rate.

47%

Percentage of the US population Republican Mitt Romney told wealthy donors were not his target because they did not pay federal income tax and believed they were "victims". The Tax Policy Centre says they are mostly poorer working families, who benefit from tax credits, and elderly people

SOURCE: REUTERS

If you earn between $100,000 and $200,000 you will be paying up to 25% effective tax rate – and that's before payroll taxes kick in. The 400 richest tax returns surveyed by the IRS paid just 18.1% in 2008. And it's got better for them. In 2001, as George W. Bush became president, that rate was 23%

So is it 99% vs 1%? The richest 1% of the US population own a third of US net worth. But an even smaller group, the 0.01% of the population, are at a record high. In fact, is it really 99.99% vs 0.01%? The top 0.01%'s share of the US national income stands at 5.37%, including capital gains. In Canada it's 3.95% and Germany, 2.9%.

Where would you fit?
Are you one of the 99.99%?
Or one of the 0.01%?

The data election: the US votes in 2012

538

Electoral college votes. The total stays the same, but population changes mean states have gained or lost votes since 2008

177,199,652

Americans registered to vote in the US. It's down 5% on 2008's 187m

$3.3bn

Amount spent on advertising during the campaign – up from $2.5bn in 2008

$11m

Spend on Spanish-language ads this campaign – eight times more than the previous general election. 10% of eligible voters are Hispanic

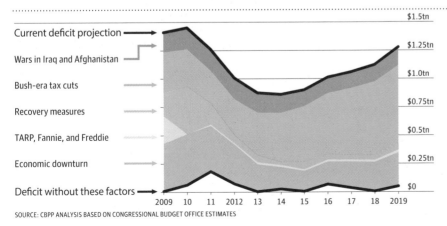

352

Days it would take to watch one million 30-second commercials

21

Record number of percentage points Obama has lagged behind Romney among white voters, according to a Washington Post/ABC News tracking poll

814,692

Number of retweets of Barack Obama's victory message – 'four more years' and the picture above – as of a week after the election. It was favourited 296,783 times during the same seven-day period

1.01m

Number of general election TV ads by both campaign teams and outside backers by late October this year, according to Kantar Media/CMAG

The big issue: economy and deficit
2009 projection and composition of deficit

Current deficit projection

Wars in Iraq and Afghanistan

Bush-era tax cuts

Recovery measures

TARP, Fannie, and Freddie

Economic downturn

Deficit without these factors

$1.5tn
$1.25tn
$1.0tn
$0.75tn
$0.5tn
$0.25tn
$0

2009 10 11 2012 13 14 15 16 17 18 2019

SOURCE: CBPP ANALYSIS BASED ON CONGRESSIONAL BUDGET OFFICE ESTIMATES

$1.16tn

The United States federal budget deficit, as of September 2012. The total is down 6% from $1.23tn in 2011

$16tn

The US federal debt in October 2012. It rose 74% in President Obama's first term

$632,177,42

Amount raised by Barack Oba
campaign by mid-October

$931.471n

Amount spent by Barack Obama and his suppor
on his campaign, according to opensecret

$17

Average donation by each of Ba
Obama's supporters to his campa

Foreign policy priorities, as reveale
word counts in the presidential del

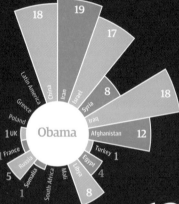

13

Field offices in Ol
the key swing st

50.1%

Ohio res

62,088,84

Votes for Obama, or 5
of the t

SOURCES: GUARDIAN ANALYSIS, PBS, KANTAR MEDIA, AP, FEC, HUFFINGTON POST, ABC NEWS?

389,088,268

...ed by Mitt Romney's campaign
... the same period

1.02bn

...ount spent by Mitt Romney and
...supporters on his campaign

617

...rage donation by each Mitt
...ney supporter to his campaign

...eign policy priorities, as revealed by
...d counts in the presidential debate

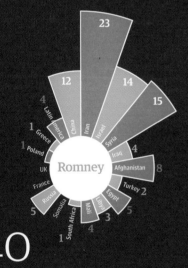

0

...d offices in Ohio,
...key swing state

8.2%

...result

8,783,137

...es for Romney, or
...7%

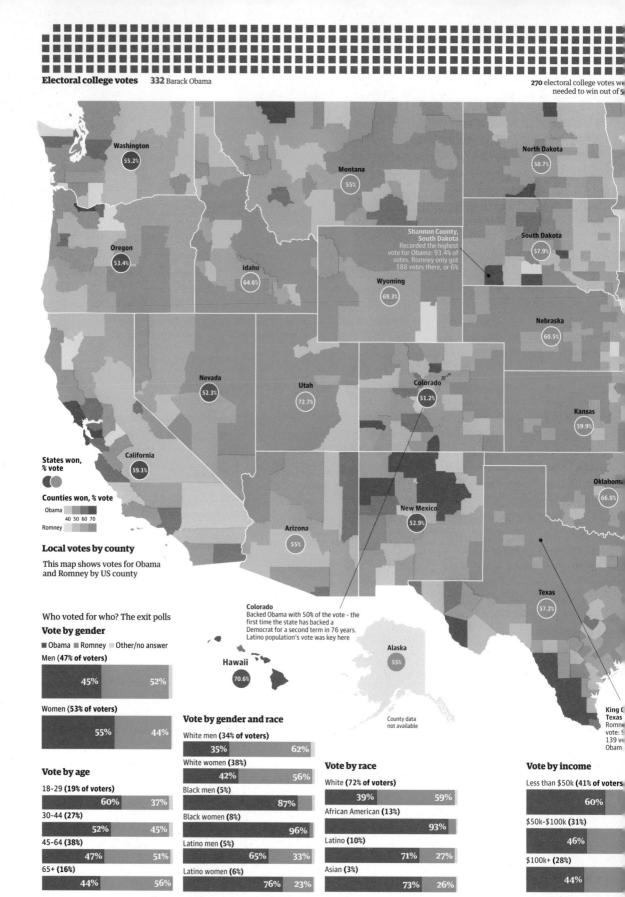

States won, % vote

Counties won, % vote

Obama

40 50 60 70

Romney

Local votes by county

This map shows votes for Obama and Romney by US county

Washington 55.2%
Oregon 53.4%
Montana 55%
North Dakota 58.7%
Idaho 64.6%
Wyoming 69.3%
South Dakota 57.9%
Nebraska 60.5%
Nevada 52.3%
Utah 72.7%
Colorado 51.2%
Kansas 59.9%
California 59.1%
New Mexico 52.9%
Oklahoma 66.8%
Arizona 55%
Texas 57.2%
Hawaii 70.6%
Alaska 55%

Shannon County, South Dakota
Recorded the highest vote for Obama: 93.4% of votes. Romney only got 188 votes there, or 6%

Colorado
Backed Obama with 50% of the vote - the first time the state has backed a Democrat for a second term in 76 years. Latino population's vote was key here

County data not available

**King C
Texas**
Romne
vote: 9
139 v
Obam

Who voted for who? The exit polls

Vote by gender

■ Obama ■ Romney ■ Other/no answer

Men **(47% of voters)**

| 45% | 52% |

Women **(53% of voters)**

| 55% | 44% |

Vote by age

18-29 **(19% of voters)**

| 60% | 37% |

30-44 **(27%)**

| 52% | 45% |

45-64 **(38%)**

| 47% | 51% |

65+ **(16%)**

| 44% | 56% |

Vote by gender and race

White men **(34% of voters)**

| 35% | 62% |

White women **(38%)**

| 42% | 56% |

Black men **(5%)**

| 87% |

Black women **(8%)**

| 96% |

Latino men **(5%)**

| 65% | 33% |

Latino women **(6%)**

| 76% | 23% |

Vote by race

White **(72% of voters)**

| 39% | 59% |

African American **(13%)**

| 93% |

Latino **(10%)**

| 71% | 27% |

Asian **(3%)**

| 73% | 26% |

Vote by income

Less than $50k **(41% of voters**

| 60% |

$50k-$100k **(31%)**

| 46% |

$100k+ **(28%)**

| 44% |

States won

Iowa
Voters gave Obama 52% of the vote. More than half of Iowa voters said the economy was the top issue facing the country, according to exit polling, and a fifth said the deficit was the top issue

Glenwood Plt, Maine
Smallest electorate with six voters. Four of them voted for Romney

New Hampshire
First battleground state win for Obama

Vermont 67%

Maine 56.3%

Wisconsin 52.7%

Michigan 53.7%

Ohio
Key swing state. Solid backing from blue collar workers after Obama's auto industry bailout

New York 62.7%

New Hampshire 52.2%

Massachusetts 60.9%

Pennsylvania 51.9%

Illinois 57.3%

Indiana 54.3%

Ohio 50.1%

Rhode Island 63.1%

Connecticut 57.9%

New Jersey 57.9%

West Virginia 62.3%

Delaware 58.6%

...ssouri 3.9%

Kentucky 60.5%

Virginia 50.7%

Maryland 61.2%

Tennessee 59.5%

North Carolina 50.6%

...kansas 60.5%

South Carolina 54.9%

Mississippi 55.4%

Alabama 60.7%

Georgia 53.4%

...siana ...5%

Electoral college votes won

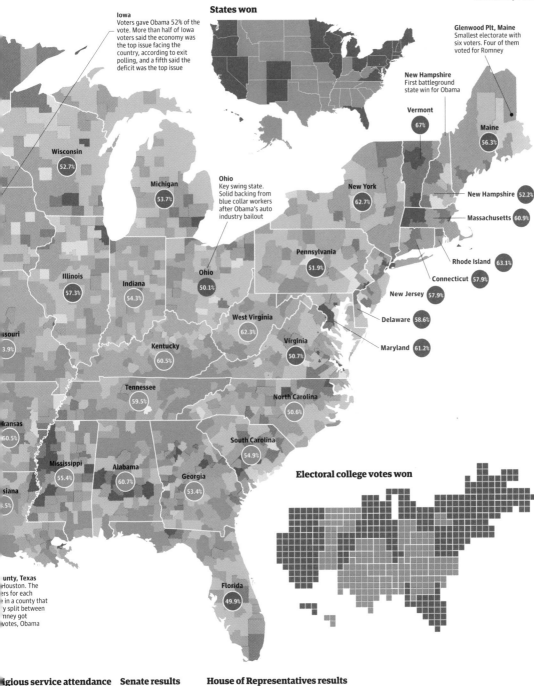

...unty, Texas
...ouston. The
...rs for each
... in a county that
... split between
...mney got
...votes, Obama

Florida 49.9%

...igious service attendance

...(42% of voters)

| 39% | 59% |

...nally (40%)

| 55% | 43% |

...17%)

| 62% | 34% |

Senate results

100 seats

53 Democratic seats
45 Republican seats
2 independents

House of Representatives results

435 seats

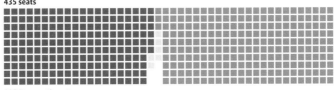

195 Democratic seats
234 Republican seats
6 open

How open journalism made our maps better

How can you get the colour scales right on maps? It's something we have spent a lot of time thinking about – and you may notice that we have tried out a huge variety of combinations. This isn't just design semantics – using the wrong colours can mean your maps are completely inaccessible to people with colour blindness, for instance, and actually obscure what you're trying to do.

It's distinct from the problems expertly faced by the Guardian graphics team – who, though they also experiment with colours, have a lot of experience of making stylish maps. But on the blog, making a Google Fusion map in a hurry, how can we get it right?

This came up when we created a map on poverty and deprivation in the capital, which was part of our London: the data series. We had been using the colour scale on the map shown right, which is a variation on the famous traffic light collection of colours: for the Guardian, this tends to go from green, meaning good or low, up to red, meaning bad or high. It's used by map makers and newspaper designers all the time. But is it any good?

This sparked a debate on Twitter, which led to a big conversation, and a mutual editing of the map's colours.

The main participants were:

● **Moritz Stefaner** (@moritz_stefaner), a freelance information visualiser, who blogs at *well-formed-data.net*;

● **Gregor Aisch** (@driven_by_data) of Driven by Data, an information visualisation architect whose work can be found at *vis4.net*;

● **Rutger van Waveren** (@RVW) who blogs at *waveren.com*

Poverty across London
The original map as it appeared online

... and a map for print using a similar colour scheme

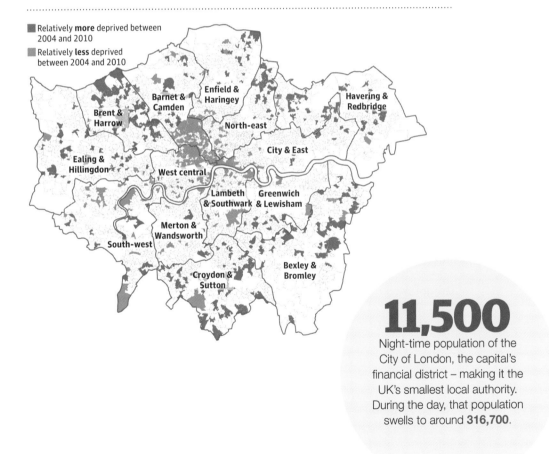

Relatively **more** deprived between 2004 and 2010

Relatively **less** deprived between 2004 and 2010

11,500
Night-time population of the City of London, the capital's financial district – making it the UK's smallest local authority. During the day, that population swells to around **316,700**.

The conversation

Gregor Aisch

Please, @datastore, take care of your choropleth maps! The colors used in the London poverty map is a complete fail

Retweeted by @ecolabs

@ljegou

RT @driven_by_data Please, @datastore, take care of your maps! The colors are a complete fail ... The white border, too.

Moritz Stefaner

@datastore @driven_by_data I am confused, too. The subleties in color choice are difficult enough, why start with failing at basics?

Simon Rogers

@driven_by_data @moritz_stefaner Actually, I really like that blend - we've been trying a lot of different scales but this is my favourite

Gregor Aisch

@smfrogers @moritz_stefaner the colors are misleading (the two reds), confusing (the blue) and not colorblind safe (green/red)

Simon Rogers

@driven_by_data @moritz_stefaner OK then, tweet me the hexcodes you would like to see for range and we'll try #opentochange

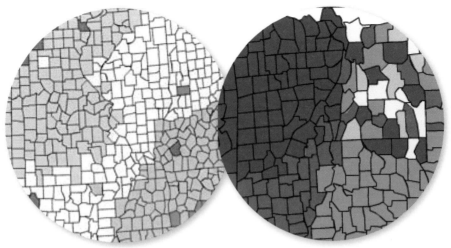

Left, the colorbrewer2.org map suggested by Gregor Aisch.
Right, a more monotone online map put forward by Rutger van Waveren

Gregor Aisch

@smfrogers @moritz_steiner this one is better #D01C8B, #F1B6DA, #F7F7F7, #B8E186, #4DAC26, taken from colorbrewer2.org

Simon Rogers

@driven_by_data I quite like it - but wouldn't the colour blind thing apply to green and pink?

Rutger van Waveren

@driven_by_data @smfrogers I don't like the colorpleth maps with many different colors. (I'm color blind) …

Rutger van Waveren

@smfrogers @driven_by_data we can see difference between green and pink ;) I'm red/green colorblind.

Gregor Aisch

@smfrogers no, according to the colour blindness simulator i'm using pink/green is fine. maybe because of the blue that's part of pink.

Simon Rogers

@driven_by_data @RVW @moritz_stefaner OK - try this … Not sure I like it as much but what does the world think?

Jérôme Cukier

@smfrogers @driven_by_data @RVW @moritz_stefaner +1 for the new version

Moritz Stefaner

@smfrogers @driven_by_data @rvw better! 2 questions remain - why a diverging scale for rank info - and why encode rank, not depr. value?

Moritz Stefaner

@smfrogers @driven_by_data @rvw 3rd: the bins have VERY different sizes.

Simon Rogers

@moritz_stefaner The value is a score, which is pretty meaningless - and is used to make the rank. It's all relative deprivation

Moritz Stefaner

@smfrogers yeah, but assuming a long tail distribution, same rank difference can correspond to quite different deprivation differences.

Simon Rogers

@moritz_stefaner The code means we can't say under 10 or over 10 - we have to pick a range, so we end up with top and bottom bins like that

Moritz Stefaner

@smfrogers Right now, the map looks like there is very little deprivation in London comp. to UK. (because of the bin size issue? or rly?)

Simon Rogers

@moritz_stefaner It's only London on this map

Gregor Aisch

@moritz_stefaner @smfrogers I'd say seq vs. diverging scale is an editorial choice. Sequential tells a different story

Moritz Stefaner

@driven_by_data @smfrogers think it is stronger indeed, but you should revert the scale on the deprivation rank map (lower rank = worse)

Gregor Aisch

@moritz_stefaner @smfrogers btw, I quite like the color choice in the original maps linked in the article

High ▬▬▬▬▬▬▬▬▬ Low

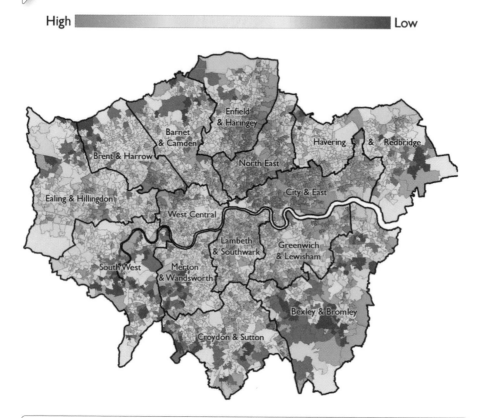

Rutger van Waveren

@datastore @driven_by_data @moritz_stefaner yes, these are better colors!

Gregor Aisch

@moritz_stefaner @smfrogers oh, that's something to avoid in general, if possible: 'a high deprivation rank means less deprived'

Tom MacInnes

@moritz_stefaner @smfrogers all else equal, 2/3 "should" be green, right (10k to 33k)? Looks a bit less than 2/3 maybe...

Nigel Hawtin

@JanWillemTulp @smfrogers @driven_by_data @RVW @moritz_stefaner agree colours +1 but too much of a difference between dark and light pink

Moritz Stefaner

@moritz_stefaner @smfrogers what do you think about just using the 'original' colors?

Simon Rogers

@driven_by_data Yep - it's better, isn't it?

Moritz Stefaner

@driven_by_data @smfrogers looking good! In an ideal world, now, the legend would be a rank-sorted chart showing the scores, and colors.

@smfrogers a la …

Moritz Stefaner

 @smfrogers @moritz_stefaner As a last tweak for today (promised) I removed the colors from the base map. More focused.

Gregor Aisch

 RT @driven_by_data: @moritz_stefaner OK, back to original - stronger, I think

Simon Rogers

 @smfrogers besides the color, the opacity of the borders (very white) is making it visually complex, @driven_by_data's version is calmer imo

Rutger van Waveren

@driven_by_data @smfrogers @moritz_stefaner
nice collaboration! The map definitely improves! :)

Jan Willem Tulp

@driven_by_data @moritz_stefaner @RVW
Thanks to all - some nice new styling I didn't
know about #openjournalism

Simon Rogers

@smfrogers @driven_by_data @rvw much better!
Thumbs up! !

Moritz Stefaner

@smfrogers @driven_by_data @moritz_stefaner
great conversation guys - there's surely a good
post in there

Mark Johnstone

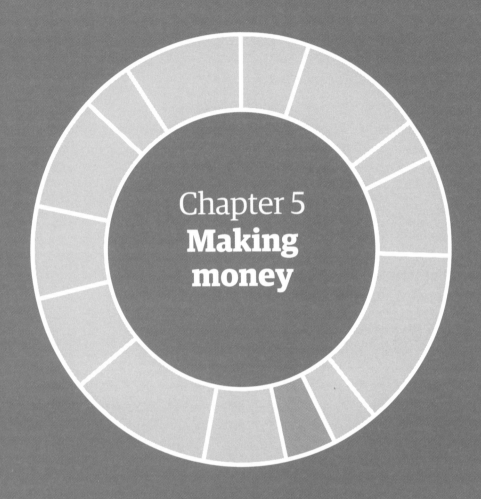

Chapter 5
Making money

Governments love data because publishing it can make them seem transparent. Big corporations, on the other hand, love it because it can make them money. While startups and new companies are desperately searching for ways to make cash from the data community, the most successful have woven it into their very existence.

It's all around the idea of big data – the huge exhaust of information that emerges from company operations. While the US Library of Congress has an enormous amount of data on its hard drives – 235 terabytes up to April 2011 – that pales into insignificance besides the amounts stored by companies. According to the latest figures, 15 out of 17 US business sectors have more data than this stored per company.

Of course, that carries risks for business: for some, data can be a threat. It was reported that Bank of America had recruited a group of lawyers as a kind of SWAT team in case WikiLeaks published secret documents it was said to have on the company. To date, nothing has emerged but the cost for the bank has obviously been a real one.

94%

Percentage of global data which was stored in digital form as of 2007. In 2000, just 25% of data was stored in analog forms – books, cassette tapes, audiotapes, video, photos. The shift to hard drives, CDs and other forms of digital storage continues

SOURCE: MCKINSEY GLOBAL INSTITUTE/SCIENCE

Every time you use a store loyalty card or download a music track or try out online dating, that information is stored and categorised. The companies that make this stuff work are those who use the data, let it lead their operations.

The numbers are huge: a disk drive that could store all the world's recorded music can now be bought for under $600; there are 5bn mobile phones in the world, which is 2bn short of enough for every man, woman and child on the planet; 30bn pieces of content are shared on Facebook every month.

Consultancy firm McKinsey provided the first official recognition of the phenomenon with a report published in spring 2011 which tried to quantify the worth of data to business – and to work out how it could grow. The firm predicted a 40% growth in global data per year. So the world of data reproduces itself every two years. If you think there's a lot of data around now, wait until the end of this decade.

The shift to internet entertainment
Online delivery tells companies about us

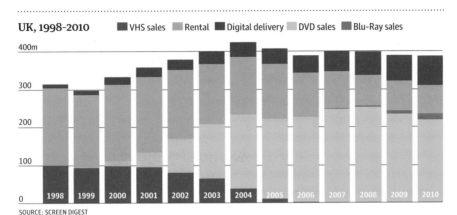

UK, 1998-2010 ■ VHS sales ■ Rental ■ Digital delivery ■ DVD sales ■ Blu-Ray sales

SOURCE: SCREEN DIGEST

"The amount of data in our world has been exploding and analyzing large data sets – so-called big data – will become a key basis of competition, underpinning new waves of productivity growth, innovation, and consumer surplus," said McKinsey. "Leaders in every sector will have to grapple with the implications of bigdata, not just a few data-oriented managers."

So where did this come from? Partly it's a result of the explosion in open data detailed in Chapter One. There is a climate now of working in information. But it's about more than that. Now we have an Internet of Things: products such as phones and tablets which collect increasing amounts of information from us as we make phone calls and use the net. It's a side-effect of Web 2.0: multimedia, social media – and business.

It's worth focusing on the McKinsey report briefly – as it has proved influential across the world of business, being passed from CEO to CEO to CEO across the world.

The group looked at the value of big data to very specific areas: US retail, where the proper use of data could increase operating margins by over 60%; US healthcare, with a potential of $300bn and an 8% cut in costs; Europe's government, which could save $149bn in efficiency improvements; and geotagged services,

2bn

Hours of movies and TV streamed by the online provider Netflix in the fourth quarter of 2011. It logs every time one of its 25m users worldwide rewinds, fast-forwards and pauses movies. **75%** of what users watch is chosen from a recommendation by the Netflix site based on its analysis of viewing patterns

SOURCE: MOHAMMAD SABAH, NETFLIX

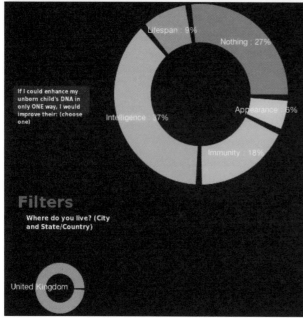

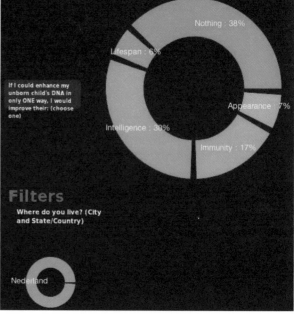

Screenshots from the Human Face of Big Data project, which uses a mobile phone app to collect data about ordinary people. It uses the passive tracking ability of phones to work out where people live and travel to, Bluetooth 'handshakes' to work out how many people they pass, and asks moral and ethical questions

Top, the constantly updating console from the website

Triangulating the results should reveal patterns of thought across the world, as well as offering the possibility of finding a 'data doppelganger' for each user – someone whose answers match yours. You can find out more at **humanfaceofbigdata.com**

Above, the mobile phone app

University Medical Practice
Tel No. 0118 9874551

Appointment Details

For: BROTHERTON, Charlotte
(Miss)
NHS #: 468 488 1415
Pt #: 1083176

Date: 12-Aug-2016
At: 5:30pm
With: Dr Anthony John Collins

Please let us know if you cannot
attend.

such as mobile phone operators, where it's worth a global $600bn. They calculated the total value of data to Europe's governments as €250bn – more than the GDP of Greece, putting the Eurozone's financial crisis into perspective.

The report has created a sensation in the business world, but will any of this actually happen?

Theoretically, yes. There's certainly enough data to go around. McKinsey reckons that every sector of the US economy had at least 200 terabytes of stored data per large company in 2009, the latest year for which data is available. By contrast, in 1999 supermarket chain Wal-Mart's data warehouse was half that size.

"The use of big data will become a key basis of competition and growth for individual firms," says McKinsey. "From the standpoint of competitiveness and the potential capture of value, all companies need to take big data seriously. In most industries, established competitors and new entrants alike will leverage data-driven strategies to innovate, compete, and capture value."

Just as governments are benefiting from greater transparency, so

2.9bn

Number of companies jointly or wholly owned by the top 100 British multinationals. 25% of them are located in jurisdictions classed as tax havens

SOURCE: ACTIONAID

Free and cheap
What net searches reveal about Britain's priorities

Most popular search terms containing "free"

1.11%	0.95	0.62	0.58	0.43	0.41	0.39	0.35	0.34	0.32
Free online games	Free games	Free music downloads	AVG free	Free SMS	Free BMD	Free	Free sex	Girls date for free	Free ads

Most popular search terms containing "cheap"

6.47%	5.47	1.11	0.60	0.46	0.38	0.36	0.34	0.30	0.30
Cheap flights	Cheap holidays	Cheap car insurance	Cheap travel insurance	Cheap hotels	Cheap laptops	Cheap package holidays	Cheap train tickets	Cheap loans	Cheap broadband

SOURCE: HITWISE

will business benefit by being open themselves. How much data stored by business really needs to be secret? The assumption that everything must be kept confidential serves no one well. It makes companies appear secretive and untrustworthy. Being open, on the other hand, only reinforces trust.

There's also an inevitable side effect of businesses storing their business financial data digitally. As the data is analysed, the nature of the business becomes more efficient, says McKinsey: "They can collect more accurate and detailed performance information on everything from product inventories to sick days."

It's about having another tool.

How does that work in practice? In Vodafone's operating centre in Newbury, Berkshire, England, the mobile phone company has a giant screen displaying every variable of its business – allowing it to know exactly how its customers use their phones. Had you been there after midnight on New Year's Eve, you would see numbers start flying across a bank of screens in a large darkened room. London: 1,170,000; Glasgow: 115,000; Manchester: 75,000; Leeds: 70,000…

A tech team clad in black look for signs that the system might not be able to cope. The figures represent the number of texts sent in the first 30 minutes of the year – pure data in action.

The company manages 90m calls and 80m texts on an average day; a typical 24 hours sees Vodafone carry 45 terabytes of data, equivalent to 11.25m music tracks.

4.4m

Tweets analysed by scientists from 630,000 Twitter users during an outbreak of flu in New York City in 2010. Their algorithm which perceived references to the outbreak and as a result analysts were able to predict up to eight days in advance who was at risk of getting flu. The success rate was 90%

SOURCE: UNIVERSITY OF
ROCHESTER, NY

Vodafone's approach is to use data to manage demand before things happen. Before the Royal Wedding in 2011 the company added extra temporary base stations to cope with heavy network usage. When Take That announced their reunion tour, and the band's official website crashed due to demand, Vodafone was prepared for the surge of fans texting one another to check whether they'd got their tickets.

One of the walls at Vodafone's operations centre shows connections to 217 countries to monitor how much traffic is coming in from abroad

901m

monthly active users by March 2012, up from just 1m in 2004. The site is now available to anyone over 12, in almost every country, in 70 languages

One in three of the estimated 2bn people in the world who are online has a Facebook account and half of these log in every day

30bn+

items of content are shared on the Facebook network, and on average every month each Facebook user creates 90 pieces of content

1 in 7

of the minutes spent online worldwide in October were spent on Facebook

23min

Facebook's users spent an average of 8.3 hours on the network per month, per person – 23 minutes per day

facebook
the data giant

1.6m

Number of top-of-the-range iPads it would take to store the 100 petabytes of information that Facebook stores

47

categories of information collected about you by Facebook so that it can sell targeted advertising. Printed out, it would total 1000+ pages for some users

15%

of users access Facebook on a mobile device. Its mobile ad business accounts for 15% of revenue. Online games such as Farmville by Zynga brought in 12% of revenues in 2011

3.74

Degrees of separation of the average user. This is down from 4.28 in 2008 – the only way in which the Facebook world is getting smaller

1 in 4

The average British 12–15-year-old has never met a quarter of their friends on Facebook, according to Ofcom research published in 2012

$1.26bn

revenues in the quarter that ended on 30 September 2012, despite a flotation on the stock market in May 2012 which disappointed financial analysts

SOURCES: FACEBOOK; OFCOM

in real time. The data shows that different cultures are "asymmetric", according to the company. Polish mothers text their sons in the UK to see if they're OK, but the sons don't text back. French people, by contrast, are almost symmetrical – as the texts go out, the replies come back in. As situations unfold in real time in Egypt or Bahrain, Vodafone can see how that affects the network too.

Even a bill being sent by email triggers a whole chain of data events: customers get bills; most open them; some have a query and call the centre. 40,000 bills go out an hour but if the centre gets hit with too many queries, billings are dialled down to reduce calls in.

And Vodafone is not alone. How does FedEx know how to get a package somewhere in the world within a day, or Amazon know to stock the right amount of each product – or run its "you might like this…" feature and not end up with a warehouse full of unsold, outdated stereos?

Other companies wouldn't exist without their data; certainly not in the same form. Experian, producer of credit ratings, is an obvious one, but rare in that its product is the raw data and its analysis. Tesco is another

You Tube

800m

Number of visitors to YouTube each month who watch more than **4bn** hours of video. **70%** of its traffic comes from outside the United States with **43** localised portals using **60** languages. **20%** of all views are on mobile devices as of 2011 and that number is increasing all the time

500

years of video are watched on Facebook each day and **700** videos are shared each minute. **72** hours of video are uploaded each minute. Targeted ads are sold based on viewing figures, location data, and the kind of content

820m

Number of plays of Gangnam Style by the Korean rapper Psy as of 25 November 2012, the weekend it broke the record for most YouTube plays ever. It is the most "liked" video of all time, inspiring scores of parodies which feature the dance, below

ALL, SOURCE: YOUTUBE TRENDS

GRAPH
MARK McCORM

Dating data
What internet sites reveal about the mating habits of the ordinary Briton, 2012

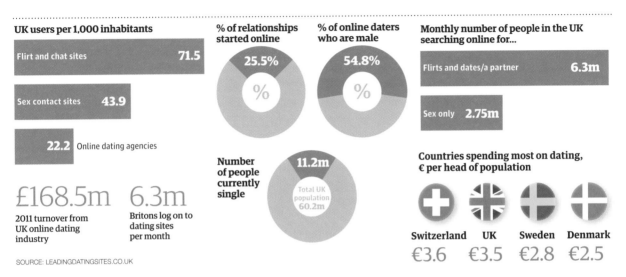

UK users per 1,000 inhabitants

Flirt and chat sites **71.5**

Sex contact sites **43.9**

22.2 Online dating agencies

£168.5m
2011 turnover from
UK online dating
industry

6.3m
Britons log on to
dating sites
per month

% of relationships started online
25.5%

Number of people currently single
11.2m
Total UK population 60.2m

% of online daters who are male
54.8%

Monthly number of people in the UK searching online for...

Flirts and dates/a partner **6.3m**

Sex only **2.75m**

Countries spending most on dating, € per head of population

Switzerland	UK	Sweden	Denmark
€3.6	€3.5	€2.8	€2.5

SOURCE: LEADINGDATINGSITES.CO.UK

example: the company records 1.5bn data points each month and its Clubcard is an example of something that makes money and changes market share.

For other newer companies, the product is based on the data instead, to create a seamless whole. Social connector LinkedIn has data woven throughout its operation, which means the company takes the personal information you enter when you create your profile and weaves it into new products and services. At one level this means the awareness to cater for how people describe themselves. In 2008, the trend was to call yourself a "guru", as in a "data guru". By 2009 that had been surpassed by "evangelist". Nowadays everyone is a "Jedi". Which are you?

The online dating company OKCupid is similarly aware of its users' activities, producing regular updates detailing which type of user pic is the most successful, the differences between male and female and black and white people's tastes. It has even worked out that iPhone users are more sexually

700,000
English language geotagged articles on Wikipedia. It compares to **24,000** in Arabic and **15,000** in Hebrew

SOURCE: OXFORD INTERNET INSTITUTE

active than either BlackBerry or Android owners.

Then you have Google, which bases its entire operation on data. The Google search, the local ads tailored to each market, Gmail's smart inbox – data is all-pervasive through the company's operations. Crucially, having access to big data means the company can start to segment its customers, i.e. tailor its services to individuals.

And with the data comes a need to make it more comprehensible. "A wealth of information creates a poverty of attention and a need to allocate that attention efficiently among the overabundance of information sources that might consume it," said the economist Herbert Simon. More sophisticated software and data visualisation techniques mean that big data gets more manageable. Combine that with new collaboration techniques which allow people in different places to work on the same information and you have a powerful combination.

Of course, the other side-effect of all this data could be something even more in demand at the moment: jobs. McKinsey reckons the US alone needs up to 190,000 deep analytical "data scientists" – the phrase of the moment for the big data analysts with the skills to exploit the numbers – by 2018. And 1.5 million data-savvy managers will be needed to make the effective decisions.

334

US astronauts trained since 1959. Although only **48** out of the 334 were female, three of the astronauts with the most hours in space are women: Peggy Whitson, Shannon Lucid and Susan J Helms have all spent more than 5,000 hours in space. Michael Fincke has spent **9,159** hours in space

SOURCE: NASA

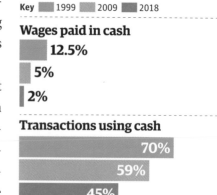

The card revolution
Changes in the way
we pay, 1999–2018

Key ■ 1999 ■ 2009 ■ 2018

Wages paid in cash

12.5%

5%

2%

Transactions using cash

70%

59%

45%

Cash spending in pubs

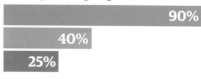

90%

40%

25%

Personal cheque transactions

6%

2%

0.8%

Debit card spending

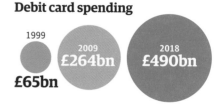

1999

2009
£264bn

2018
£490bn

£65bn

In practice: big data and its uses

J ournalists get size out of all proportion. To a hassled reporter, a spreadsheet with 1,000 lines can be overwhelming. But for a serious data analyst, something that size would barely raise an eyebrow. This is the rise of big data – and we're talking large datasets which often require sophisticated analysis to get the basics to emerge. So how big does it have to be to count as Big data?

Some analysts have a very simple rule of thumb: "if it's too big to go on one machine, then it's big data," says one.

McKinsey defines big data as "datasets whose size is beyond the ability of typical database software tools to capture, store, manage, and analyse."

This definition changes over time, too. We used to need a computer the size of a house to process the functions that can now be carried out on a smartphone – so the idea of what constitutes big data in future will be very different from today. A Sinclair ZX81, the home computer that thousands upon thousands of people had in the early 1980s, came with 1KB of memory – in 20 years, we will potentially be processing terabytes in our own home offices too.

McDonald's
420,000
employees worldwide, working in more than 34,000 restaurants in 120 countries. McDonald's Corp is headquartered in Oak Brook, Illinois, and was founded in 1940

Apple
72,000
employees worldwide, most of them working in the 250+ Apple stores in the US and the 140+ stores internationally *(as of 2012).* **It was founded in 1976 and has shifted from a computer maker to a producer of consumer electronics and a retailer. It is based in Cupertino, California**

Amazon
56,000+
employees worldwide, boosted by seasonal workers during the holiday period. It is the world's largest online retailer and has branched out into consumer electronics and film streaming. It was founded in 1994 and is headquartered in Seattle

Google
53,500+
employees worldwide, based out of Mountain View in California in a group of buildings called the 'googleplex'. It was founded in 1998

Starbucks
160,000
employees around the world, in more than 20,300 stores, 64% in the US, around 4% (793) in the UK *(2012).* **It was founded in 1971 and is headquartered in Seattle**

Facebook
4,330+
employees worldwide. Based in Menlo Park, California. Founded in 2004 by Harvard students

Big corporations and tax
US giants criticised by the public accounts committee for avoiding UK tax, 2012

McDonald's
£1,248.5m

● UK turnover, 201
● Profit before tax
● Tax paid
● Tax as % of turn

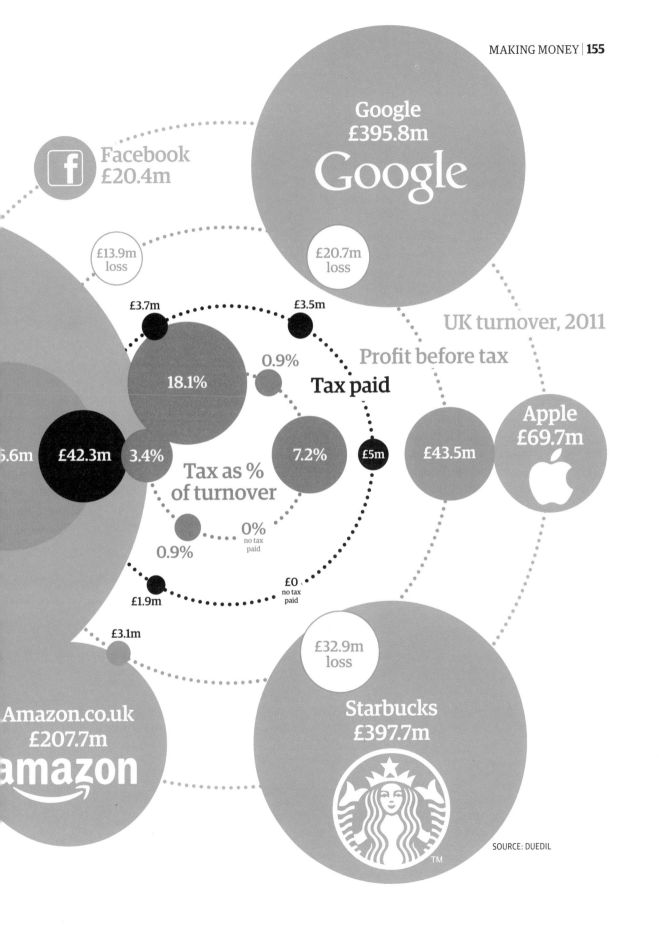

Facebook
£20.4m

Google
£395.8m
Google

£13.9m
loss

£20.7m
loss

UK turnover, 2011

Profit before tax

£3.7m

£3.5m

0.9%

Tax paid

18.1%

£42.3m

3.4%

7.2%

£5m

£43.5m

Apple
£69.7m

Tax as %
of turnover

0%
no tax
paid

0.9%

£1.9m

£0
no tax
paid

£3.1m

£32.9m
loss

Amazon.co.uk
£207.7m
amazon

Starbucks
£397.7m

SOURCE: DUEDIL

Chapter 6
**Measuring
happiness**

**What you'll find out
in this chapter:**

» Why GDP is a poor
measure of well-being
» Why the government
is spending £2m per
year to find out how
satisfied we are » The
gloomiest place in the
UK - and the happiest

Teaching British civil servants how to be happy is not what you'd expect from a Pennsylvania professor of psychology. But helping Whitehall understand well-being is precisely what Marty Seligman was doing in London.

Seligman has a history of getting into tricky places. The expert in positive psychology was hired by the US army to develop a "resilience program" to help soldiers cope better with the stress of combat. Now he's trying to help the rest of the world become content and satisfied. And governments are listening.

> You cannot capture happiness on a spreadsheet any more than you can bottle it ... if anyone was trying to reduce the whole spectrum of human happiness into one snapshot statistic I would be the first to roll my eyes
>
> **David Cameron, 2010 speech**

As recession bites the major economies hard, governments are trying to find new ways of judging their societies, not by the amount of money they generate but by the happiness and contentment of their citizens. The brightest minds are spending time, money and effort on trying to make something work they don't fully understand yet. "You cannot capture happiness on a spreadsheet," said the British Prime Minister David Cameron. But why bother?

Our lives are ruled by one measure, after all: Gross Domestic Product, or GDP. A recession, for instance, is defined as two consecutive quarterly falls in GDP – but what does that actually mean?

The idea of a single number to show a country's economic power

Britain's GDP
GDP per person, adjusted
for inflation 1955-2008

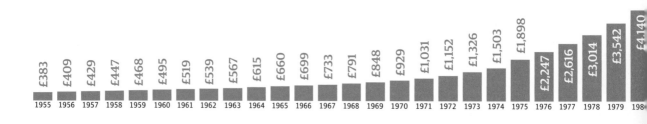

1955	1956	1957	1958	1959	1960	1961	1962	1963	1964	1965	1966	1967	1968	1969	1970	1971	1972	1973	1974	1975	1976	1977	1978	1979	198
£383	£409	£429	£447	£468	£495	£519	£539	£567	£615	£660	£699	£733	£791	£848	£929	£1,031	£1,152	£1,326	£1,503	£1,898	£2,247	£2,616	£3,014	£3,542	£4,140

came from one man, US economist Simon Kuznets. It was 1937, and the US was emerging from the hell of the Great Depression. Kuznets' idea, presented to Congress that year, was simple: measure all production by companies, people and government. That would produce a big number which represents everything the economy produces, so the US is worth $15 trillion, the UK $2.3 trillion and so on. It would go up in good times, and down in bad.

What GDP misses is almost more important than what it includes. Robert Kennedy said that GDP "does not allow for the health of our children, the quality of their education, or the joy of their play … It measures neither our wisdom nor our learning; neither our compassion nor our devotion to our country; it measures everything, in short, except that which makes life worthwhile."

Even Kuznets agreed that "the welfare of a nation can scarcely be inferred from a measure of national income."

And it is a perverse measure. Because it's all about production, GDP doesn't take account of the

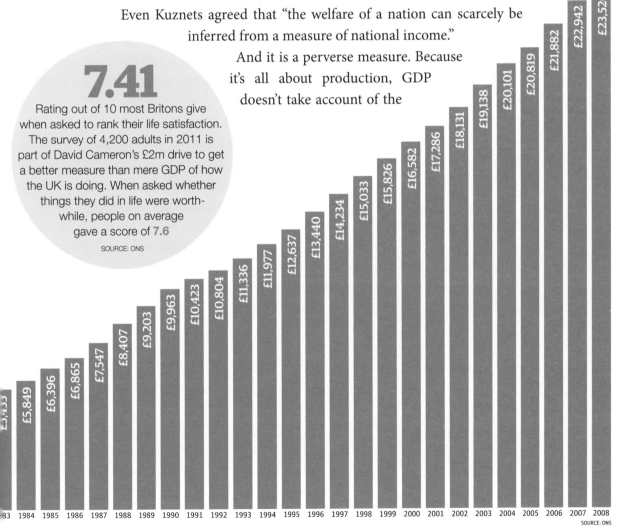

7.41

Rating out of 10 most Britons give when asked to rank their life satisfaction. The survey of 4,200 adults in 2011 is part of David Cameron's £2m drive to get a better measure than mere GDP of how the UK is doing. When asked whether things they did in life were worthwhile, people on average gave a score of **7.6**

SOURCE: ONS

£5,849 £6,396 £6,865 £7,547 £8,407 £9,203 £9,963 £10,423 £10,804 £11,336 £11,977 £12,637 £13,440 £14,234 £15,033 £15,826 £16,582 £17,286 £18,131 £19,138 £20,101 £20,819 £21,882 £22,942 £23,520

83 1984 1985 1986 1987 1988 1989 1990 1991 1992 1993 1994 1995 1996 1997 1998 1999 2000 2001 2002 2003 2004 2005 2006 2007 2008

SOURCE: ONS

Ranking the G20 for well-being
The Happy Planet Index vs GDP per person, $

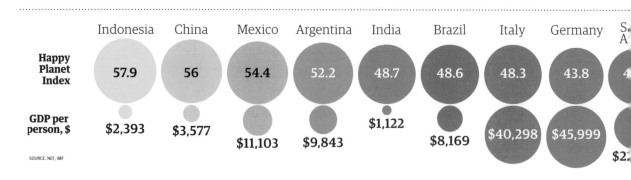

	Indonesia	China	Mexico	Argentina	India	Brazil	Italy	Germany	S A
Happy Planet Index	57.9	56	54.4	52.2	48.7	48.6	48.3	43.8	4
GDP per person, $	$2,393	$3,577	$11,103	$9,843	$1,122	$8,169	$40,298	$45,999	$2.

SOURCE: NEF, IMF

state of the environment, inequality between rich and poor, the value of each economy's assets, and how sustainable the growth actually is. If you have a major disaster, such as the BP spill in the Gulf of Mexico, it will have a positive effect on GDP as the economy works to recover.

It is the baleful influence of GDP that motivates the father of well-being, Professor Joseph Stiglitz. The Nobel Prize-winning former World Bank chief economist and Columbia professor points out that an obsession with GDP actually helped push the US into the housing bubble which has burst so spectacularly.

"In the years before the crisis many people in Europe were saying they ought to follow the American model as the GDP growth was greater. And, as an American, I was a little bit sensitive to some of the weak points, the fact that most Americans were worse off year by year and our growth was based on a bubble and prices were so distorted," he says.

"That was quite a dramatic illustration because now people realise the growth the US had was not sustainable and was going to only a small group of the population. Today you don't hear that argument much."

The answer is to measure something else – but something broader than "happiness". Happiness is intangible; well-being is

29th
Ranking of Norway, the Western European nation which appears highest on the New Economics Foundation's Happy Planet Index with a score of 51.4. The highest ranked country is Costa Rica, with a score of 64. Its high ranking is due to a small ecological footprint and high life expectancy

SOURCE: NEF

The New Economics Foundation's Happy Planet
Index measures several indicators: experienced well-
being, ecological footprint and life expectancy

apan	Turkey	S Korea	UK	Canada	France	Australia	US	S Africa	Russia
41.7	41.4	41.1	40.3	39.8	36.4	34.1	28.8	27.8	22.8
7,644	$11,194	$20,955	$44,720	$46,799	$48,293	$50,053	$47,335	$6,648	$14,688

measurable in the same way that our economy is.

Nicolas Sarkozy asked Stiglitz to look at other ways to measure how well a nation was doing as part of the French presidency of Europe.

Well-being is now being examined in the US, Canada, Australia, France, Italy and Spain. There are parliamentary commissions into the issue in Germany, Norway and Denmark.

The OECD has also just launched its Better Life index, where users can go online to create their own measurements of the success of each country and how they compare across a range of indicators from wealth and crime to housing and inequality.

In the UK, David Cameron has taken a personal interest in the issue, ordering the national statistician, Jil Matheson of the Office for National Statistics, to lead a £2m-a-year project to work out how to measure well-being. The UK project is led by a key part of Cameron's world inside Downing Street, the Behavioural Insight Team, headed by policy wonk David Halpern, who also worked for the previous Labour administration.

While Tony Blair had debated the issue and ordered research on it, very little actually happened. But Cameron, watching from the Opposition benches, certainly took it all in. Halpern says the project

36,300

homes repossessed in England and Wales in 2010. Around three homes for every 1,000 in England has a repossession claim made against it

SOURCE: MINISTRY OF JUSTICE

The map of happiness
A global projection of subjective well-being, 2006

1 Denmark

4 Iceland

2 Switzerland

3 Austria

23 United States

5 Bahamas

This map was one of the first global happiness maps to be created. Adrian White, an analytic social psychologist from the University of Leicester, took data from Unesco, the World Health Organisation, UN Human Development Report, the CIA, the New Economics Foundation, the Veenhoven database, the Latinbarometer and the Afrobarometer to create a picture of the world's well-being

Happy   **Average**   **Unhappy**

The lowest ranked country was Burundi at 178th.

41st

Where the United Kingdom ranked on the 2006 survey

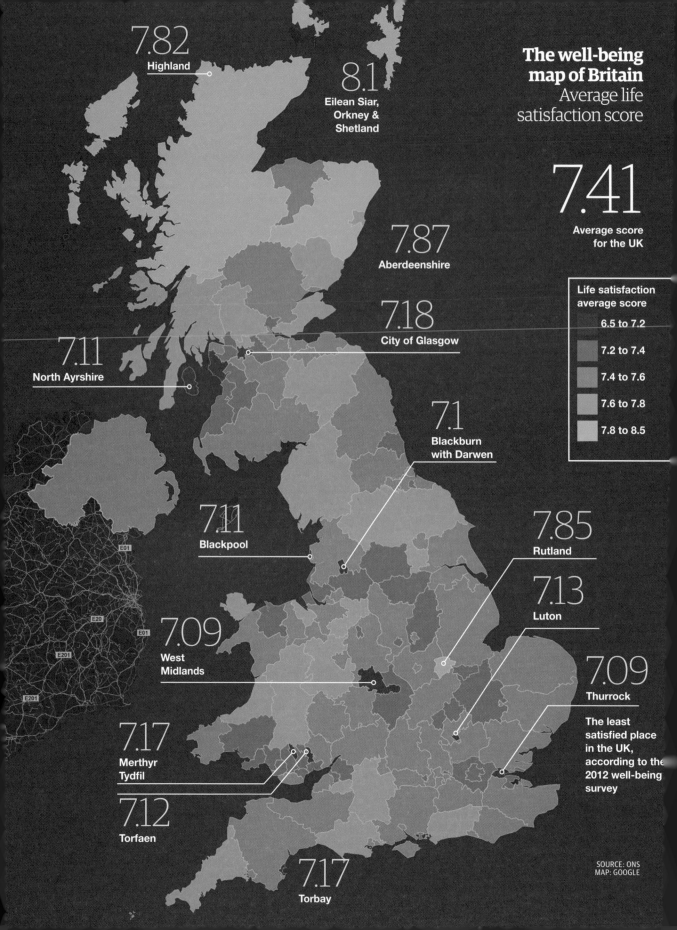

The well-being map of Britain
Average life satisfaction score

7.41
Average score for the UK

7.82
Highland

8.1
Eilean Siar, Orkney & Shetland

7.87
Aberdeenshire

7.18
City of Glasgow

7.11
North Ayrshire

7.1
Blackburn with Darwen

7.11
Blackpool

7.85
Rutland

7.13
Luton

7.09
West Midlands

7.09
Thurrock
The least satisfied place in the UK, according to the 2012 well-being survey

7.17
Merthyr Tydfil

7.12
Torfaen

7.17
Torbay

Life satisfaction average score
- 6.5 to 7.2
- 7.2 to 7.4
- 7.4 to 7.6
- 7.6 to 7.8
- 7.8 to 8.5

SOURCE: ONS
MAP: GOOGLE

How are you feeling?
% difference from the average, by social grade, UK

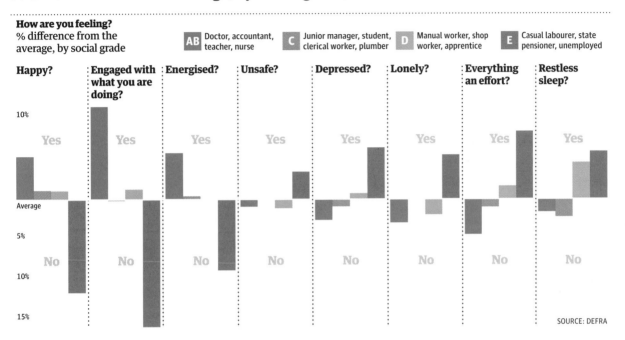

How are you feeling?
% difference from the
average, by social grade

AB Doctor, accountant, teacher, nurse **C** Junior manager, student, clerical worker, plumber **D** Manual worker, shop worker, apprentice **E** Casual labourer, state pensioner, unemployed

SOURCE: DEFRA

"has a profoundly democratic element to it because it's driven by what people really want".

"Only a small part of your life is spent in paid employment," says Halpern. "When we spend time with our friends or watch TV, those things are very consequential but we don't measure them."

For Jil Matheson, it's a chance to make a difference. The ONS has already started surveying 200,000 people in its huge annual Integrated Household Survey (IHS) about their level of fulfilment, anxiety and stress – the so-called 'subjective' measures. She has also produced a major report into how to look at 'objective' measures – wealth, income, childhood and inequality.

Matheson dismisses the media's verdict that this subject is "woolly". "I'm conscious of the word 'woolly' and it puzzles me," she says. "I don't know what is woolly about asking people

Only a small part of your life is spent in paid employment. When we spend time with our friends or watch TV, those things are very consequential but we don't measure them

David Halpern, Behavioural Insight Team, No 10

World rankings
The UN human development report, 2012

The UN's human development report
ranks 169 countries by how developed
they are in education, health,
and inequality

Top five			2005 rank
1	Norway	0.938	1
2	Australia	0.937	2
3	New Zealand	0.907	3
4	United States	0.902	4
5	Ireland	0.895	5
26	UK	0.849	22

Bottom five		
165	0.284 Mozambique	165
166	0.282 Burundi	167
167	0.261 Niger	166
168	0.239 Dem Rep Congo	168
169	0.14 Zimbabwe	169

about their lives; you can measure these things … When people start seeing results, that label will disappear."

Marty Seligman agrees that it can be measured "about as well as schizophrenia, depression, alcoholism … far from perfect, but psychometrically respectable."

But it seems unlikely that we will ever get a single "happiness index", one number which can show how happy we all are, in the way the GDP shows how wealthy. Not least because the international community could never agree on one. "We're a long way off from a single indicator," says Matheson.

Stiglitz agrees – and doesn't believe there should ever be one. "No single indicator would be adequate to describe really what's going on," he says. "If you're driving, you might want to know two things: how fast you're going, say 50 miles per hour, and how far you can go without running out of gasoline, say 150 miles. If you added the two numbers you would have a figure that was totally meaningless. While each of those two numbers is actually individually very meaningful, if you add them together, you would get gibberish."

But how can you make politicians and – more importantly – their treasuries, take notice? David Halpern says having a well-being measure could be a powerful influence on policy. Take moves by central government in the UK to cut costs by closing post offices. "Post offices are expensive, so the answer has been to shut them down. But do they do something else, which we don't capture?"

Isn't the well-being debate just an idea for the rich world? Stiglitz argues that it is even more important for developing countries. For instance, a

6,385
Civil partnerships across the UK in 2010. The Civil Partnerships Act came into force on the 5 December 2005 and has allowed same-sex couples aged over 16 to obtain legal recognition of their relationship but campaigners are now fighting for legislation to change, in a bid to open up marriage to gay couples

SOURCE: ONS

Are we thriving?
The happiest countries by % who say they are thriving, 2010

Happiness index, by % thriving

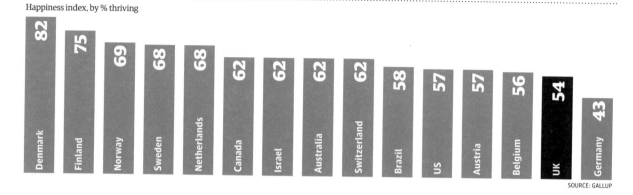

SOURCE: GALLUP

company destroying the environment could help pump up that country's GDP, leaving very little money going back into the economy which could be damaging to the national well-being. He says: "Some of the biggest disparities between GDP and well-being occur in developing countries."

Marty Seligman, whose positive psychology theories are also being trialled in three British schools, says the moves are encouraging but may not go far enough. Talking about the UK in particular, he says: "Number 10 [Downing Street] is seriously interested in the measurement of well-being and the possibility of judging public policy by its effect … It is scientifically informed, which is a good first step. But well-being or flourishing for a nation or an individual is more than just the subjective judgment of life satisfaction." This is Seligman's PERMA theory: Positive Emotion, Engagement, Relationships, Meaning and Accomplishment.

Ask the well-being experts what makes them happy and the answers are diverse. For Jil Matheson it's going to see her football team, Derby County, win. "Which probably implies that I'm a pretty miserable bugger."

For Marty Seligman it's the fact that he is about to watch the Sound

82%
People in marriages or civil partnerships who say they are satisfied or very satisfied with their lives. **80%** of people gave a rating of seven or more when asked whether the things they did in their lives were "worthwhile". The happiest segments of society were aged 16-19 and those over 65

SOURCE: ONS

Happiness by age and gender
Life satisfaction in the UK, 2011–12

● Overall, how satisfied are you with your life?

○ Overall, to what extent do you feel the things you do in your life are worthwhile?

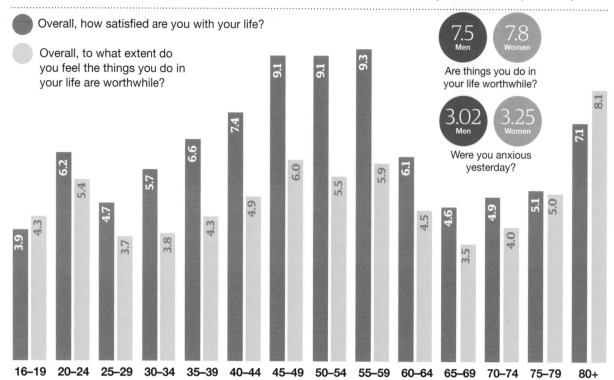

7.4 Men   **7.5** Women
Average life satisfaction (0–10 scale)

7.5 Men   **7.8** Women
Are things you do in your life worthwhile?

3.02 Men   **3.25** Women
Were you anxious yesterday?

Age	Satisfied	Worthwhile
16–19	3.9	4.3
20–24	6.2	5.4
25–29	4.7	3.7
30–34	5.7	3.8
35–39	6.6	4.3
40–44	7.4	4.9
45–49	9.1	6.0
50–54	9.1	5.5
55–59	9.3	5.9
60–64	6.1	4.5
65–69	4.6	3.5
70–74	4.9	4.0
75–79	5.1	5.0
80+	7.1	8.1

10%
Drop in the populations of the Baltic Republics since the break-up of the Soviet Union in 1990. Only Estonia has seen a sharp increase in life expectancy. Democratic records are exemplary, but the countries sit surprisingly low on international measures for well-being and happiness

of Music at home with his family and then play internet bridge.

And Joseph Stiglitz? Family, of course. And work – he is just back from a high-level visit to crisis-ridden Greece, Egypt and Spain when we speak. "When I think about money, one of the things it contributes to my well-being most is the security that it gives me. Especially when I see myself compared to people that I know who are at the margin and you see the anxieties they feel and the constant struggle to make ends meet, and how absorbing it is of their energies."

But what does he do to relax? Photography, it turns out. "I like taking pictures," he says. "But I don't have time."

A version of this chapter first appeared in Google Think Quarterly

Happiness by race, marital status, health and employment
Life satisfaction in the UK, 2011-12

How life satisfaction varies from the average depending on **racial background**

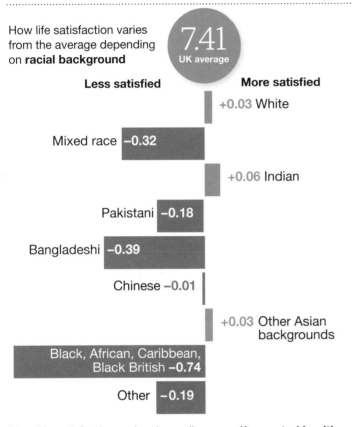

7.41 UK average

Less satisfied — **More satisfied**

+0.03 White

Mixed race −0.32

+0.06 Indian

Pakistani −0.18

Bangladeshi −0.39

Chinese −0.01

+0.03 Other Asian backgrounds

Black, African, Caribbean, Black British −0.74

Other −0.19

Life satisfaction by **marital status**

Married/ civil partnership	**7.72**
Cohabiting	**7.51**
Single	**7.14**
Widowed	**7.26**
Divorced, separated	**7.72**

Life satisfaction by employment status

7.53 Employed 6.47 Unemployed 7.37 Economically inactive

How life satisfaction varies depending on **self-reported health**

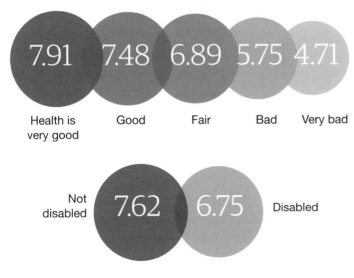

7.91 Health is very good 7.48 Good 6.89 Fair 5.75 Bad 4.71 Very bad

Not disabled 7.62 6.75 Disabled

Life satisfaction by **occupation**

Very low 0–4	Low 5–6	Medium 7–8	High 9–10

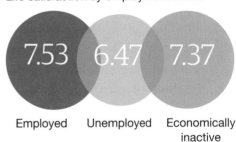

Managers, directors, senior officials	**average** 7.66
Professional occupations	7.69
Associate professional, technical occupations	7.56
Administrative and secretarial	7.55
Skilled trades	7.50
Caring, leisure and other service occupations	7.48
Sales and customer services	7.37
Process, plant and machine operatives	7.34

How we die, 2011
Primary cause of death as recorded
on death certificates

2010 figures

England and Wales

Circulatory system diseases	158,084
Neoplasms	141,446
Respiratory system diseases	67,276
Digestive system diseases	25,662
Mental & behavioural disorders	19,916
Nervous system diseases	18,483
External causes of morbidity & mortality	17,201
Genitourinary system diseases	12,406
Endocrine, nutritional & metabolic diseases	7,185
Certain infectious & parasitic diseases	5,037
Musculoskeletal system & connective tissue diseases	4,165

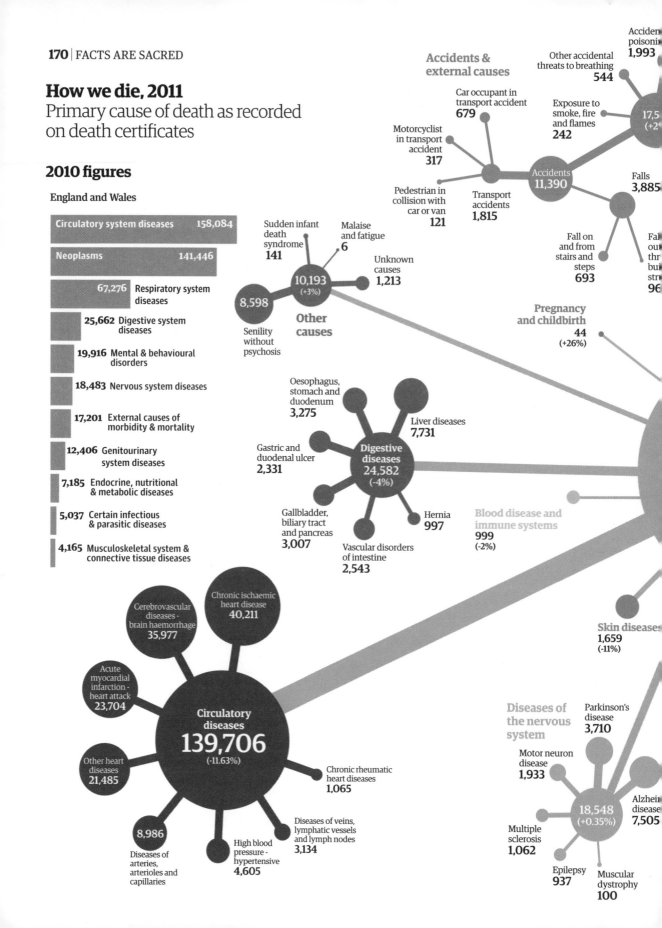

**Accidents &
external causes**

Car occupant in
transport accident
679

Motorcyclist
in transport
accident
317

Pedestrian in
collision with
car or van
121

Transport
accidents
1,815

Other accidental
threats to breathing
544

Exposure to
smoke, fire
and flames
242

Acciden
poisoni
1,993

**17,5
(+2**

Accidents
11,390

Falls
3,885

Fall on
and from
stairs and
steps
693

Fal
ou
thr
bui
str
96

Sudden infant
death
syndrome
141

Malaise
and fatigue
6

Unknown
causes
1,213

10,193
(+3%)

8,598

Senility
without
psychosis

**Other
causes**

**Pregnancy
and childbirth
44
(+26%)**

Oesophagus,
stomach and
duodenum
3,275

Liver diseases
7,731

Gastric and
duodenal ulcer
2,331

**Digestive
diseases
24,582
(-4%)**

Gallbladder,
biliary tract
and pancreas
3,007

Hernia
997

Vascular disorders
of intestine
2,543

**Blood disease and
immune systems
999
(-2%)**

**Skin diseases
1,659
(-11%)**

Cerebrovascular
diseases -
brain haemorrhage
35,977

Chronic ischaemic
heart disease
40,211

Acute
myocardial
infarction -
heart attack
23,704

**Circulatory
diseases
139,706
(-11.63%)**

Other heart
diseases
21,485

Chronic rheumatic
heart diseases
1,065

8,986

Diseases of
arteries,
arterioles and
capillaries

High blood
pressure -
hypertensive
4,605

Diseases of veins,
lymphatic vessels
and lymph nodes
3,134

**Diseases of
the nervous
system**

Parkinson's
disease
3,710

Motor neuron
disease
1,933

**18,548
(+0.35%)**

Alzhei
disease
7,505

Multiple
sclerosis
1,062

Epilepsy
937

Muscular
dystrophy
100

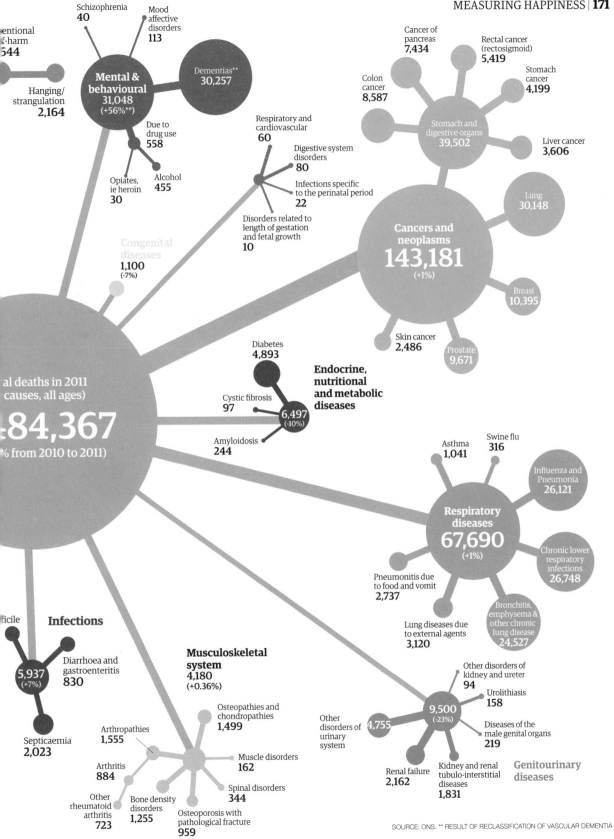

Schizophrenia
40

Mood
affective
disorders
113

entional
-harm
544

Hanging/
strangulation
2,164

**Mental &
behavioural
31,048**
(+56%**)

Dementias
30,257**

Due to
drug use
558

Opiates,
ie heroin
30

Alcohol
455

Respiratory and
cardiovascular
60

Digestive system
disorders
80

Infections specific
to the perinatal period
22

Disorders related to
length of gestation
and fetal growth
10

Congenital
diseases
1,100
(-7%)

Cancer of
pancreas
7,434

Rectal cancer
(rectosigmoid)
5,419

Stomach
cancer
4,199

Colon
cancer
8,587

Stomach and
digestive organs
39,502

Liver cancer
3,606

Lung
30,148

**Cancers and
neoplasms
143,181**
(+1%)

Breast
10,395

Skin cancer
2,486

Prostate
9,671

Diabetes
4,893

**Endocrine,
nutritional
and metabolic
diseases**

Cystic fibrosis
97

6,497
(-10%)

Amyloidosis
244

al deaths in 2011
causes, all ages)

84,367

% from 2010 to 2011)

Asthma
1,041

Swine flu
316

Influenza and
Pneumonia
26,121

**Respiratory
diseases
67,690**
(+1%)

Chronic lower
respiratory
infections
26,748

Pneumonitis due
to food and vomit
2,737

Lung diseases due
to external agents
3,120

Bronchitis,
emphysema &
other chronic
lung disease
24,527

ficile

Infections

5,937
(+7%)

Diarrhoea and
gastroenteritis
830

Septicaemia
2,023

**Musculoskeletal
system
4,180**
(+0.36%)

Osteopathies and
chondropathies
1,499

Arthropathies
1,555

Muscle disorders
162

Arthritis
884

Spinal disorders
344

Other
rheumatoid
arthritis
723

Bone density
disorders
1,255

Osteoporosis with
pathological fracture
959

Other disorders of
kidney and ureter
94

Urolithiasis
158

Other
disorders of
urinary
system

4,755

9,500
(-23%)

Diseases of the
male genital organs
219

Renal failure
2,162

Kidney and renal
tubulo-interstitial
diseases
1,831

Genitourinary
diseases

SOURCE: ONS. ** RESULT OF RECLASSIFICATION OF VASCULAR DEMENTIA

Coronation Britain vs Golden Jubilee Britain
Changes during the 60 years of Queen Elizabeth II's reign

When Elizabeth became Queen, Churchill was prime minister and Britain still had a sizeable number of overseas territories. See how 60 years has changed the world

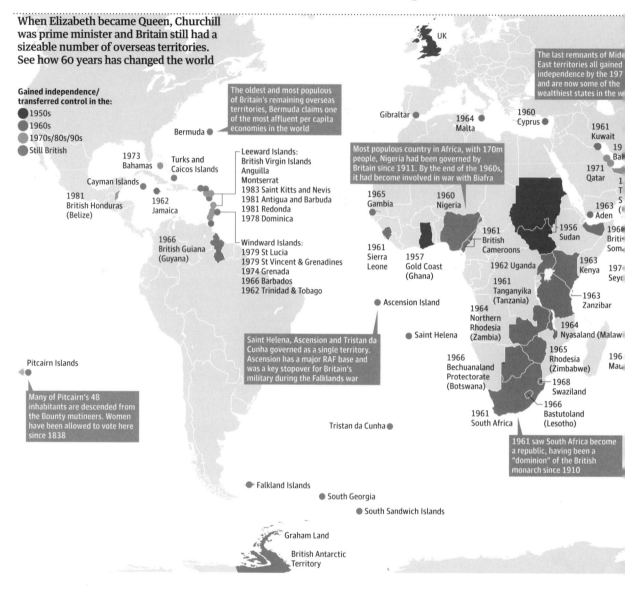

Gained independence/ transferred control in the:
- 1950s
- 1960s
- 1970s/80s/90s
- Still British

UK

The last remnants of Middle East territories all gained independence by the 197... and are now some of the wealthiest states in the w...

Gibraltar

1964 Malta

1960 Cyprus

1961 Kuwait

19... Ba...

1971 Qatar

The oldest and most populous of Britain's remaining overseas territories, Bermuda claims one of the most affluent per capita economies in the world

Bermuda

Most populous country in Africa, with 170m people, Nigeria had been governed by Britain since 1911. By the end of the 1960s, it had become involved in war with Biafra

1973 Bahamas

Turks and Caicos Islands

Leeward Islands:
British Virgin Islands
Anguilla
Montserrat
1983 Saint Kitts and Nevis
1981 Antigua and Barbuda
1981 Redonda
1978 Dominica

1965 Gambia

1960 Nigeria

1963 Aden

1956 Sudan

196... Briti... Som...

Cayman Islands

1981 British Honduras (Belize)

1962 Jamaica

1961 British Cameroons

1962 Uganda

1963 Kenya

197... Sey...

1966 British Guiana (Guyana)

Windward Islands:
1979 St Lucia
1979 St Vincent & Grenadines
1974 Grenada
1966 Barbados
1962 Trinidad & Tobago

1961 Sierra Leone

1957 Gold Coast (Ghana)

1961 Tanganyika (Tanzania)

1963 Zanzibar

Ascension Island

1964 Northern Rhodesia (Zambia)

1964 Nyasaland (Malaw...

Saint Helena

1965 Rhodesia (Zimbabwe)

196... Mau...

Pitcairn Islands

Saint Helena, Ascension and Tristan da Cunha governed as a single territory. Ascension has a major RAF base and was a key stopover for Britain's military during the Falklands war

1966 Bechuanaland Protectorate (Botswana)

1968 Swaziland

Many of Pitcairn's 48 inhabitants are descended from the Bounty mutineers. Women have been allowed to vote here since 1838

1966 Bastutoland (Lesotho)

Tristan da Cunha

1961 South Africa

1961 saw South Africa become a republic, having been a "dominion" of the British monarch since 1910

Falkland Islands

South Georgia

South Sandwich Islands

Graham Land

British Antarctic Territory

Average age at marriage
All couples who married in 1952 and 2009*

24.2 26.5 30 36.2

Then   Now

SOURCE: ONS, DWP *MOST RECENT FIGURE AVAILABLE

Couples getting married or divorced
All couples, 1952 and 2009*

Then

Now

349,308   231,490

33,922   119,589

Population of the UK in 1952

50.3m

2012

63.1m

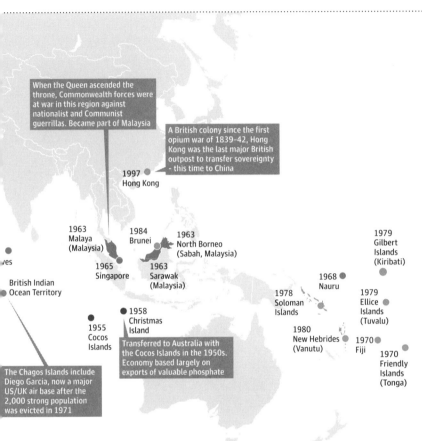

When the Queen ascended the throne, Commonwealth forces were at war in this region against nationalist and Communist guerrillas. Became part of Malaysia

A British colony since the first opium war of 1839–42, Hong Kong was the last major British outpost to transfer sovereignty – this time to China

1997
Hong Kong

1963
Malaya
(Malaysia)

1984
Brunei

1963
North Borneo
(Sabah, Malaysia)

1979
Gilbert
Islands
(Kiribati)

1965
Singapore

1963
Sarawak
(Malaysia)

1968
Nauru

1978
Soloman
Islands

1979
Ellice
Islands
(Tuvalu)

British Indian
Ocean Territory

1958
Christmas
Island

1980
New Hebrides
(Vanutu)

1970
Fiji

1970
Friendly
Islands
(Tonga)

1955
Cocos
Islands

Transferred to Australia with the Cocos Islands in the 1950s. Economy based largely on exports of valuable phosphate

The Chagos Islands include Diego Garcia, now a major US/UK air base after the 2,000 strong population was evicted in 1971

UK GDP
In 2012 prices, including inflation

Now
£1,561bn

Then
£377bn

Average income per person
In 2012 prices, including inflation

Then
£7,500

Now
£24,700

Top rate of income tax in 1952

97.5%

2012 50%

Cars on the road, 1952

3m or 1 in 5 households

2012 31.26m

or 4 in 5 households

Size of the civil service, 1952

972,174

2012
498,433

Public spending

Education
Health
9
7
Defence
25
Then
%
17
Benefits
42
Other

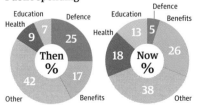

Education
13
Defence
5
Benefits
26
Now
%
18
Health
Other
38

SOURCE: ONS *MOST RECENT FIGURE AVAILABLE

Unemployment   Now 2.65m

Then
379,000

SOURCE: ONS *MOST RECENT FIGURE AVAILABLE

The Queen's wealth and what she does with it

The money she gets from the state...   and how she spend

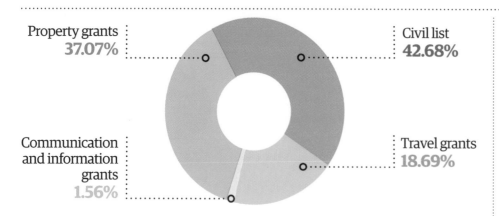

Property grants
37.07%

Civil list
42.68%

Communication
and information
grants
1.56%

Travel grants
18.69%

Prince Philip's income from civil list

£359,000

Annual income from the civil list

£7.9m

Total official spending by the Queen
which was paid for by the state in
grants and the civil list, 2011

£32.1m

According to Forbes
magazine, the Queen's
personal fortune is about

£310m

Catering a
hospitali
3

1,200	Staff in the royal household
450	Paid for by the state
76,000	Guests at official events at the palaces last year
1.86m	paying visitors to royal palaces last year

This includes property holdings,
such as Balmoral Castle and
Sandringham, but does not
include the Crown Estates, which
belong to the sovereign but
which cannot be sold

£10bn

Estimated wealth of the Royal Art
Collection, some 130,000 objects
including works by Da Vinci, Titian,
Michelangelo, Holbein and Fabergé

£7bn

Value of the Crown Estate's property
portfolio, which includes Regent
Street and stakes in Bluewater
shopping centre

£90m

Value of the
Queen's personal
share portfolio

Out of every £10 from the public purse, she spends **£3.71** on the upkeep of property

Admin costs
37p

Ceremonial functions
12p

Communications
16p

Royal travel: helicopters
75p

Royal travel: trains
28p

Housekeeping & furnishing
16p

Royal travel: lease of civil planes
69p

Other
22p

£1.05bn

ural estate, including
06,000 hectares of
rming land

19,680

pages of stamps in the 328
albums that comprise the
Royal Philatelic Collection

£587m

Value of the marine estate – the
seabed out to 12 nautical miles
and much of the foreshore –
including revenue from offshore
wind farms

MO FARAH WINS THE OLYMPIC
5,000M TITLE. PHOTOGRAPH:
TOM JENKINS FOR THE GUARDIAN

Keeping a watch on London's Games

Was 2012 the first open data Olympics? It should have been – we have access to better data analysis and visualisation tools than ever before, many of them free. There is also a culture of open data around the world that just wasn't there at the time of Beijing in 2008. Governments have thrown open the doors to their data vaults and numbers are everywhere.

And what is open data? It is data published as a spreadsheet or a CSV or some other machine-readable format which allows analysts to do something with it. It's what our Free our Data campaign called for.

Open data has won the big argument, since the McKinsey report, which pointed out that open data means money for those who can build apps and services off the back of it. And with it has come the rise in data journalism – the art/craft/slog of getting stories out of numbers.

And these Olympics were a gift for data journalism. Every day brought us a story that cried out for analysis.

This happened around the web – not least the excellent BBC guide, Your Olympic Body Match or the New York Times results page, the Telegraph's Olympic Viz blog – or the live medal counter from France-Info. The ever-fantastic La Nación data blog in Argentina took our Olympic medal-winner data and turned it into a Spanish-language interactive graphic online.

A lot of these were small data projects which we could easily update as the Games went on. They were certainly not big data projects requiring weeks of development time; but rather quick hits which we could fit around the news agenda.

But how open was the data around these Olympic Games? At the beginning, we asked the International Olympic Committee if they would be providing results data in an open format.

1

The number of gold medals won at the 1996 Atlanta summer Olympics, Team GB's nadir. There were just 15 medals in total, and Britain finished 36th in the medal table – below Belgium, Algeria and Kazakhstan. In the wake of the humiliation, the Major government started National Lottery funding for the development of elite athletes

The herald of the Games
The 70-day Olympic torch relay in numbers

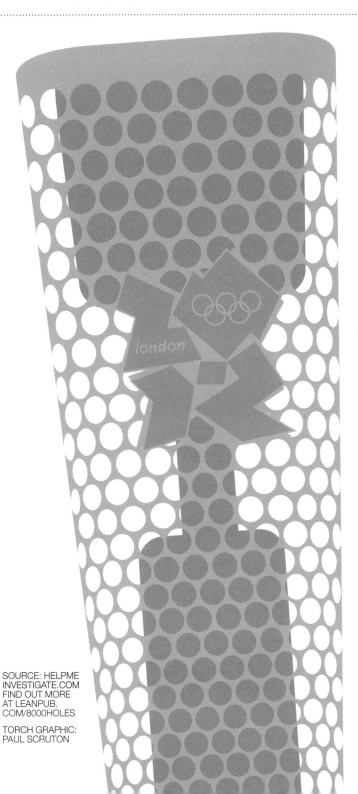

80cm

Height of the torch. It has **8,000** holes punched into it, one for each torchbearer

3

sides to the torch design, marking the three-word Olympic motto – *citius, altius fortius* or faster, higher stronger; the Olympic values of respect, excellence and friendship; and London's three times as host city – in 1908, 1948 and 2012

8,000

the number of torchbearers, and the distance in miles of the torch relay. The torchbearers were:

1,360

chosen by Coca-Cola, **1,300** under the Future Flames scheme

2,012

nominated by the public, chosen by Locog under the Moment to Shine programme

1,360

chosen by sponsor Samsung, **80%** of these from public campaigns

1,360

chosen by sponsors Lloyds TSB, **15%** of places given to internal candidates

919

distributed by Locog, the IOC and the British Olympic Association

913

distributed by commercial partners, including EDF

The rest are not known

SOURCE: HELPME INVESTIGATE.COM FIND OUT MORE AT LEANPUB. COM/8000HOLES

TORCH GRAPHIC: PAUL SCRUTON

Olympic nations
Which countries top the all-time medals tables?

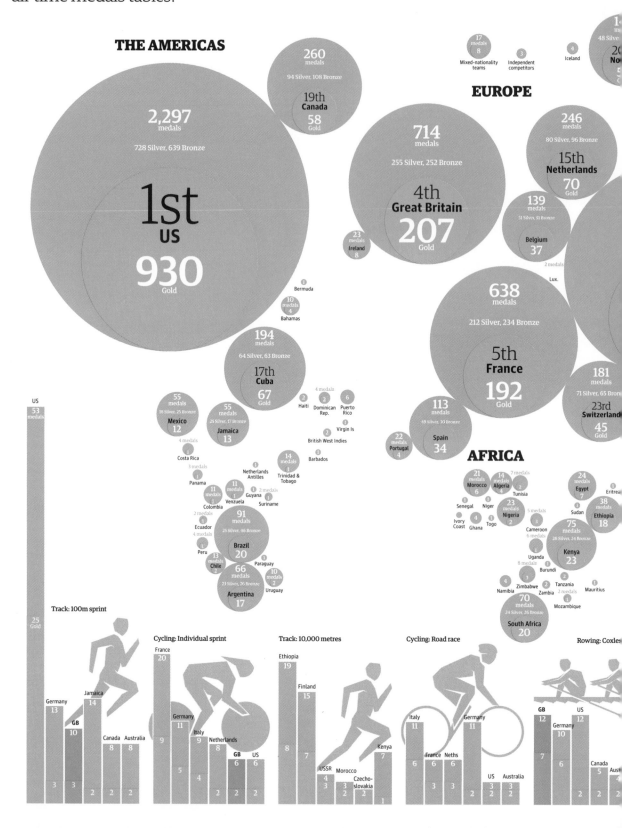

THE AMERICAS

260 medals
94 Silver, 108 Bronze
19th Canada
58 Gold

2,297 medals
728 Silver, 639 Bronze
1st US
930 Gold

Bermuda 1
Bahamas 10 medals 4

194 medals
64 Silver, 63 Bronze
17th Cuba
67 Gold

Haiti 2
Dominican Rep. 2
Puerto Rico 6
4 medals
Virgin Is 2
British West Indies 1

55 medals
18 Silver, 25 Bronze
Mexico 12

55 medals
25 Silver, 17 Bronze
Jamaica 13

Barbados 1

Costa Rica 1 4 medals
Panama 1 3 medals
Colombia 11 medals 1
Venezuela 11 medals 1
Guyana 1
Suriname 2 medals 1
Netherlands Antilles 1
Trinidad & Tobago 14 medals 1

Ecuador 2 medals 1
Peru 4 medals 1
Chile 13 medals

91 medals
25 Silver, 46 Bronze
Brazil 20

Paraguay

66 medals
23 Silver, 26 Bronze
Argentina 17

Uruguay 10 medals 2

---

17 medals 8
Mixed-nationality teams

Independent competitors 3

Iceland 4

1 48 Silver 20 **No**

EUROPE

714 medals
255 Silver, 252 Bronze
4th Great Britain
207 Gold

Ireland 23 medals 8

246 medals
80 Silver, 96 Bronze
15th Netherlands
70 Gold

139 medals
51 Silver, 51 Bronze
Belgium 37

Lux. 2 medals

638 medals
212 Silver, 234 Bronze
5th France
192 Gold

113 medals
49 Silver, 30 Bronze
Spain 34

Portugal 22 medals 4

181 medals
71 Silver, 65 Bron
23rd Switzerland
45 Gold

AFRICA

Morocco 21 medals 6
Algeria 14 medals 4
Tunisia 7 medals

Egypt 24 medals 7
Eritrea 1
Ethiopia 38 medals 18

Senegal 1
Niger 1
Nigeria 23 medals 2
Sudan 5 medals 1

Ivory Coast 4
Ghana 1
Togo 1
Cameroon 6 medals 3

Kenya 75 medals
28 Silver, 24 Bronze
23

Uganda 8 medals
Burundi 2
Tanzania 2
Mauritius 1
Namibia 4
Zimbabwe 3
Zambia 2 medals 1
Mozambique 2 medals 1

South Africa 70 medals
24 Silver, 26 Bronze
20

US 53 medals

25 Gold

Track: 100m sprint

Germany 13
GB 10
Jamaica 14
Canada 8
Australia 8
3 3 2 2

Cycling: Individual sprint

France 20
Germany 11
Italy 9
Netherlands 8
GB 6
US 6
9 7 5 4 2 2

Track: 10,000 metres

Ethiopia 19
Finland 15
Kenya 7
8 7
USSR 4 3
Morocco 3 2
Czecho-slovakia 2 1

Cycling: Road race

Italy 11
Germany 11
France 6
Neths 6
US 3
Australia 3
6 6 3 3 2 2

Rowing: Coxles

GB 12
US 12
Germany 10
7 6
Canada 5
Aus 4
2 2

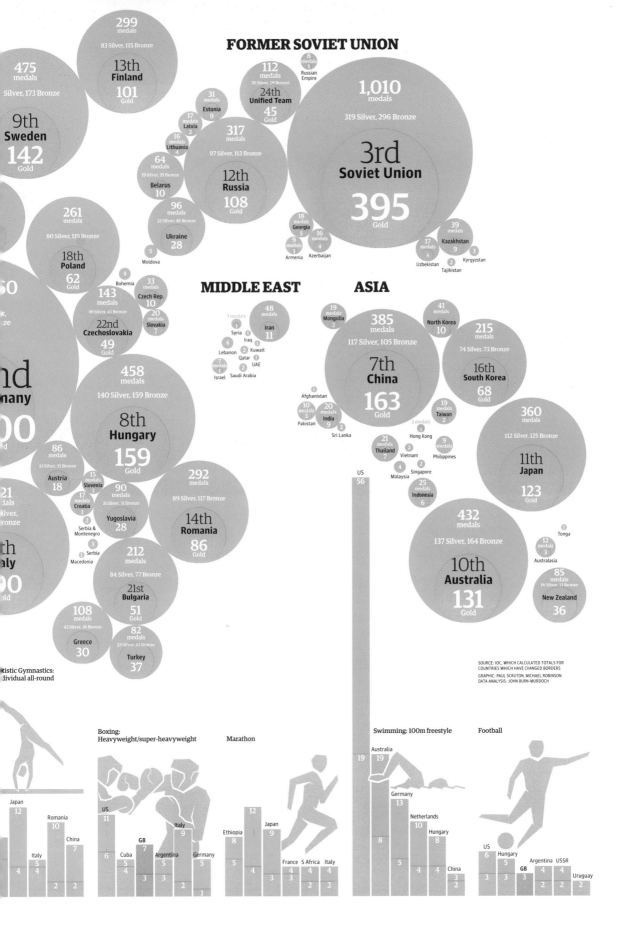

This was the response:

"Can you please clarify what you mean by 'open data'?"

And that's not to say that we didn't get any raw data from the IOC – the list of every medal won at an Olympic Games was a real example, although a historical one. And we also got the full list of team GB athletes from London 2012 as a spreadsheet, which must be the first time that has happened. It's interesting data and it allows all sorts of analysis.

But is that the key data we need? There were two obvious datasets which should be published in an open data format: the full list of all athletes and the live results.

The first should have been simple: every athlete coming to London for the Games was registered by London 2012 and their details published on the official website. It was deliberately set up to be almost impossible to scrape, even

Gold **29** Silver **17** Bronze **19**

65

The number of gold medals by Team GB at London 20 its best performance since London Olympiad of 1908, only 22 countries competed modern era record of 19 g medals was surpassed on final Tuesday of the Gam

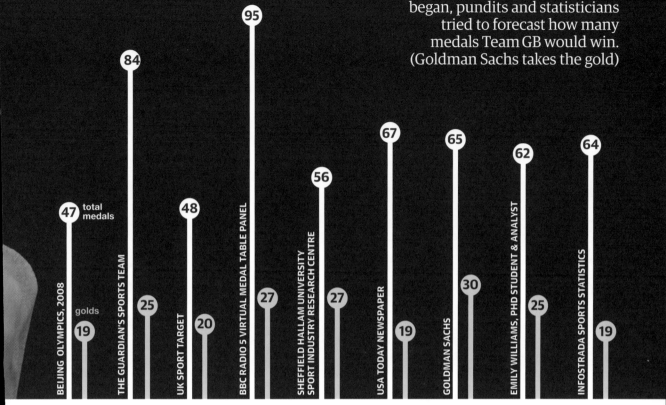

began, pundits and statisticians tried to forecast how many medals Team GB would win. (Goldman Sachs takes the gold)

95

84

67

65

62

64

56

47 total medals

48

30

27

27

25

25

19 golds

20

19

19

BEIJING OLYMPICS, 2008

THE GUARDIAN'S SPORTS TEAM

UK SPORT TARGET

BBC RADIO 5 VIRTUAL MEDAL TABLE PANEL

SHEFFIELD HALLAM UNIVERSITY SPORT INDUSTRY RESEARCH CENTRE

USA TODAY NEWSPAPER

GOLDMAN SACHS

EMILY WILLIAMS, PHD STUDENT & ANALYST

INFOSTRADA SPORTS STATISTICS

for our own pretty experienced team. But the data it recorded is really useful: age, sex, event, height and weight. It allowed us to look at which kinds of athletes were coming from where – what sex they were and which events they were competing in.

We asked London 2012 for the data – and we were told it did not exist as a spreadsheet, which seemed unlikely, but that we were free to cut and paste it from the official press site. So that's what we did. That's not exactly open data – although we made it so.

As for live results, it may be broadcast in front of your eyes but re-using and reproducing it was a no-go, largely because it still costs money to get the data in the first place. We had a live feed from the New York Times at the Guardian, for instance – and republishing that as downloadable data was explicitly forbidden. The BBC similarly had a live feed – and you could get results from London 2012 too. But not as live open data. So, what could we do?

We tried to apply everything we knew to the medals table.

Alternative medal tables
If medals were awarded by GDP, population or team size, who would top the table?

	Official IOC ranking	By size of team	By population	By GDP rank
1	USA	China	Grenada	Grenada
2	China	Jamaica	Jamaica	Jamaica
3	Great Britain	Iran	Bahamas	North Korea
4	Russia	Botswana	New Zealand	Mongolia
5	South Korea	USA	Trin & Tobago	Georgia
6	Germany	Ethiopia	Montenegro	Kenya
7	France	Kenya	Cyprus	Montenegro
8	Italy	Russia	Hungary	Belarus
9	Hungary	Grenada	Slovenia	Armenia
10	Australia	Georgia	Denmark	Ethiopia
11	Japan	Azerbaijan	Australia	Cuba
12	Kazakhstan	North Korea	Lithuania	Bahamas
13	Netherlands	Great Britain	Georgia	Moldova
14	Ukraine	Kazakhstan	Mongolia	Hungary
15	New Zealand	South Korea	Croatia	Azerbaijan
16	Cuba	Hungary	Belarus	Trin & Tobago
17	Iran	Uganda	Estonia	Lithuania
18	Jamaica	Germany	Cuba	Ukraine
19	Czech Republic	Netherlands	Netherlands	Croatia
20	North Korea	Japan	Great Britain	New Zealand
				40 Great Britain

SOURCE: GUARDIAN DATA & IMPERIAL COLLEGE;
MEDAL SCORES IN ALL BUT FIRST COLUMN WEIGHTED FOR RANKINGS, GOLD = 3, SILVER = 2, BRONZE = 1

How do you measure a team's performance in the Olympics? The traditional way is to just count up the number of medals won. And the result? The biggest countries always come top: the Olympic "superpowers" of the US, China, Russia, UK, Australia and Germany.

But what if the totals took account of factors that must have an influence, such as the size of a country's population or its economic power, or compared it to the size of the athletic team in London?

The Royal Statistical Society and the Datablog teamed up with four statisticians at Imperial College, London, to help us work out how those key factors might change the league table. By "weighting" the medals, what happened to the results?

The team, Christoforos Anagnostopoulos, Giovanni Montana, Axel Gandy and Daniel Mortlock, looked at previous Olympics and traditional indicators such as the output of a country's economy (GDP), the size of its population – and also ways to weight the score by the size of each country's Olympic team.

What's the rationale? Take the 2008 results. The Bahamas had a population of approximately 334,000 in 2008, whereas the USA had 304,000,000 – almost 1,000 times larger. And yet the Bahamas won two medals, whereas the US won 110 – 55 times as many. "Taking population into account," says Anagnostopoulos, "It no longer seems obvious that the US should rank higher than the Bahamas. The intuition is that the US had a larger pool of possible athletes to choose from, and consequently it makes sense that it should do better too."

So, what would the results look like?

Says Anagnostopoulos: "The simplest approach is to divide the number of medals by the population

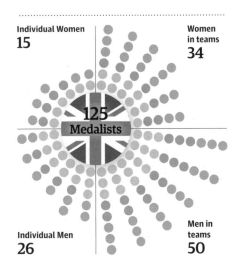

Men vs women
How do Team GB's
125 medalists divide up?

Individual Women
15

Women
in teams
34

125
Medalists

Individual Men
26

Men in
teams
50

62m
passenger journeys were made on the Tube during London 2012, up 35% on normal levels. Tuesday 7 August was the busiest day in the history of the London Underground with 4.57m passenger journeys

SOURCE: GETAHEADOFTHEGAMES.COM

£428m The estimated cost of the Olympic Stadium. The total cost of the venues was an estimated £1.1bn

TOM JENKINS FOR
THE GUARDIAN

of each country. We will however look at other types of indices that might be harder to interpret directly. Consequently, to make the league table interpretable without reference to the underlying index, we express the results as a (weighted) medal count.

"As the Games progress, for each medal type (Bronze/Silver/Gold), we redistribute the medals that have been already won, taking into account the country's population: for a small country, one medal will be worth more than for a larger country, and it may therefore end up with two or three medals, whereas the larger country 'loses' some of its medals in order to correct for the advantage afforded to it by way of its larger population. The resulting medal count will depend on the relative sizes of the countries of the medal winners, and may change as more

10,903
Number of athletes who took part in the Games, competing in **26** different sports across 39 disciplines over 19 days of competition (the football tournaments started before the opening ceremony)

SOURCE: IOC

medals are added onto the database. We do the same for Silvers and Golds, as well as for total medal count."

GDP is another obvious one to re-size on, particularly when you consider how expensive sport equipment and training is. Moreover, since GDP also grows with population size, it implicitly also takes into account population size.

Although penalising larger wealthier countries may seem intuitively "fair", our statistical team invited us to think harder about the potential arbitrariness of penalties and how they can be selected objectively. Anagnostopoulos explains: "We have been thinking of GDP (or population) as an 'advantage' that needs to be 'corrected for' by penalising. This however involves an arbitrary decision of how much to penalise by. A statistician would take a different, more objective view, where GDP is a factor that can, to some extent, explain the performance of various countries.

Sitting vs standing
Britons are better at sports where you sit down

Number of medals won sitting or 'standing' sports

Sitting (cycling, rowing)

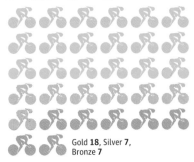

Gold **18**, Silver **7**, Bronze **7**

Standing (includes swimming)

Gold **11**, Silver **10**, Bronze **12**

*IOC count for team sports

"A different, more objective view, would interpret GDP as a factor that can, to some extent, explain the performance of various countries. Once this explanatory potential is exhausted, what 'is left' (the statistical jargon for this is 'residual') can be interpreted as 'GDP-corrected' athletic skill – a purer measure. Crucially, we may then rely on sound principles of statistical modelling to determine fairly conclusively which index is the one that maximises the explanatory power of GDP (and/or population) in this context. The resulting measure is no longer a simple ratio, but a variant of a log scale, which carefully balances the numbers in a fairly complicated way. When the Games are over, we will be able to analyse the results based on this work."

Team size is also a factor – and one which our team said could be a

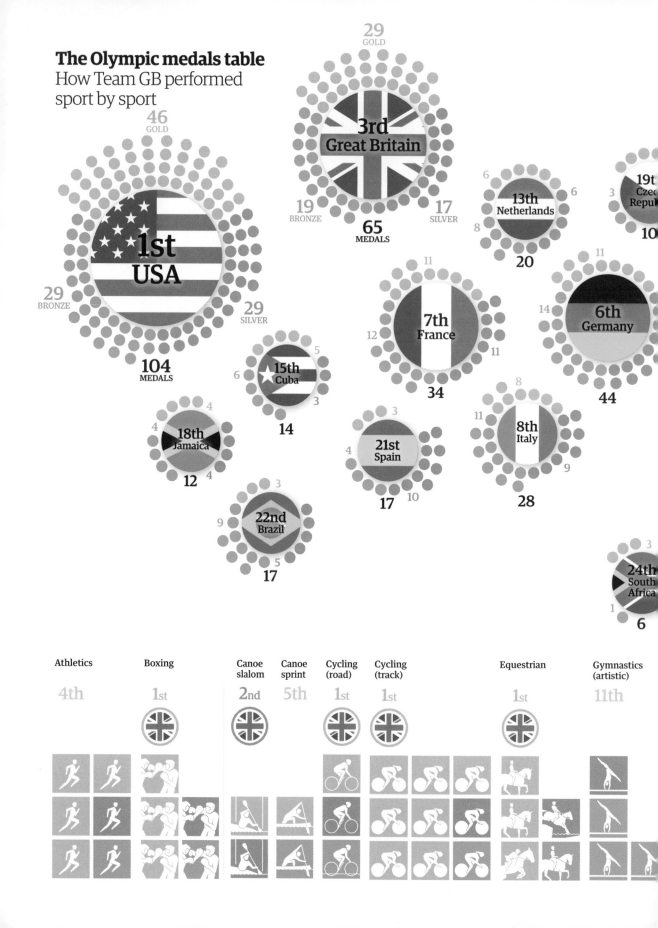

The Olympic medals table
How Team GB performed
sport by sport

46 GOLD

29 BRONZE

1st USA

29 SILVER

104 MEDALS

29 GOLD

3rd Great Britain

19 BRONZE

17 SILVER

65 MEDALS

6

13th Netherlands

6

8

20

3

19th Czech Republic

10

11

7th France

12

11

34

11

6th Germany

14

44

5

15th Cuba

6

3

14

8

8th Italy

11

9

28

4

18th Jamaica

4

4

4

12

3

21st Spain

4

10

17

3

22nd Brazil

9

5

17

3

24th South Africa

1

6

Athletics	Boxing	Canoe slalom	Canoe sprint	Cycling (road)	Cycling (track)	Equestrian	Gymnastics (artistic)
4th	1st	2nd	5th	1st	1st	1st	11th

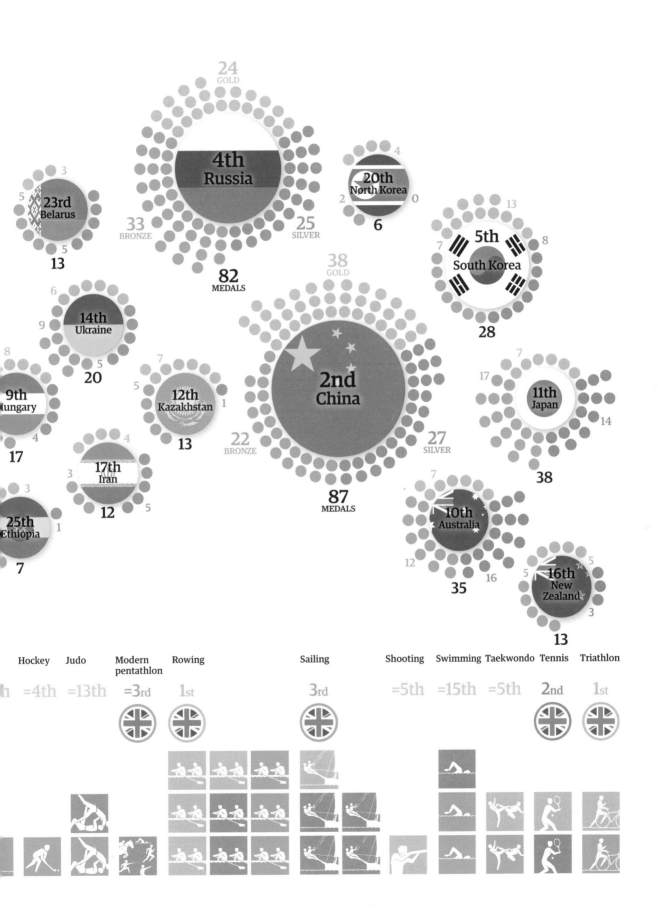

24
GOLD

4th
Russia

33
BRONZE

25
SILVER

82
MEDALS

3

5

23rd
Belarus

5

13

4
2 0

20th
North Korea

6

13
GOLD

8

5th
South Korea

28

6

14th
Ukraine

9

8

5

20

38
GOLD

7

5

12th
Kazakhstan

1

13

2nd
China

22
BRONZE

27
SILVER

87
MEDALS

7

17

11th
Japan

14

38

9th
Hungary

4

17

4

3

17th
Iran

5

12

7

10th
Australia

12

16

35

3

25th
Ethiopia

1

7

5

5

16th
New
Zealand

3

13

Hockey	Judo	Modern pentathlon	Rowing		Sailing	Shooting	Swimming	Taekwondo	Tennis	Triathlon
h	=4th	=13th	=3rd	1st	3rd	=5th	=15th	=5th	2nd	1st

Michael Phelps – the greatest Olympian
The swimmer with twice as many golds as his nearest rivals

| 18 | 2 | 2 |

Michael Phelps
US

| 9 | 5 | 4 |

Larisa Latynina
USSR

| 9 | 1 | 1 |

Mark Spitz
US

47th
Where Michael Phelps would appear in the all-time medals table with his 18 golds – he would be above India and Indonesia, combined population 1.48bn

8
Number of gold medals Phelps won in Beijing, breaking Mark Spitz's record for the most golds won in one Olympics. In seven of the eight events he broke the world record

6
The number of medals he won in London, making him the most successful individual Olympian in three consecutive Games. His total at London 2012 would put him at 20th in the medals table, above Spain, Brazil and South Africa

4 -	**9 1** -	**8 3 1**	**8 2 1**	**8 3 1**	**8 4** -

vo
mi
and

**Carl
Lewis**
US

**Jenny
Thompson**
US

**Matt
Biondi**
US

**Sawao
Kato**
Japan

**Birgit
Fischer**
E Germany

.4m

number of Twitter followers
amassed by Phelps, an
e Tweeter; he also has
m Facebook likes

15

The age at which Michael Phelps
broke his first world record and
swam in his first Olympics. He
did not win a medal in Sydney in
2000 but he was the youngest
male swimmer in the US team
for more than 60 years

$1m

The amount that sponsors
Speedo gave to Phelps after
his eight golds at the Beijing
Olympics. He is worth an
estimated $40m, according to
Forbes magazine

better indicator than either GDP or population as it has already taken that into account by team selection.

So, what happened at the end of the Games? We had a winner: Russia.

The figures initially were based on separate rankings for GDP, population and team size. The team then combined them all into one index.

Says Anagnostopoulos: "We employ GDP per capita rather than GDP, since we are already taking population into account in this approach."

Each country was then scored based on the number of extra medals it would win if those medals were weighted according to our new ranking – this is known as a "residual" in statistical jargon.

"We propose this as a purer measure of athletic skill. For countries that under-performed, this number can be negative," says Anagnostopoulos.

So, the final ranking was:

	2012	In 2008
1	**Russia**	China
2	**UK**	Russia
3	**China**	Australia
4	**Hungary**	United States
5	**South Korea**	UK
6	**Ukraine**	Cuba
7	**Australia**	South Korea
8	**Cuba**	Ukraine
9	**Jamaica**	Belarus
10	**Belarus**	Kenya

Youth vs maturity
How old were Team GB's medal winners?

Age breakdown by sport of medal winning athletes in Team GB

● 19 or under ● 20-24 ● 25-29 ● 30-39 ● 40+

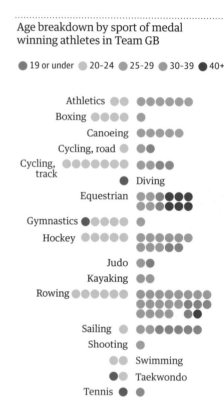

26.3

The average age of Team GB's athletes at London 2012. The youngest large team (100 members or more) was China, which had an average age of 24.3 years. The oldest of the large teams was Sweden, with an average age of 28.4

SOURCE: IOC

So Team GB had moved way up the table.

The UK was ahead of Russia on golds, but Russia did better on other medals. If this statistical model only measured gold medals, Team GB would come top.

31

The number of events in which Team GB came last or was in the bottom three. This can be explained by the fact that Britain had the largest team at the Games, with 542 members, and the country made an effort to enter a team in events such as handball, in which Britain does not usually compete

And Anagnostopoulos posed some words of warning for UK celebrants: "Although the UK has every right to be proud of its performance, this enthusiasm must be somewhat moderated against the fact that past Olympics have shown a clear presence of a home advantage effect."

In 2008, the home team came top. In 2004, Greece ranked 12th according to this model. "A far superior performance to both before and after it hosted the Olympics."

Which was the best indicator? Says Anagnostopoulos: "The team size indeed proved to be a fairly good predictor of performance in the Games. However, we do not allow this factor to affect a country's ranking here, since in principle a poor, small country can still produce a relatively large team size, and should not be penalised for that."

So, it is possible to do interesting things by creating your own data in combining the existing and the new.

In some ways, the interesting stuff took place outside anyway – the way Emoto analysed Twitter sentiment, for instance, is revolutionary and will change the way we see the Games.

Will that be the case at Rio in 2016? The economics mean it probably will be. But is it sustainable?

We have seen how hackers have reclaimed elections around the world, opening up the data for everyone to use. At the end of July, as the Games got under way, developers took part in the first Olympic hackday. It's hard to see that by 2016 this won't emerge as data we can all use.

50.2m

The number of people who watched at least 15 minutes of the Olympics coverage in Britain, some **87%** of the population. The opening ceremony attracted **26.9m** viewers at its height in the UK and in the US it broke the previous record for the Olympics, attracting **40.7m** viewers

So, was it the first open data Olympics? Not this time.

But it was the first data Olympics.

12 things we learned about London 2012

TOM JENKINS FOR THE GUARDIAN

Olympics are always judged on who gets the most medals and which country wins the most golds. Which normally means the attention focuses on the traditional Olympic winners: the US, China, Russia and the UK.

But what if there was another way to see the Olympic medals table?

We worked with statisticians at Imperial College to produce this alternative medal table, where countries are judged not simply on how many medals they won but how it compares to each country's GDP, or population, or team size.

And the final winner on these measures? Russia.

16.3m

people in the UK watched Jessica Ennis (above) win the heptathlon gold on Super Saturday – 4 August – rising to 17.1m later that evening when Mo Farah won the first of his two golds, in the 10,000m. The highest audience of the Games was on Sunday 5, when 20m people watched Usain Bolt win the 100m final.

SOURCE: BBC

1

There's more than one way to read a medals table

2

We can compare performances with Beijing 2008

It may be hard to believe now, but after a couple of days questions were raised about how well the team was doing, compared to 2008 in Beijing. By day three, Team GB was placed 20th in the league table, compared to seventh at the same stage in 2008. The Guardian updated its interactive graphic every day to allow users to see exactly how the six biggest teams were doing measured against 2008's performance. In the final analysis, Team GB, Russia and Germany all did better than they did in 2008; Australia and China did worse. Team USA got more golds but fewer medals overall.

The figures are controversial: according to Lord Moynihan, head of the British Olympic Authority, in 2008, 50% of Team GB's gold medals were won by privately educated athletes. However, it looks as if the real figure in Beijing was lower than that. And that figure seems to have held steady or even increased slightly in 2012.

As the Games progressed, we were interested in who the athletes were who were winning for Team GB – what they won for and where they went to school. Malcolm Tozer, the expert on British medal success and education, says that these games saw 37% of medals being won by privately educated athletes. Their number increased from 26 in 2008 to 44 in 2012.

Tozer adds: "Independent schools as a country (not including a gold from Ruta Meilutyte of Plymouth College, representing Lithuania) would have finished 12th in the medal table."

This is up four places on Beijing.

3

Almost 40% of Team GB medalists went to private school

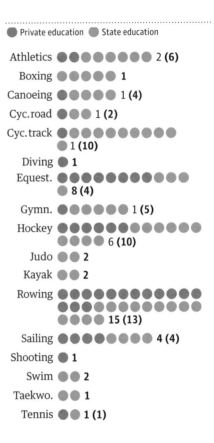

State vs private
Educational breakdown of Team GB medal winners

● Private education   ● State education

Athletics ●●●●●●●● 2 **(6)**
Boxing ●●●●● 1
Canoeing ●●●●● 1 **(4)**
Cyc.road ●●● 1 **(2)**
Cyc.track ●●●●●●●●●
●● 1 **(10)**
Diving ● 1
Equest. ●●●●●●●●●
● 8 **(4)**
Gymn. ●●●●●● 1 **(5)**
Hockey ●●●●●●●●●●
●●●● 6 **(10)**
Judo ●● 2
Kayak ●● 2
Rowing ●●●●●●●●●●
●●●●●●●●●●
●●●● 15 **(13)**
Sailing ●●●●●●● 4 **(4)**
Shooting ● 1
Swim ●● 2
Taekwo. ●● 1
Tennis ●● 1 **(1)**

4

The world's athletes are shaped by their chosen sport

Do you look like an Olympic athlete? If you are aged 26, weigh 72.8kg and are 176.9cm tall then the answer is yes.

Thanks to the first comprehensive scrape of every London 2012 Olympic athlete we can create a real picture of what kinds of people compete in the Games. We analysed more than 10,000 Olympians taking part in the London 2012 Games to see the spread of ages, heights and weights across the sports for men and women. And if you think you know what it takes to compete in the Games, you may find some of the results surprising.

If you imagine that all Olympic athletes are young, for instance, then you would be wrong – while the average is 26, there were 187 athletes over 40 at this year's games, including the eldest, Hiroshi Hoketsu, who competed in the dressage for Japan at the age of 71.

Britain and the United States have the largest two teams in the Olympics with over 1,000 athletes between them – but how do they compare?

Team GB is younger, lighter and smaller than their transatlantic counterparts. Its average age is 26.3, compared to 27.1 for the US – a gap of 3%. It is also 2% lighter at an average of 74.5kg, compared to 75.9kg.

5

Team GB is not as far behind Team USA as we thought

But Team GB, although it has fewer medals, compares well to its transatlantic ally, with a wider spread of gold medals in different sports. Swimming dominates the US medal table – with a total of 31 medals in all, including 16 golds (with Michael Phelps contributing three of them). That is followed by 29 track and field medals, including nine golds.

31

Number of US medals won in swimming alone. Team USA's women won 58 of the team's 104 medals – 29 of them gold – and were a dominant part of the victorious track and field team. Team GB, by contrast, won medals over a wider spread of sports, with the cycling and rowing teams the most dominant

6

Chinese prodigy
Ye Shiwen is a very
fast swimmer

Ye Shiwen swam the last 50m of her 400m individual medley final quicker than the winner of the men's race. How 'unbelievable' is this in statistical terms?

Dozens of arguments have been made as to why Ye Shiwen's sensational swim evening should or shouldn't be viewed with suspicion, many of them ill-conceived, but one that stands up to scrutiny concerns a particular statistic.

Ye Shiwen flew down the final length of Saturday's 400m individual medley final in 28.93 seconds, seventeen-hundredths of a second faster than Ryan Lochte, the winner of the equivalent mens' race.

This fact is significant not because swimming aficionados are sexist and believe that a women cannot naturally swim faster than a man, but because it is a clear statistical anomaly.

The fastest men in history
How past champions compare to Usain Bolt

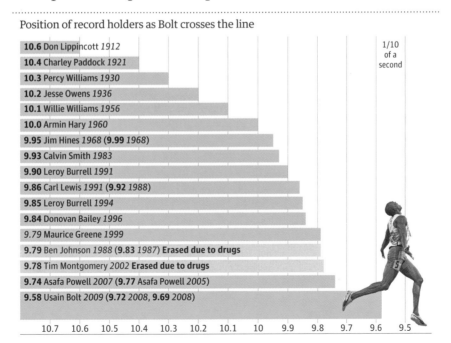

Position of record holders as Bolt crosses the line

10.6 Don Lippincott *1912*
10.4 Charley Paddock *1921*
10.3 Percy Williams *1930*
10.2 Jesse Owens *1936*
10.1 Willie Williams *1956*
10.0 Armin Hary *1960*
9.95 Jim Hines *1968* (**9.99** *1968*)
9.93 Calvin Smith *1983*
9.90 Leroy Burrell *1991*
9.86 Carl Lewis *1991* (**9.92** *1988*)
9.85 Leroy Burrell *1994*
9.84 Donovan Bailey *1996*
9.79 Maurice Greene *1999*
9.79 Ben Johnson *1988* (**9.83** *1987*) **Erased due to drugs**
9.78 Tim Montgomery *2002* **Erased due to drugs**
9.74 Asafa Powell *2007* (**9.77** Asafa Powell *2005*)
9.58 Usain Bolt *2009* (**9.72** *2008*, **9.69** *2008*)

1/10 of a second

10.7 10.6 10.5 10.4 10.3 10.2 10.1 10 9.9 9.8 9.7 9.6 9.5

The cost of an Olympic medal
UK Sport funding per medal at London 2012

Athletics

Target 5–8 medals
Achieved 4 1 1
Funding
£25.148m
£ per medal
£4.19m

Boxing

Target 3–5 medals
Achieved 3 1 1
Funding
£9.55m
£ per medal
£1.91m

Canoeing

Target 3–4 medals
Achieved 2 1 1
Funding
£16.18m
£ per medal
£4.04m

Cycling

Target 6–10 medals
Achieved 8 2 2
Funding
£26.03m
£ per medal
£2.17m

Equestrian

Target 3–4 medals
Achieved 3 1 1
Funding
£13.395m
£ per medal
£2.68m

ABOVE, THREE-DAY EVENTER MARY KING; BELOW, DOUBLE CYCLING GOLD MEDALLIST LAURA TROTT, PHOTOGRAPHS: TOM JENKINS FOR THE GUARDIAN

Diving

Target 1–3 medals
Achieved 0 0 1
Funding
£6.54m
£ per medal
£6.54m

Gymnastics

Target 1–2 medals
Achieved 0 1 3
Funding
£10.77m
£ per medal
£2.69m

Hockey

Target 1–2 medals
Achieved 0 0 1
Funding
£15.01m
£ per medal
£15.01m

Judo

Target 0–1 medals
Achieved 0 1 1
Funding
£7.498m
£ per medal
£3.749m

Triathlon

Target 1–2 medals

Achieved (1) (0) (1)

Funding

£5.29m

£ per medal

£2.65m

ALISTAIR BROWNLEE,
TRIATHLON WINNER,
BY TOM JENKINS
FOR THE GUARDIAN

Sailing

Target 3–5 medals

Achieved (1) (4) (0)

Funding

£22.94m

£ per medal

£4.59m

Shooting

Target 0–1 medals

Achieved (1) (0) (0)

Funding

£2.46m

£ per medal

£2.46m

Rowing

Target 6 medals

Achieved (4) (2) (3)

Funding

£27.29m

£ per medal

£3.03m

Total UK Sport funding

£264.14m

for London 2012, up from

£235.1m

spent on the 2008 Beijing Olympics

Since 2008, a total of around

£100m

per year has been invested in 1,200 athletes competing across 47 different sports in the Olympic and Paralympic Games

Swimming

Target 5–7 medals

Achieved (0) (1) (2)

Funding

£25.14m

£ per medal

£8.38m

Modern pentathlon

Target 1–2 medals

Achieved (0) (1) (0)

Funding

£6.29m

£ per medal

£6.29m

Taekwondo

Target 1–3 medals

Achieved (1) (0) (1)

Funding

£4.83

£ per medal

£2.42m

7

We can work out who really paid for the Olympics

Think you know how much London 2012's Olympic Games cost? Think again. The £9bn figure that we have seen is just the largest part of a complicated set of arrangements involving public and private finance. We thought it would be a good idea to gather all that data together in one place – to provide a definitive guide to the funding of London 2012.

We pulled together data published by the Olympic Delivery Authority (ODA), the Department for Culture, Media and Sport (DCMS) – and what we know of the London Organising Committee of the Olympic and Paralympic Games (Locog) to piece together a detailed picture of funding and spending.

The difference between Locog and the ODA is, as a Locog spokeswoman put it to me: "The ODA is building the theatre; we put on the show." The ODA has spent £6.248bn of public money on getting the grounds and venues ready, with another £2.537bn coming via other bodies such as local authorities and direct from the DCMS itself. Locog had budgeted the smallest amount: £2bn.

So, how did we get there? We identified spending of around £11bn – which is essentially the government's £9bn plus Locog's published budget of £2bn. The final reckoning of spending totals will not come out until May 2013, so we have divided up its funding using what we know, which is that Locog is paying for half the budget for ceremonies, half the budget for the Paralympics and, obviously, the cost of running the events themselves.

Paralympics success
How London 2012 broke ticket sales records

Tickets sold

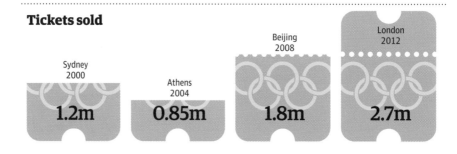

Sydney 2000 — 1.2m
Athens 2004 — 0.85m
Beijing 2008 — 1.8m
London 2012 — 2.7m

8

Twitter can provide a barometer of how we felt about the Games

Who were the social media stars of London 2012? We had never had such access to detailed data about social media – and about how we use it. And the Olympics is ultimately an emotional event. At London 2012, we had some genuinely innovative approaches. Emoto 2012 for instance, provided a real-time guide to Twitter sentiment, as tweets were being posted. Infomous monitored all social media – again live as it was happening.

9

Michael Phelps's achievement is astonishing

If he were a country he would be ahead of Georgia, Uzbekistan, Croatia, Chile, the old Russian Empire, Israel and Tunisia in the all-time medals table. He's won more golds than India, Taiwan, Portugal, Nigeria, Thailand and North Korea ever have.

London is the first city ever to have hosted three Olympics. In 1908, at the height of the British Empire, it was a last-minute choice, stepping in for Rome after the eruption of Mount Vesuvius. In 1948, Germany and Japan were banned following their wartime defeat, the Soviet Union was absent

Yorkshire vs the UK
Yorkshire, Scotland and London top medals table

Team GB medal breakdown by county or region

● 1 medal ● 2 ● 3 ● 4 ● 5+

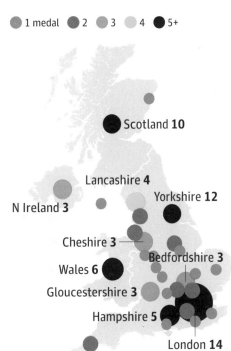

Scotland **10**

Lancashire **4**

Yorkshire **12**

N Ireland **3**

Cheshire **3**

Bedfordshire **3**

Wales **6**

Gloucestershire **3**

Hampshire **5**

London **14**

10

Contrasting London's three Games provides a snapshot of change

Who competed in the Paralympic Games?

Teams by size and by gender

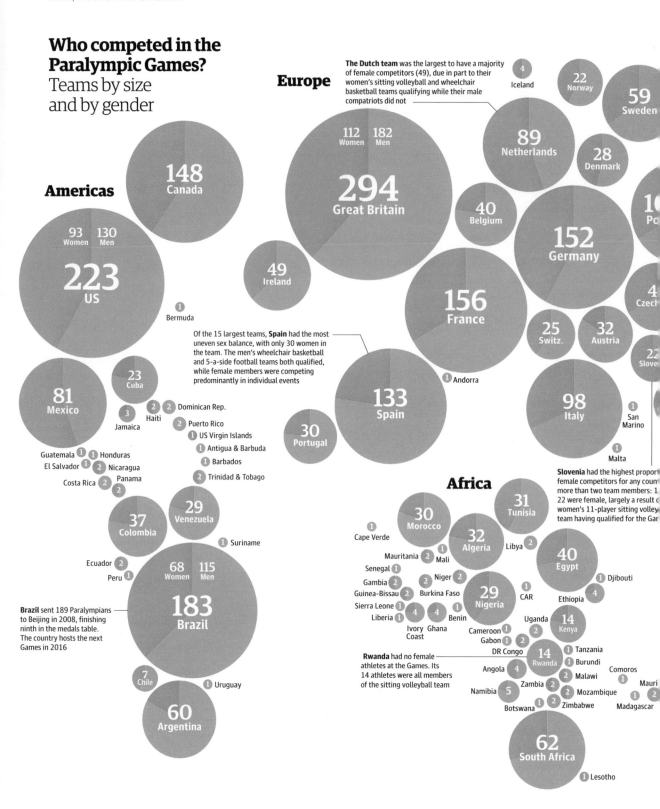

Europe

The Dutch team was the largest to have a majority of female competitors (49), due in part to their women's sitting volleyball and wheelchair basketball teams qualifying while their male compatriots did not

4 Iceland

22 Norway

59 Sweden

89 Netherlands

28 Denmark

112 Women **182** Men

294 Great Britain

40 Belgium

152 Germany

1 Po

49 Ireland

40 Belgium

156 France

25 Switz.

32 Austria

4 Czech

22 Slove

Americas

148 Canada

93 Women **130** Men

223 US

1 Bermuda

Of the 15 largest teams, **Spain** had the most uneven sex balance, with only 30 women in the team. The men's wheelchair basketball and 5-a-side football teams both qualified, while female members were competing predominantly in individual events

1 Andorra

133 Spain

98 Italy

1 San Marino

81 Mexico

23 Cuba

2 **2** Dominican Rep.

3 Haiti

2 Puerto Rico

Jamaica

1 US Virgin Islands

1 Antigua & Barbuda

Guatemala **1** **1** Honduras

El Salvador **1** **2** Nicaragua

Costa Rica **2** Panama **2**

1 Barbados

2 Trinidad & Tobago

30 Portugal

1 Malta

Slovenia had the highest propor female competitors for any coun more than two team members: 1 22 were female, largely a result o women's 11-player sitting volley team having qualified for the Gar

37 Colombia

29 Venezuela

1 Suriname

Ecuador **2**

Peru **1**

68 Women **115** Men

183 Brazil

Brazil sent 189 Paralympians to Beijing in 2008, finishing ninth in the medals table. The country hosts the next Games in 2016

7 Chile

1 Uruguay

60 Argentina

Africa

30 Morocco

31 Tunisia

1 Cape Verde

32 Algeria

Libya **2**

Mauritania **2** Mali **1**

40 Egypt

Senegal **1**

Niger **2**

1 Djibouti

Gambia **2**

Burkina Faso **2**

1 CAR

Ethiopia **4**

Guinea-Bissau **2**

29 Nigeria

14 Kenya

Sierra Leone **1**

Liberia **1**

4 **4** Benin

Uganda **2**

Ivory Coast Ghana

Cameroon **1**

1 Tanzania

Gabon **1** **2**

1 Burundi

DR Congo

14 Rwanda

Comoros **1**

Rwanda had no female athletes at the Games. Its 14 athletes were all members of the sitting volleyball team

Angola **4**

Malawi **2**

Mauri

Zambia **2**

Namibia **5**

Mozambique **2**

1 **2**

Botswana **1** Zimbabwe **2** Madagascar

62 South Africa

1 Lesotho

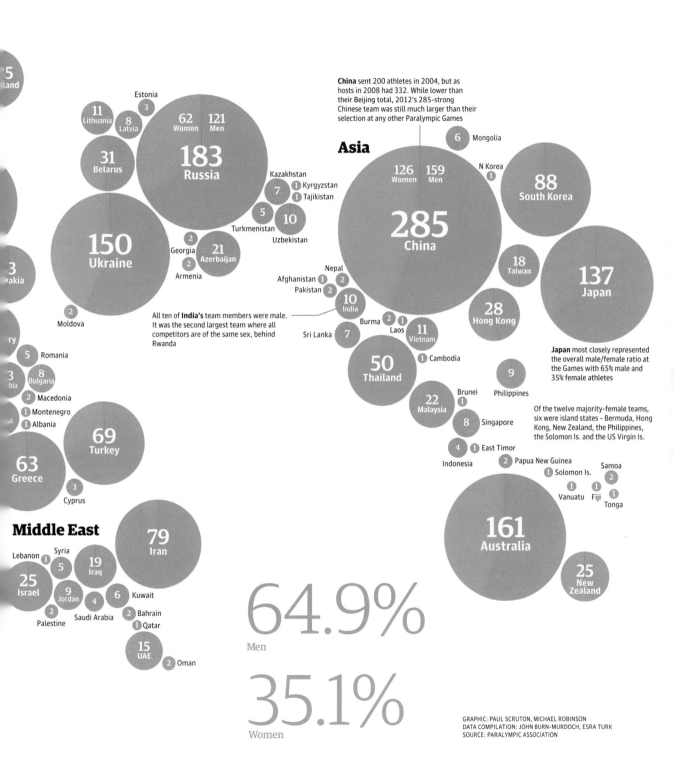

5
land

Estonia
3

11
Lithuania

8
Latvia

31
Belarus

62
Women

121
Men

183
Russia

Kazakhstan

1 Kyrgyzstan

7

1 Tajikistan

5

10

Turkmenistan

Uzbekistan

150
Ukraine

2
Georgia

21
Azerbaijan

2
Armenia

2
Moldova

All ten of **India's** team members were male.
It was the second largest team where all
competitors are of the same sex, behind
Rwanda

China sent 200 athletes in 2004, but as
hosts in 2008 had 332. While lower than
their Beijing total, 2012's 285-strong
Chinese team was still much larger than their
selection at any other Paralympic Games

Asia

6 Mongolia

126
Women

159
Men

N Korea
1

88
South Korea

285
China

18
Taiwan

137
Japan

Nepal

Afghanistan 1

2

Pakistan 2

10
India

28
Hong Kong

Burma

2 1

Sri Lanka

7

Laos

11
Vietnam

1 Cambodia

50
Thailand

9
Philippines

Japan most closely represented
the overall male/female ratio at
the Games with 65% male and
35% female athletes

Of the twelve majority-female teams,
six were island states - Bermuda, Hong
Kong, New Zealand, the Philippines,
the Solomon Is. and the US Virgin Is.

ry

5 Romania

3
bia

8
Bulgaria

1 Macedonia

1 Montenegro

a

1 Albania

69
Turkey

63
Greece

3
Cyprus

22
Malaysia

Brunei
1

8 Singapore

4 1 East Timor

Indonesia

2 Papua New Guinea

1 Solomon Is.

Samoa
2

1 1 1

Vanuatu Fiji

Tonga

161
Australia

25
New
Zealand

Middle East

Lebanon 1

Syria

5

19
Iraq

79
Iran

25
Israel

9
Jordan

4

6 Kuwait

2 Bahrain

Saudi Arabia

1 Qatar

Palestine

15
UAE

2 Oman

64.9%
Men

35.1%
Women

GRAPHIC: PAUL SCRUTON, MICHAEL ROBINSON
DATA COMPILATION: JOHN BURN-MURDOCH, ESRA TURK
SOURCE: PARALYMPIC ASSOCIATION

4,269

Number of athletes who competed at the Paralympic Games in London, taking part in 21 different disciplines

164

Number of countries which sent athletes; the biggest delegation was from Paralympics GB, which had 294 members

40

GB athletes won gold in 34 events, 22 of them women. The most successful Britons were cyclist Sarah Storey (pictured) and wheelchair racer David Weir, who both won four gold medals

8

The number of gold medals won by swimmer Jacquelin Freney of Australia. She ha won three bronzes in Beiji as a 16-year-old

and this was the "austerity Olympics" in a broke country. So, how does 2012 compare?

The House of Commons Library, which usually supplies MPs with the answers to tricky research questions, has published the ultimate statistical guide to how Britain, London and the Olympic Games themselves have changed. Olympic Britain charts how the world the Olympians of 1908 knew would seem unrecogniseable today. And how we got there.

In 1908, the first modern Olympics of 1896 was still a live memory, and this was quite a different world. The majority of the competitors came from the empires of Britain, Russia, Germany, the Austro-Hungarians and France, plus the new power: America. The five rings of the Olympic symbol weren't invented until Baron Pierre de Coubertin presented it to the world in 1914. Although the colonies were allowed to participate, it was hardly encouraged for fear it would lead to national identity and

6.3m
The number of Channel 4 viewers who saw at least five minutes of the T43/T44 100m final, won by Jonnie Peacock. 11.2m saw at least five minutes of the opening ceremony

176
The number of classifications for different levels of impairment within the Paralympic disciplines. There are 57 classifications within athletics alone

1,992
Total number of medals awarded in the London Paralympic Games

565
Records broken at the Games, of which 232 were world records and 333 were Paralympic records

undermine their European masters. Two indigenous Africans from South Africa had been allowed to compete in the St Louis Games of 1904, featuring in "athletic games for savages", although they were allowed to enter the marathon, finishing ninth and twelfth out of 36. It wasn't until 1952 that any other sub-Saharan country participated, Ghana, although it didn't win a medal until Clement Quartey won a boxing silver in 1960.

11
Providing the raw data is as important as writing about it

When an event produces as much information as the Olympic Games – but the data is as closed off as this, then there is a role in simply making that data easy to find. We included most statistics and schedules on a London Olympics data special site. Here are some of the raw data highlights we produced:

The Paralympic medals table
How Paralympics GB performed sport by sport

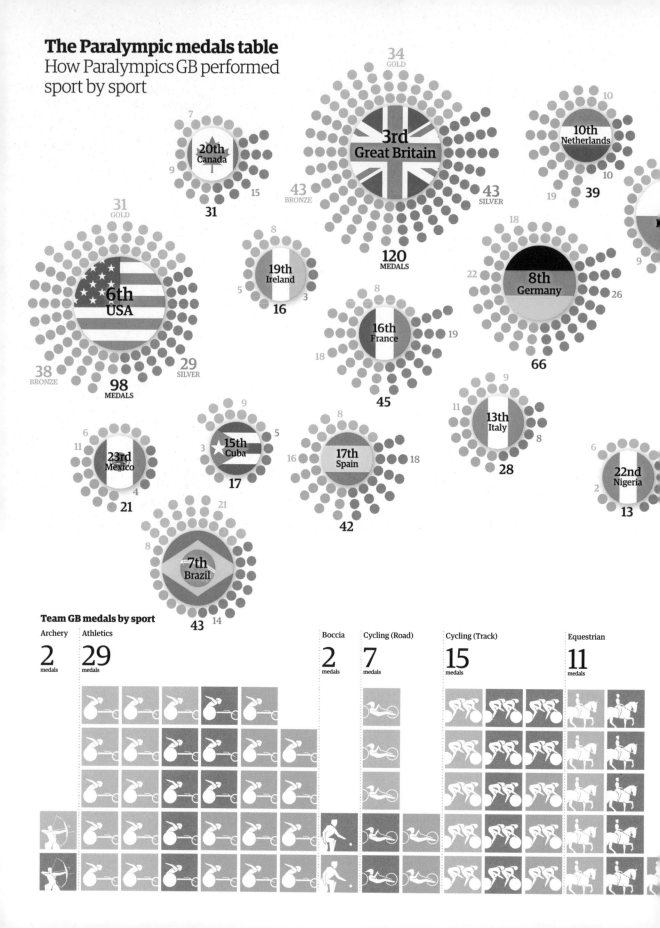

20th Canada — 7 · 9 · 15 — **31**

3rd Great Britain — 34 GOLD · 43 BRONZE · 43 SILVER — **120 MEDALS**

10th Netherlands — 10 · 10 · 19 — **39**

31 GOLD **6th** USA **38 BRONZE** · **29 SILVER** — **98 MEDALS**

19th Ireland — 8 · 5 · 3 — **16**

8th Germany — 18 · 22 · 26 — **66**

16th France — 8 · 18 · 19 — **45**

13th Italy — 9 · 11 · 8 — **28**

23rd Mexico — 6 · 11 · 4 — **21**

15th Cuba — 9 · 3 · 5 — **17**

17th Spain — 8 · 16 · 18 — **42**

22nd Nigeria — 6 · 2 — **13**

7th Brazil — 8 · 21 · 14 — **43**

Team GB medals by sport

Archery	Athletics	Boccia	Cycling (Road)	Cycling (Track)	Equestrian
2 medals	**29** medals	**2** medals	**7** medals	**15** medals	**11** medals

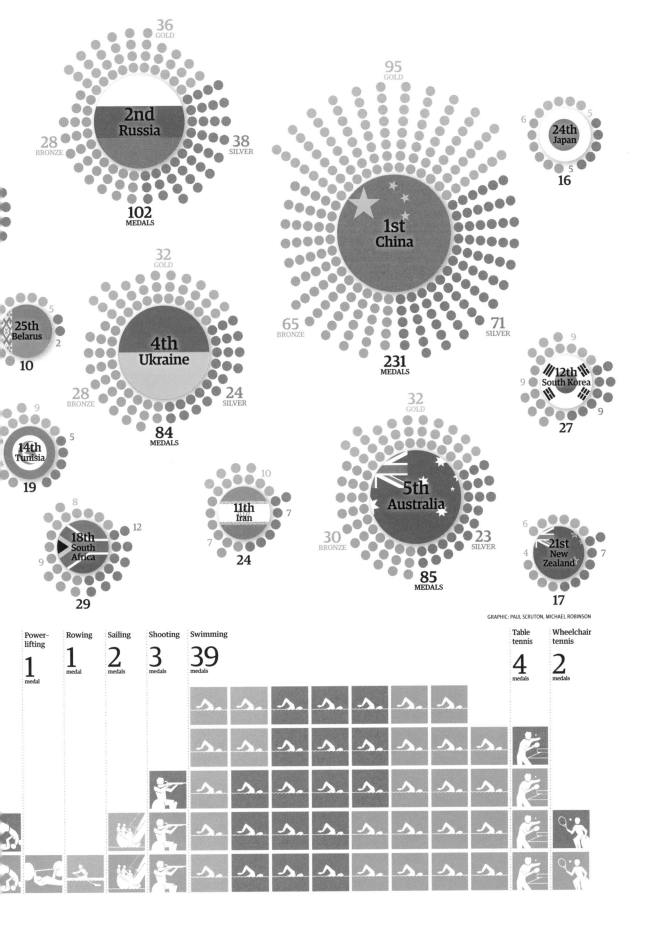

36
GOLD

2nd
Russia

28
BRONZE

38
SILVER

102
MEDALS

95
GOLD

1st
China

65
BRONZE

71
SILVER

231
MEDALS

6   5

24th
Japan

5

16

32
GOLD

4th
Ukraine

28
BRONZE

24
SILVER

84
MEDALS

5

25th
Belarus

2

10

9

12th
South Korea

9   9

9

27

9

5

14th
Tunisia

19

10

11th
Iran

7

7

24

32
GOLD

5th
Australia

30
BRONZE

23
SILVER

85
MEDALS

8

18th
South
Africa

12

9

29

6

21st
New
Zealand

7

4

17

GRAPHIC: PAUL SCRUTON, MICHAEL ROBINSON

Power-lifting	Rowing	Sailing	Shooting	Swimming		Table tennis	Wheelchair tennis
1 medal	**1** medal	**2** medals	**3** medals	**39** medals		**4** medals	**2** medals

● Every medal won in the 2012 Games
● Every record broken at London 2012
● Every athlete competing at London 2012
● Every result for every athlete in every event
● The schedule as open data.

76.3%
of Olympic tickets and 91% of Paralympics tickets were sold to the UK public. However, for some blue riband sessions, the proportion of tickets sold to the public was much lower. For example, only 51.1% of those who watched Usain Bolt win the 100m final were holding tickets sold to the UK public
SOURCE: LOCOG

When an event dominates the news, costs as much and involves as many people as the Olympics did, there will always be data to analyse and generate stories from. It's more than just reporting results.

As the Games developed, the big question of the day became how to interpret the stream of numbers emanating from Stratford's Olympic Park and the other Olympic venues. It became less about using other people's data and more about generating our own.

12

Major news events always produce data journalism

When the 8,000 runners started carrying the Olympic torch around the country, data journalists started to work at breaking down the numbers behind the news. An investigation by Help Me Investigate, which was published on the Datablog, looked into the hundreds of "ghost runners", who were not on the official list but were instead placed there by sponsors. The 25% of places outside of public nomination campaigns were allocated through internal processes at commercial partners, the International Olympic Committee, sporting bodies, direct invitation from Locog, and the relay's sponsors – one of whom allocated 15% of its 1,360 places for its own staff. Some data on places is still missing.

The fact that this information was closed and required a major investigative effort reflects a lot of what we know about the Olympics: the stuff you really want to know isn't necessarily the information that's open and published freely. It's much more likely to be hidden right around the corner.

And if data journalism is about anything, it's about turning that corner and telling that story.

Additional material by John Burn-Murdoch and Nicola Hughes

Chapter 7
Data around the world

What you'll find out in this chapter:

» How you can analyse data at street level » The revolution the internet has sparked in Africa » The most dangerous countries, according to the murder map of the world

The world may be in recession but the Open Data movement is blossoming, with governments and organisations freeing data around the globe. From national-level efforts in the US, Australia, New Zealand, Spain, to local government in California, San Francisco, New York … the list expands every day.

And it's not just governments: the European Union has become one of the latest bodies to throw open the doors of its data vaults, following the World Bank, with the Organisation for Economic Co-operation and Development (OECD) said to be not far behind. But how does it work in practice? What actually happens when you free the data?

Toronto and Nairobi could not be much further apart but both have dived into the open data fray with enthusiasm. How has it worked for them?

Toronto, Canada

Imagine if you took the historic records of everyone who died in the first world war. Then you matched them to one area to see how it had been affected. Or if you wanted to see if one part of your city had an epidemic of bedbugs. Or if you wanted to find out where the most guns are.

This is the work of data journalist Patrick Cain, quietly and methodically producing strikingly interesting maps of his home city of Toronto.

It's the pinnacle of what data journalism is supposed to be about. And, if you're looking for innovative data reporting, vast open data resources and the latest open data apps, Canada is a good place to start.

Enthralled by open data initiatives around the world, Canadians from Ottawa to Vancouver are embracing spreadsheets as never before – and producing great work which you don't often hear about outside the country.

Patrick Cain works by doggedly pursuing datasets, often from official sources which don't want to know, but bolstered by a powerful freedom of information system:

"If something is uncontroversial (like dog

171%
Increase in Chinese carbon emissions since the year 2000. China emits more CO_2 than the US and Canada put together

SOURCE: US ENERGY INFORMATION ADMINISTRATION

Mapping Toronto's mother tongues
How Patrick Cain uses 2011 census data

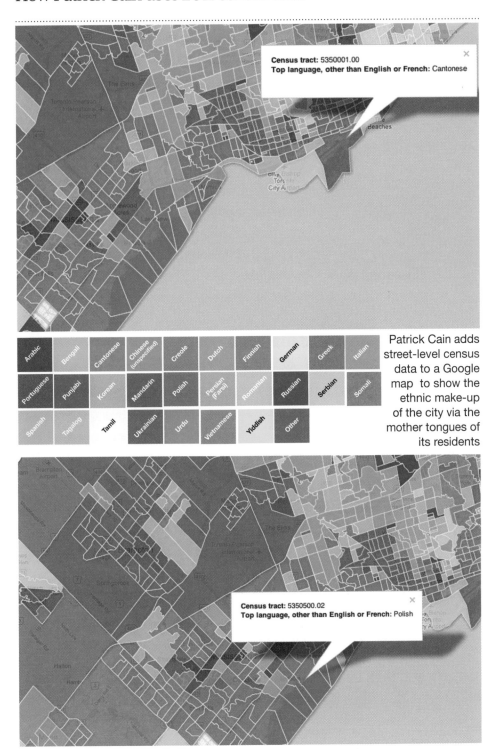

Census tract: 5350001.00
Top language, other than English or French: Cantonese

Patrick Cain adds street-level census data to a Google map to show the ethnic make-up of the city via the mother tongues of its residents

Census tract: 5350500.02
Top language, other than English or French: Polish

licences by postal code) there are often no issues about releasing it. On the other side, we have the sex offender database, which I've been trying to get access to since the spring in 2008. Sometimes there is ineffective resistance, like the landlord and tenant appeal board that tried to get me to sign a non-disclosure agreement. Mostly I get things in the mail as the law demands … Everybody (including me) likes the rage-against-the-machine stories, but in the majority of cases the system works more or less as intended."

Cain is one of the most established of the new breed. Names mentioned by those in the know include Chad Skelton on the Vancouver Sun, Rob Cribb at the Toronto Star; David McKie at CBC and Glen McGregor at the Ottawa Citizen.

Toronto's open data initiative is run by a small team of enthusiasts

> 66
> Mostly I get things in the mail as the law demands. Everybody (including me) likes the rage-against-the-machine stories, but in the majority of cases, the system works more or less as intended
>
> **Patrick Cain, data journalist**
> 99

Toronto's war dead mapped
Old records and Google maps give insight into history

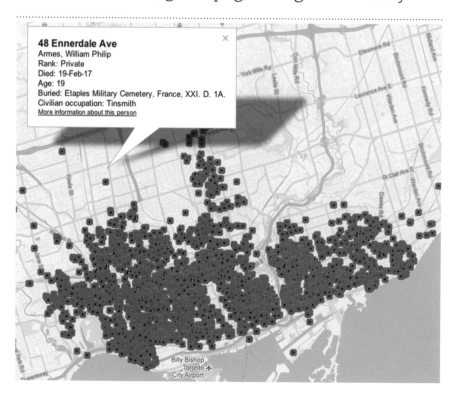

in the city authority's web department. Led by Trish Garner, the unit updates the site every day with raw datasets from local election results to detailed boundary mapping. And all in addition to their day job of keeping the city's tech running. She's inspired by the worldwide open data movement.

3.05m

Refugees from Afghanistan in 2011, followed by Iraq and Somalia. Pakistan hosted the largest number of refugees in relation to the size of its economy, with **710** refugees per $1 of GDP (PPP) per capita

SOURCE: UN

"I think there's a large community of developers in Toronto and across Canada which is inspired by what's going on in the UK and in the US under the Obama administration and want to see change here at home. A good majority have registered with us and are quite avidly following what we're doing."

Politically, she says, support is growing: "There has been solid support from the very top – our Mayor – and from the City Clerk and the CIO [Chief Information Officer] … this is key for us. I have to say, too, that it wouldn't be possible to carry on without the constructive feedback and support we've received from the developer community, and the dedication and enthusiasm of a bright, highly motivated, energetic team. They love what they do and they have fun."

The Canadian government is consulting on an open data policy and recently, Canada's biggest open data sites – Toronto, Vancouver, Ottawa and Edmonton – have started getting together to set a series of open data standards. Jury Konga, who has been helping to create the G4 Open Data Framework, which links cities all over Canada, says the country is jumping onto the open data train: "Canada is a hive of activity in Open Government and Open Data and I only see it increasing … We have also seen Open Data surface in the political realm where the Liberal Party of Canada recently put forward a new policy of Open Gov–Open Data and mayoral candidates in Toronto advocated increasing the Open Data program in Toronto … I am ecstatic with the progress we've made but there is much more to do."

34,612

Deaths in Mexico's drug war, up until the end of 2010, by far the most violent year so far with **15,273** people killed

SOURCE: GOVERNMENT OF MEXICO

The conflict in Syria, 2012
Using multiple sources to build up a complex picture

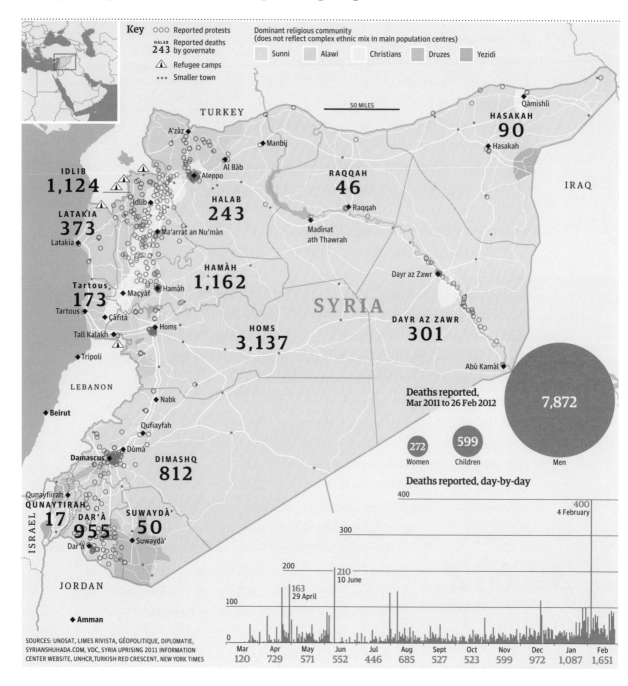

Key
○○○ Reported protests
HALAB Reported deaths
243 by governate
△ Refugee camps
••• Smaller town

Dominant religious community
(does not reflect complex ethnic mix in main population centres)
Sunni   Alawi   Christians   Druzes   Yezidi

TURKEY

50 MILES

A'zàz
Manbij
Al Bàb
Aleppo
IDLIB
1,124
Idlib
HALAB
243
LATAKIA
373
Latakia
Ma'arrat an Nu'màn
HAMÀH
HASAKAH
90
Hasakah
RAQQAH
46
Raqqah
Madinat
ath Thawrah
IRAQ

Tartous
173
Tartous
Çâfità
Tall Kalakh
Tripoli
Maçyàf   Hamàh
Homs
HAMÀH
1,162
SYRIA
Dayr az Zawr
DAYR AZ ZAWR
301
HOMS
3,137

LEBANON
Nabk
Beirut
Qufiayfah
Dùmà
Abù Kamàl

Damascus
DIMASHQ
812

Qunayfiirah
QUNAYTIRAH
17   **DAR'À**
955
Dar'à
SUWAYDÀ'
50
Suwaydà'

ISRAEL

JORDAN

Amman

Deaths reported,
Mar 2011 to 26 Feb 2012

272
Women
599
Children
7,872
Men

Deaths reported, day-by-day
400

400
4 February

300

210
10 June

200

163
29 April

100

0

Mar	Apr	May	Jun	Jul	Aug	Sept	Oct	Nov	Dec	Jan	Feb
120	729	571	552	446	685	527	523	599	972	1,087	1,651

SOURCES: UNOSAT, LIMES RIVISTA, GÉOPOLITIQUE, DIPLOMATIE, SYRIANSHUHADA.COM, VDC, SYRIA UPRISING 2011 INFORMATION CENTER WEBSITE, UNHCR, TURKISH RED CRESCENT, NEW YORK TIMES

Nairobi, Kenya

Claire Provost

When violence erupted after the 2007 Kenyan elections, a team of activists produced Ushahidi – a digital open-source platform to monitor crises in near real-time. Taking its name from the Kiswahili word for testimony, or witness, Ushahidi has since been deployed to monitor unrest in the Democratic Republic of Congo, track violence in Gaza and gather global reports about the spread of swine flu. Around the same time, a partnership between Vodafone and Safaricom, Kenya's largest mobile operator, produced M-PESA, the mobile banking system that has revolutionised the way many Kenyans manage their money.

Projects from Ushahidi to M-PESA have put Kenya firmly

133

Countries in the world rated as "significantly corrupt" by Transparency International in its Corruption Index – out of 184. The index scores countries on a scale of zero (low) to 10 (high). Afghanistan and Myanmar both have a score of 1.5, with Somalia and North Korea – measured for the first time – coming in last with a score of 1

Ushahidi's open-source, collaborative approach has helped it spread across Africa, where millions of people are gaining internet access through phones every year

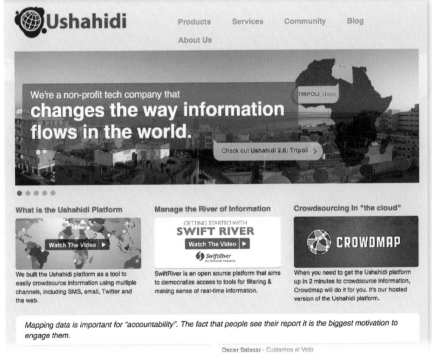

on the map of ICT innovation in international development – a position and a trend the Kenyan government now seems eager to promote.

Kenya has become the first sub-Saharan African country to launch a national open data initiative, opening the books on public expenditure, parliamentary proceedings and the locations of public services.

The Kenya Open Data Initiative (KODI) – which can be found at opendata.go.ke holds more than 160 datasets organised under six sub-headings: education, energy, health, population, poverty and water and sanitation.

Users can explore data at the country level, but also by county or constituency. The platform includes newly created geospatial boundaries for Kenya's 47 counties and geocoded datasets can be visualised quickly using simple built-in tools. Data is pulled in from the national census and government ministries as well as from the World Bank.

79

countries will have a million or more Muslim inhabitants in 2030, up from **72** countries today. If current trends continue, Muslims will make up **26.4%** of the world's total projected population of **8.3bn** in 2030. From 1990 to 2010, the global Muslim population increased at an average annual rate of **2.2%**

SOURCE: PEW RESEARCH

"Our information is a national asset, and it's time it was shared: this data is key to improving transparency; unlocking social and economic value; and building Government 2.0 in Kenya," says the KODI website.

The initiative, launched by the Kenyan government, aims to promote data-driven decision making and help improve government transparency and accountability.

Users of the open data portal can create interactive charts and tables, and developers can download the raw data via an API to analyse and build applications for web and mobile. There's also a "suggest a dataset" button that collects requests for new data. Demands have already piled in, with requests for data on youth unemployment, libraries, crime and the locations of primary and secondary schools.

Writing for the East African, Charles Onyango-Obbo, Nation Media Group's executive editor for Africa and digital media, suggests that the Kenyan president Mwai Kibaki's acceptance of the open data initiative is linked to the "enlightened malice" of an outgoing leader putting measures in place "that make it harder for their predecessors to govern with as

Africa's top Tweeters
Mobile technology reveals spread of wealth in Africa

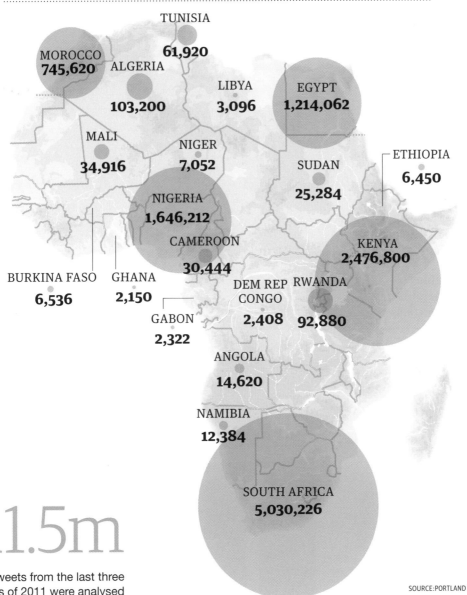

TUNISIA
61,920

MOROCCO
745,620 ALGERIA

LIBYA
3,096

EGYPT
1,214,062

103,200

MALI
34,916

NIGER
7,052

SUDAN
25,284

ETHIOPIA
6,450

NIGERIA
1,646,212

CAMEROON
30,444

KENYA
2,476,800

BURKINA FASO
6,536

GHANA
2,150

DEM REP
CONGO
2,408

RWANDA
92,880

GABON
2,322

ANGOLA
14,620

NAMIBIA
12,384

SOUTH AFRICA
5,030,226

SOURCE:PORTLAND

11.5m

Tweets from the last three months of 2011 were analysed by Portland and Tweetminster to reveal the spread of technology and Twitter in the continent. Some 68% of users said they used the social networking platform to monitor the news

Wiring up Africa
The undersea internet infrastructure, 2012

Mediterranean undersea cables
— **Atlas Offshore:** 320 gigabits (Active)
— **SAS-1:** 1280 gigabits (Active)
— **SEA-ME-WE 4:** 1280 gigabits (Active)
— **I-ME-WE:** 3840 gigabits (Active)
— **EIG:** 3840 gigabits (Active)

West coast cables
— **SAT3/SAFE:** 340 gigabits (Active)
— **MaIN OnE:** 1920 gigabits (Active)
— **GLO-1:** 2500 gigabits (Active)
— **WACS:** 5120 gigabits (Q2 2012)
— **ACE:** 5120 gigabits (Q2 2012)
— **SAex:** 12.8 terabits (2014)
— **WASACE:** 40 terabits (2014)

East coast cables
— **SEAS:** 320 gigabits (Q3 2012)
— **TEAMs** 1280 gigabits (Active)
— **Seacom:** 1280 gigabits (Active)
— **Lion2:** 1280 gigabits (Active)
— **Lion:** 1300 gigabits (Active)
— **EASSy:** 4720 gigabits (Active)
— **BRICS:** 12.8 terabits (2014)

KEY
— 0-2,000gb
— 2,000-4,000gb
— 4,000-6,000gb
— 12.8tb
— 40tb

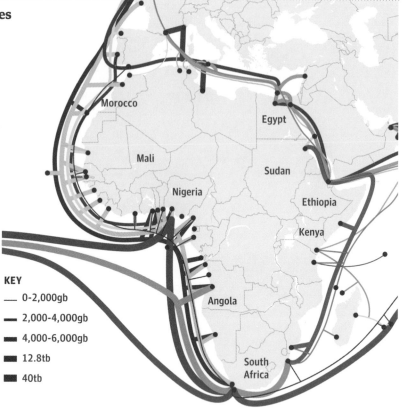

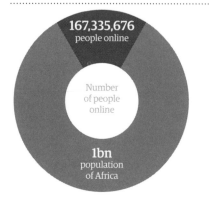

167,335,676
people online

Number of people online

1bn
population of Africa

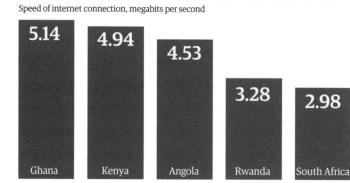

Speed of internet connection, megabits per second

5.14	4.94	4.53	3.28	2.98
Ghana	Kenya	Angola	Rwanda	South Africa

7%
of the world's internet users are in Africa

15.6%
of Africa's population is on the internet

37.7%
of the rest of the world is on the internet

48m
Facebook users in Africa as of September 2012

Internet users
By country and mobile phone penetration, 2012

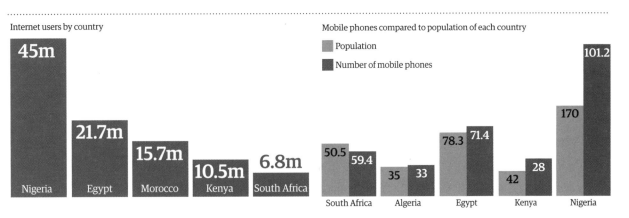

Internet users by country

45m Nigeria
21.7m Egypt
15.7m Morocco
10.5m Kenya
6.8m South Africa

Mobile phones compared to population of each country
- Population
- Number of mobile phones

	South Africa	Algeria	Egypt	Kenya	Nigeria
Population	50.5	35	78.3	42	170
Number of mobile phones	59.4	33	71.4	28	101.2

free a hand as they did". Kenya currently ranks 154 out of the 178 countries listed in Transparency International's annual corruption index.

"For the first time ever, people in our communities will be empowered to choose the best schools for their children, locate the nearest health facility that meets their needs, and use regional statistics to lobby their constituency representative for better infrastructure and services in their county," said Paul Kubuko, CEO of the Kenya ICT Board, to mark the launch.

The data portal is managed by the Kenya ICT Board in partnership with the World Bank, and is powered by Socrata, a Seattle-based startup that has worked on open data projects with partners such as the City of Chicago and Medicare, the US government social insurance programme for those over 65 and for people living with disabilities.

But with the still-low proportion of people connected to the internet in Kenya, does a digital platform for government data really make that information more accessible? According to Socrata, only 25.9% of Kenyans have access to the internet. But, the developer is quick to point out, the majority of Kenyans – 63.2% –

7,853
tonnes of global opium production in 2009 – Afghanistan produced just under 7,000 metric tonnes of this. 460–480 mt of heroin was trafficked and 375 mt are estimated to have reach consumers
SOURCE: UN

2.7m

New HIV cases in 2010, down from **3.2m** in 2001. Since 1999, the year in which it is thought the HIV epidemic peaked globally, the number of new infections has fallen by **19%**

SOURCE: UNAIDS

have mobile access, and the open data portal should be seen as an important first step towards the development of mobile applications to improve the lives of ordinary Kenyans.

"It now falls to Kenya's dynamic and entrepreneurial citizens to create user-friendly and relevant applications that will benefit Kenyans by identifying development solutions and improving development outcomes," said World Bank country director Johannes Zutt at the launch event in Nairobi.

To promote the new platform, the Kenya ICT Board is awarding grants to developers to create "high-impact" apps using the data. Already, the team behind the Ushahidi-powered platform, Huduma – Kiswahili for "services" – has used the data to map and explore access

Comparing healthcare systems
Showing the strengths and weaknesses of Cuba, the UK and the United States

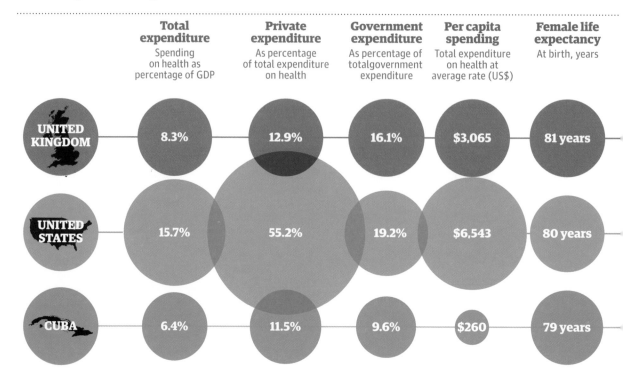

	Total expenditure Spending on health as percentage of GDP	**Private expenditure** As percentage of total expenditure on health	**Government expenditure** As percentage of total government expenditure	**Per capita spending** Total expenditure on health at average rate (US$)	**Female life expectancy** At birth, years
UNITED KINGDOM	8.3%	12.9%	16.1%	$3,065	81 years
UNITED STATES	15.7%	55.2%	19.2%	$6,543	80 years
CUBA	6.4%	11.5%	9.6%	$260	79 years

to health, infrastructure and education. Virtual Kenya has built an application mapping counties where MPs have refused to pay taxes. The Nairobi-based Business Daily has announced plans to publish a series of articles on the newly released data.

The right to information was enshrined in the 2010 Kenyan Constitution, which also requires the government to publish and publicise any important information affecting the country. But progress on translating words into action has been slow and the government has yet to enact freedom of information legislation. An open data initiative, though, is a big step for any country – and how the newly accessible datasets will affect the relationships between Kenyans and their government is certainly something to watch.

15.8m

The size of Lagos in Nigeria by the year 2025, making it Africa's largest city. The other largest cities will be Cairo (**11m** now; **13.5m** by 2025); Alexandria (**4.4m** now, **5.6m** in 2025); Kinshasa in DRC (**8.7m** now, **15m** by 2025); and Luanda, Angola (**4.8m** now, **8m** by 2025

SOURCE: UN-HABITAT

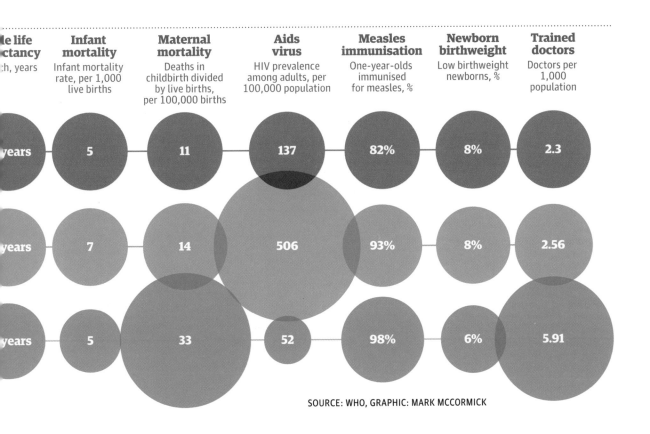

Life expectancy	Infant mortality	Maternal mortality	Aids virus	Measles immunisation	Newborn birthweight	Trained doctors
birth, years	Infant mortality rate, per 1,000 live births	Deaths in childbirth divided by live births, per 100,000 births	HIV prevalence among adults, per 100,000 population	One-year-olds immunised for measles, %	Low birthweight newborns, %	Doctors per 1,000 population
years	5	11	137	82%	8%	2.3
years	7	14	506	93%	8%	2.56
years	5	33	52	98%	6%	5.91

SOURCE: WHO, GRAPHIC: MARK McCORMICK

Murder map of the world

Murder rates per million people, 2006

Different countries record crimes in different ways – and some are better at it than others. The numbers are full of variables – how many crimes are actually reported to the police, and even what counts as a crime. Murder is obviously an offence in every country in the world – and tends to be reported. These numbers come from the United Nations Survey of Crime Trends. Afghanistan's rate may seem low; this is because the number dates from before the surge in roadside bombings. Somalia's low rate is likely a reflection of the poor functioning of the government until very recently.

Statisticians use a rate so that we can compare different countries in a meaningful way – 100 murders in one country is proportionally more severe than in the other. So, the number of murders per 100,000 population – or per 1 million population in this case – allows a fair comparison.

SOURCE: UNODC

Europe

Iceland 10
Scotland
Norway 8
Sweden 12
Finland 28
Northern Ireland 24
England & Wales 16
Netherlands 11
Denmark
Germany 14
Belgium 10
Poland 17
Ireland 11
France 21
Lux
Czech Rep 22
Andorra 14
Switz 29
Liecht 29
Slovakia 23
Hungary 21
Portugal 14
Spain 12
Monaco 31
Italy 7
Austria
Slovenia 12
Romania 24
Croatia 20
Serbia 14
Bulgaria 31
Malta 17
Bosnia 18
Turkey 69
Montenegro 36
Albania 66
Greece 10
Macedonia 24
Cyprus 18

Eurasia

Lithuania 91
Belarus 83
Moldova 72

North America

Canada 15
US 59
Mexico 109

Caribbean and South America

Bermuda 11
Bahamas 225
Cuba 60
Haiti 53
Dominican Republic 168
Puerto Rico 189
Anguilla 83
Saint Kitts and Nevis 227
Antigua and Barbuda 77
Dominica 103
Jamaica 337
Saint Lucia 213
Guatemala 263
Belize 301
Honduras 138
Saint Vincent and the Grenadines 160
Barbados 151
El Salvador 564
Nicaragua 174
Grenada 49
Trinidad and Tobago 137
Costa Rica 73
Panama 134
Venezuela 325
Colombia 611
Guyana 192
Brazil 308
Suriname 118
Ecuador 168
Peru 30
Bolivia 53
Chile 55
Paraguay 178
Argentina 53
Uruguay 47

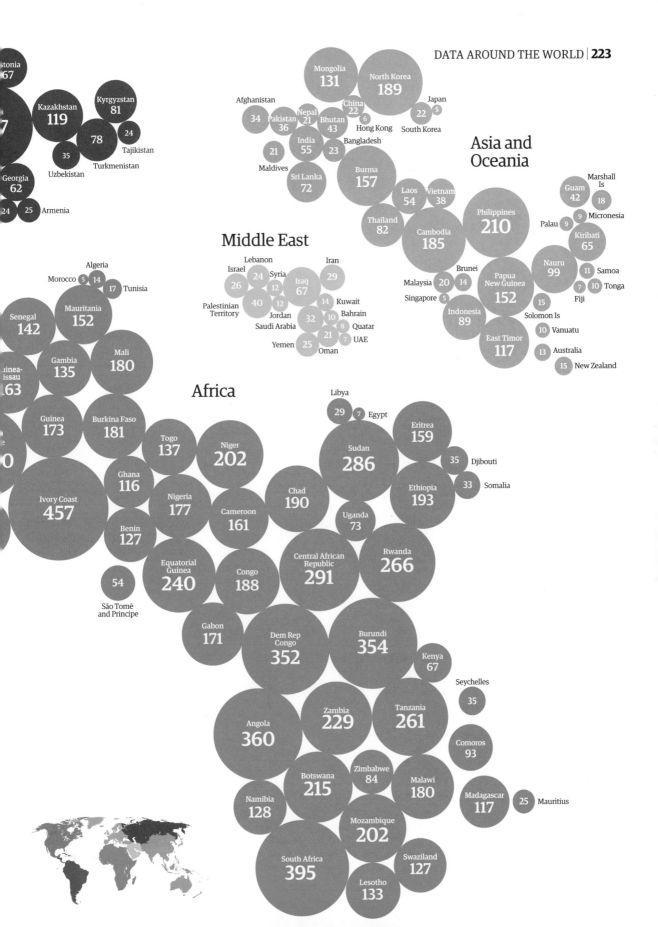

stonia
67

Kazakhstan
119

Kyrgyzstan
81

78

24
Tajikistan

35

Uzbekistan

Turkmenistan

Georgia
62

24

25 Armenia

Asia and Oceania

Mongolia
131

North Korea
189

Japan

22

5

South Korea

Afghanistan

34

Pakistan
36

Nepal
21

Bhutan
43

China
22

Hong Kong
6

India
55

Bangladesh
23

21

Maldives

Sri Lanka
72

Burma
157

Laos
54

Vietnam
38

Thailand
82

Cambodia
185

Philippines
210

Guam
42

Marshall
Is
18

Palau
9

9
Micronesia

Kiribati
65

Brunei

Malaysia
20

14

Singapore
5

Papua
New Guinea
152

Nauru
99

11
Samoa

7

10 Tonga

Fiji

Indonesia
89

Solomon Is
15

10 Vanuatu

East Timor
117

13 Australia

15 New Zealand

Middle East

Lebanon

Israel

24

Syria

Iran

26

40

12

Iraq
67

29

12

Kuwait
14

Palestinian
Territory

Jordan

Saudi Arabia

32

10 Bahrain

8 Quatar

21

7 UAE

Yemen
25

Oman

Africa

Algeria

Morocco
5

14

17 Tunisia

Senegal
142

Mauritania
152

Guinea-
issau
63

Gambia
135

Mali
180

Guinea
173

Burkina Faso
181

Togo
137

Niger
202

Ghana
116

Libya

29

7 Egypt

Sudan
286

Eritrea
159

35 Djibouti

Ivory Coast
457

Nigeria
177

Cameroon
161

Chad
190

Ethiopia
193

33 Somalia

Benin
127

Uganda
73

Equatorial
Guinea
240

Congo
188

Central African
Republic
291

Rwanda
266

54

São Tomé
and Príncipe

Gabon
171

Dem Rep
Congo
352

Burundi
354

Kenya
67

Seychelles
35

Angola
360

Zambia
229

Tanzania
261

Comoros
93

Botswana
215

Zimbabwe
84

Malawi
180

Madagascar
117

25 Mauritius

Namibia
128

Mozambique
202

South Africa
395

Swaziland
127

Lesotho
133

US$ billionaires

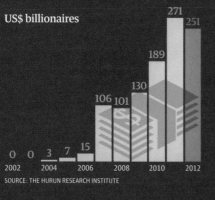

| 0 | 0 | 3 | 7 | 15 | 106 | 101 | 130 | 189 | 271 | 251 |

2002   2004   2006   2008   2010   2012

SOURCE: THE HURUN RESEARCH INSTITUTE

BMW sales
(excluding MINI)

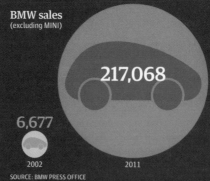

217,068

6,677

2002   2011

SOURCE: BMW PRESS OFFICE

Divorces

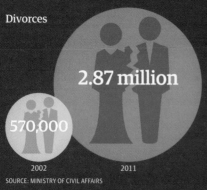

2.87 million

570,000

2002   2011

SOURCE: MINISTRY OF CIVIL AFFAIRS

Number of internet users

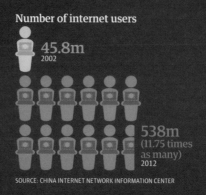

45.8m
2002

538m
(11.75 times
as many)
2012

SOURCE: CHINA INTERNET NETWORK INFORMATION CENTER

Cement consumption
tons

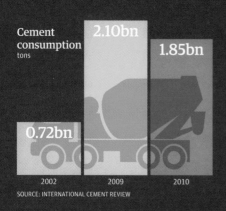

2.10bn

1.85bn

0.72bn

2002   2009   2010

SOURCE: INTERNATIONAL CEMENT REVIEW

KFC outlets

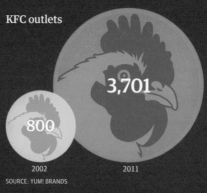

3,701

800

2002   2011

SOURCE: YUM! BRANDS

Bottles of wine consumed

1,600m
(est)

700m

2002   2011

SOURCE: CNN

International tourism
Number of departures

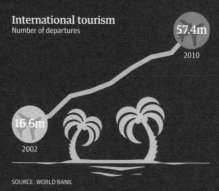

57.4m
2010

16.6m
2002

SOURCE: WORLD BANK

GDP gro
Q3 2010

Diplomacy
Embassies, consulates
and missions

289   251

GDP
per capita
2009

$45,989.18

Social
media
Facebook/
Qzone users
worldwide
31 Jan 2009

500m

9.4%

Unemployment
China = Sept 2009 est.

Wal
$40

Top brand
Revenue

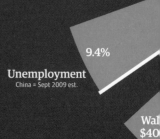

Ratio of workers to retirees (age
2000

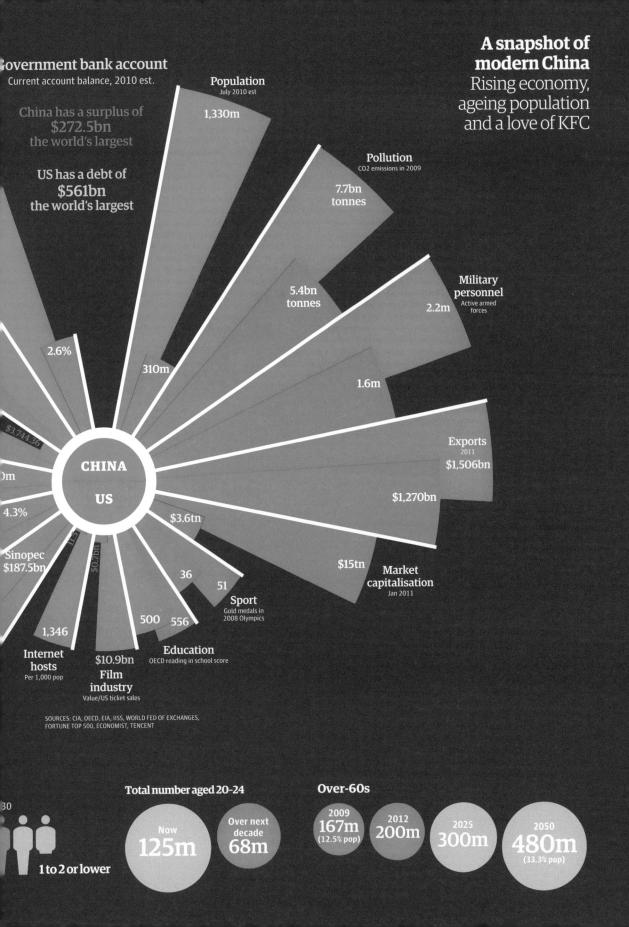

A snapshot of modern China
Rising economy, ageing population and a love of KFC

Government bank account
Current account balance, 2010 est.

China has a surplus of
$272.5bn
the world's largest

US has a debt of
$561bn
the world's largest

Population
July 2010 est
1,330m

Pollution
CO2 emissions in 2009
7.7bn tonnes

5.4bn tonnes

Military personnel
Active armed forces
2.2m

2.6%

310m

1.6m

$3,744.36

0m

4.3%

Exports
2011
$1,506bn

$1,270bn

Sinopec
$187.5bn

$3.6tn

CHINA

US

$15tn

Market capitalisation
Jan 2011

36

51

Sport
Gold medals in 2008 Olympics

500   556

1,346

Internet hosts
Per 1,000 pop

$10.9bn
Film industry
Value/US ticket sales

Education
OECD reading in school score

SOURCES: CIA, OECD, EIA, IISS, WORLD FED OF EXCHANGES,
FORTUNE TOP 500, ECONOMIST, TENCENT

30

1 to 2 or lower

Total number aged 20-24

Now
125m

Over next decade
68m

Over-60s

2009
167m
(12.5% pop)

2012
200m

2025
300m

2050
480m
(33.3% pop)

Extinctions and critically endangered species in numbers

● Extinct ○ Critically endangered

North America

246
Plants, insects & other

27
Fish

19
Birds

5 Mammals

4 Reptiles

2 Amphibians

261
Extinctions

27
in 2012

303
Critically endangered

33
in 2012

Europe

319
Plants, insects & other

63
Fish

7 Reptiles

5 Mammals

2 Birds

2 Amphibian

398
Critically endangered

30
Extinctions

2
in 2012

5
in 2012

Caribbean islands

66
Amphibians

128
Plants, insects & other

23
Reptiles

14
Birds

6 Mammals

5 Fish

242
Critically endangered

50
Extinctions

10
in 2012

17
in 2012

North Africa

28
Plants, insects & other

12
Fish

6

52
1996-2012

16
in 2012

4
in 2012

Mesoamerica

168
Amphibians

41
Fish

35
Mammals

118
Plants, insects & other

12
Reptiles

9
Birds

383
Critically endangered

30
Extinctions

3
in 2012

10
in 2012

Sub-Saharan Africa

381
Plants, insects & other

97
Extinctions

33
in 2012

South America

155
Amphibians

398
Plants, insects & other

51
Birds

32
Mammals

14
Fish

9
Reptiles

659
Critically endangered

33
Extinctions

1 in 2012

53
in 2012

3,879
species
are on the
critically
endangered
list

European eel

Amur leopard

Chinese giant salamander

Sumatran elephant

Greater bamboo lemur

French Polynesia

Kakapo parrot

Species listed as 'critically endangered'

	1-3
	4-10
	11-20
	21-50
	51-100
	101-200
	201+

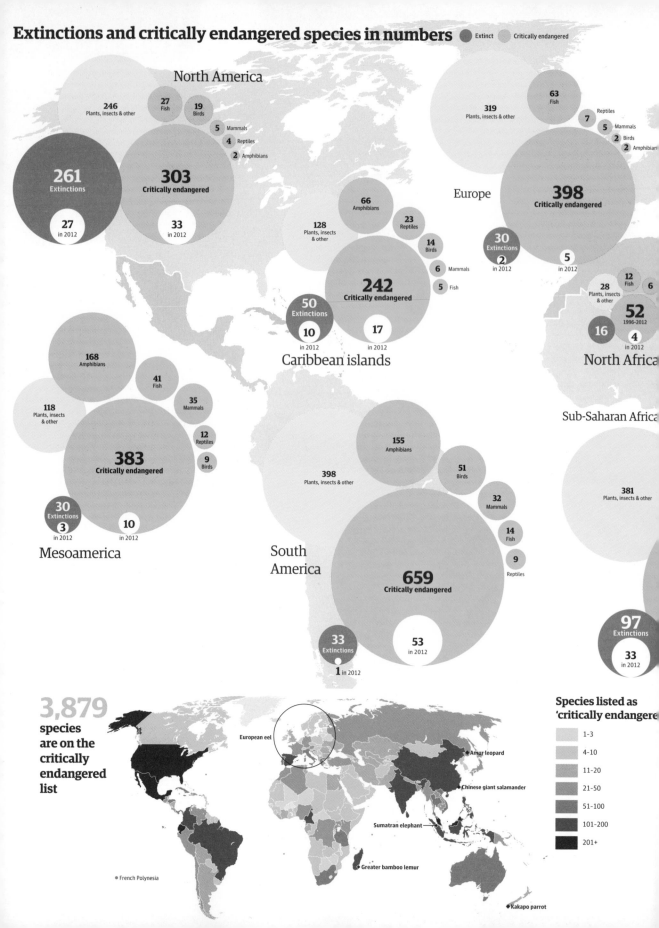

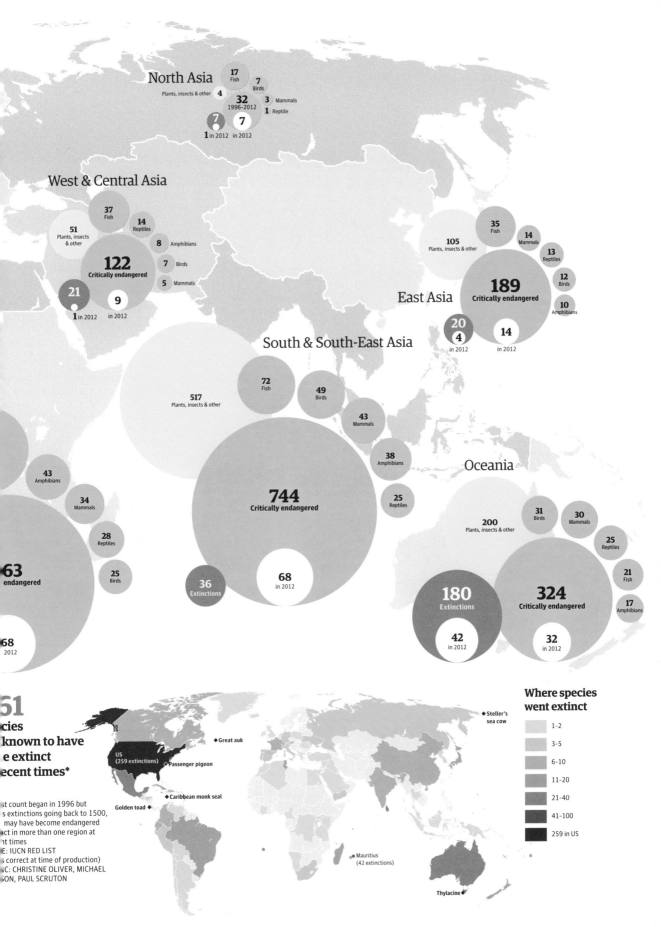

North Asia

17 Fish

7 Birds

4 Plants, insects & other

32 1996–2012

3 Mammals

1 Reptile

7 **1** in 2012

7 in 2012

West & Central Asia

37 Fish

14 Reptiles

51 Plants, insects & other

8 Amphibians

7 Birds

5 Mammals

122 Critically endangered

21 **1** in 2012

9 in 2012

East Asia

35 Fish

14 Mammals

105 Plants, insects & other

13 Reptiles

12 Birds

10 Amphibians

189 Critically endangered

20 **4** in 2012

14 in 2012

South & South-East Asia

72 Fish

49 Birds

517 Plants, insects & other

43 Mammals

38 Amphibians

25 Reptiles

744 Critically endangered

36 Extinctions

68 in 2012

43 Amphibians

34 Mammals

28 Reptiles

63 endangered

25 Birds

68 2012

Oceania

200 Plants, insects & other

31 Birds

30 Mammals

25 Reptiles

21 Fish

17 Amphibians

180 Extinctions

324 Critically endangered

42 in 2012

32 in 2012

51 cies known to have e extinct ecent times*

st count began in 1996 but s extinctions going back to 1500, may have become endangered ct in more than one region at nt times
E: IUCN RED LIST
s correct at time of production)
C: CHRISTINE OLIVER, MICHAEL SON, PAUL SCRUTON

◆ Steller's sea cow

◆ Great auk

US (259 extinctions) ◇ Passenger pigeon

◆ Caribbean monk seal

Golden toad ◆

● Mauritius (42 extinctions)

Thylacine ◆

Where species went extinct

	1–2
	3–5
	6–10
	11–20
	21–40
	41–100
	259 in US

Chapter 8
Crowdsourcing

What you'll find out in this chapter:

》How we used readers to analyse large numbers of documents
》The first country in the world to have a majority of women in parliament
》Why you should never mess with Doctor Who fans

If data journalism is trendy right now, then crowdsourcing comes right behind. What news organisations used to call "surveys" now get called crowdsourcing to make them sound current and "now". It's a way for websites to encourage community engagement – which matters. But does it produce data?

It comes from the fact that we are not the experts any more. It's not so long ago that the limit of a journalist's engagement with their readers was to calmly hand out pearls of wisdom which would then be gratefully accepted.

Those days are long gone. Taking that approach now would mean missing out on stories every day.

The Guardian's first big crowdsourcing exercise was looking into the expenses of Members of the UK Parliament in 2009.

The way MPs had claimed expenses and, in particular, the running of the second home allowance, supposed to cover members who have to travel to Westminster, shocked the public. It was the scandal of the year, and resulted in the resignations of cabinet ministers, MPs and even the Speaker of the House of Commons.

For months, the Daily Telegraph had the benefit of unrestricted access to leaked Parliamentary documents detailing each MP's individual receipts. We would have access to the full database and be expected to analyse it in one day.

Then-Guardian developer Simon Willison came up with the solution: get our readers to help. So when the 458,000 documents were released, that's what we did, here: **mps-expenses.guardian.co.uk**

Under a system that has now been replaced by an independent watchdog, the House of Commons released thousands of MPs' receipts – 700,000 individual documents contained within 5,500 PDF files covering all 646 members of parliament. It was an enormous dataset – four years' worth of expenses and every claim. Each MP's information could be up to 7MB of receipts covering their mortgages, second home purchases, duck houses and soft furnishings.

20%

Number of UK graduates earning £9.92 per hour – less than the median wage of £10 per hour for those educated to an A-level standard. 1.34m graduates make up the 20% on the lower wages

SOURCE: ONS

MPs' expenses
2008-09

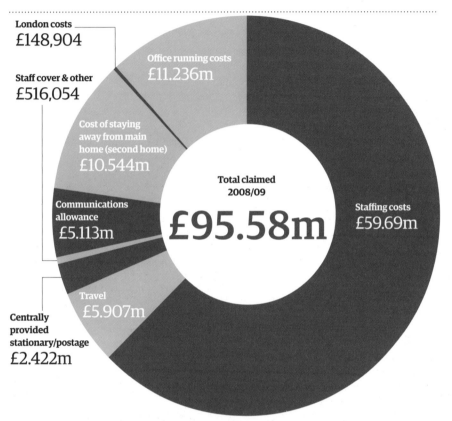

London costs
£148,904

Staff cover & other
£516,054

Office running costs
£11.236m

Cost of staying away from main home (second home)
£10.544m

Communications allowance
£5.113m

Total claimed 2008/09

£95.58m

Staffing costs
£59.69m

Travel
£5.907m

Centrally provided stationary/postage
£2.422m

How many MPs claimed how much second home allowance

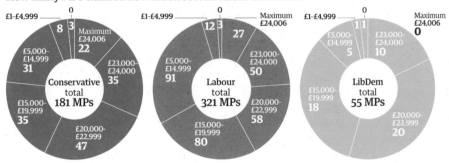

£1-£4,999   0

8   3

Maximum £24,006   **22**

£5,000-£14,999   **31**

£23,000-£24,000   **35**

Conservative total 181 MPs

£15,000-£19,999   **35**

£20,000-£22,999   **47**

£1-£4,999   0

12   3

Maximum £24,006

27

£5,000-£14,999   **91**

£23,000-£24,000   **50**

Labour total 321 MPs

£20,000-£22,999   **58**

£15,000-£19,999   **80**

£1-£4,999   0

1   1

£5,000-£14,999

£23,000-£24,000   **10**

Maximum £24,006   **0**

5

LibDem total 55 MPs

£15,000-£19,999   **18**

£20,000-£22,999   **20**

NOTE: EXCLUDES LONDON MPS WHO ARE NOT ELIGIBLE

Average claims by party for different allowances

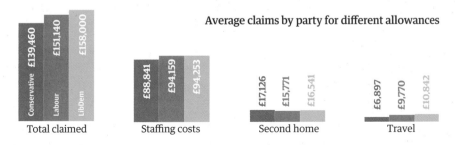

Conservative £139,460   Labour £151,140   LibDem £158,000
Total claimed

£88,841   £94,159   £94,253
Staffing costs

£17,126   £15,771   £16,541
Second home

£6,897   £9,770   £10,842
Travel

Our democracy in numbers

650
Number of MPs elected. However, due to deaths and nomination to specialist roles such as the Speaker, there are seldom 650 MPs sitting at any one time

144
Number of women MPs as of October 2012, four times the number the UK had in 1987

27
MPs came from an ethnic minority in the 2010 election. This represents a near-doubling of the total

35%
of the 2010 intake went to fee-paying schools, compared with 7% of the population. 20 went to Eton College, including David Cameron, one of 18 old Etonian prime ministers

50
The average age of the MPs in the 2010 parliamentary intake. The youngest is Pamela Nash, Labour MP for Airdrie and Shotts, who was 25 when elected

146
Numbers of MPs who stood down in the 2010 election, creating one of the biggest turnovers in history. Most retired, some were hit by the expenses scandal

£1.16m
Cost of the inquiry into MPs' expenses

£1.12m
Amount that was eventually paid back

–15%
Drop in claims after a new expenses regime was introduced

£65,738
Annual salary of an MP as of 2010. The prime minister earns £142,500; a cabinet member £134,565 and a select committee chair £80,320. MPs salaries in the UK are lower than in the US Senate (£120,000+) and the German Bundestag (£80,000+)

£110,000
Amount paid by the Telegraph to its source for the details of MPs' expenses in 2009, according to the paper's assistant editor, Andrew Pierce

SOURCES: IPSA; SUTTON TRUST
PHOTOGRAPH: DAN CHUNG
FOR THE GUARDIAN

After the scandal
Expenses claims by MPs, May to August 2010

Total Conservative claims
£1.6m

Total Liberal
Democrat claims
£0.3m

Total Labour claims
£1.1m

£184.13

Average for each
Conservative claim
8,972 claims

£140.73

Average for each
Liberal Democrat claim
1,924 claims

£138.13

Average for each
Labour claim
8,113 claims

SOURCE: IPSA

In practice, the data managed to be both open and closed at the same time. Open because it allowed us unprecedented access to MPs' claims over a huge amount of time. Closed because key address and personal details were blacked out – or 'redacted' in official parlance – and impossible to analyse.

We wanted to open up this data to as many people as possible and get our readers to help analyse it and find the stories buried within the photocopied handwritten receipts. Users could find their MP, or any other member – and look at their records directly. For every page for every MP you would be able to: comment on individual expenses; highlight ones of interest; tell us how interesting that receipt was; and, crucially, help by entering the numbers on the page.

51%
of top parliamentarians in Rwanda are women – the highest figure in the world. It was the first country in the world to have a majority female parliament. By law, 30% of its MPs must be women. Half of its supreme court justices are also women

SOURCE: UN

How British do we feel?
Crowdsourcing the strength of the union

6,594
Respondents said they were British ●

Two conflicting tides are pulling at many of the citizens of the UK - their identity as Britons and their identity as people from one of the constituent regions of the British Isles. The conflict is most pointed in Scotland, which will vote on independence in 2014. Will the groundswell of support for Great Britain during London 2012 have a lasting legacy or will attitudes continue to reflect this internet survey of Guardian readers in October 2011?

Northern Ire
Perhaps the
complex part o
UK when it c
to national ide
Responses were
between Br
Northern
and

British

6,594

DATA MAPPING: ALEX GRAUL

948
pondents
n't

hern Irish

29

6

Shetland
Could these "others"
view themselves as
more Nordic than
Scottish?

Scottish

2,874

English

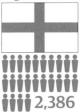

2,386

Corby
It may be decades
since Scots began
moving there to work
in the steel mills
but the cultural link
remains strong

Welsh

1,355

Other

1,309

Cornwall A strong
turnout for "others"

Using that information, we would then begin to be able to piece together a unique picture of how MPs' claims have changed over time.

Some information was easy to work out. We could see quite easily what different MPs had done – some had filed nearly 2,000 pieces of paper over four years; others less than 40. It also helped us find stories – readers dug through the PDFs to find stories such as one MP's £200 propelling pencil or another's imported Indian rugs. But in terms of generating data, it was less successful, highlighting a side effect of getting lots of people to help you with stories: you need lots of people at the other end to go through what it means. So, while we got stories from the information, we didn't get the raw data to allow us to work out how different MPs in different parties claimed their expenses. But it did show the power of putting raw data into the public arena. One user reviewed over 29,000 pages. They possibly know more about MPs' expenses now than the entire Guardian newsdesk.

The second time we repeated the exercise, it was more like a game

1,301

People commended in the Queen's Birthday honours in 2011. For the 945 where we could identify the reason for the honour, the biggest single reason given was "community service", followed by charitable or voluntary work

Rise of the undecideds
ICM polling from Thatcher to the 2010 general election

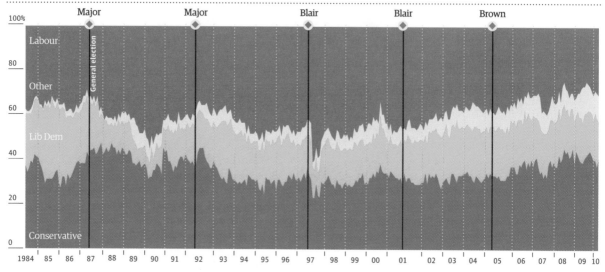

SOURCE: GUARDIAN/ICM

and we asked less of our readers. The entire set of documents was reviewed twice over, but we didn't ask for data, just to help us find interesting stuff.

That sharing of experiences is something crowdsourcing is perfect for, especially if the subject is one which people care about. In one recent exercise for the Datablog, people from around the world identified the locations of the Occupy protests taking place across the globe – a cause they cared about.

Old Weather is an example of where it can work well. The project, organised by crowdsourcing experts Zooniverse, is investigating the data in old Royal Naval log books from the beginning of the century. The data the site's users collect will help meteorologists learn more about how the climate has changed over the last century.

On a less formal basis, of course, we crowdsource all the time, engaging our users in the news process, whether it's helping us with the published emails of former Alaska governor and US vice-presidential hopeful Sarah Palin or users helping us identify missing demonstrators in Iran.

The Datablog now has an active community of users who visualise the data we publish, in turn publishing their views on a Flickr page (Guardian Datastore) and commenting on what they have done. And that's not all – the data posts we produce are subject to intense scrutiny. If we get anything wrong, someone lets us know about it.

The power of the web has made data analysis a collaborative process, which for us means better stories and more scrutiny.

Distrust of institutions
Party membership and public life, 2010

Membership of the UK's three main political parties, thousands

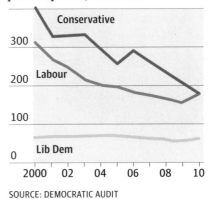

SOURCE: DEMOCRATIC AUDIT

Overall perception of standards of conduct in public life, UK, 2010, %

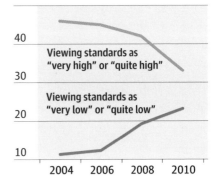

In numbers
Women and inequality

139

constitutions around the world guarantee gender equality, and 115 countries give women equal property rights

117

countries have equal pay laws

53%

of working women are in vulnerable employment, and in some countries women are paid 30% less than men

603m

women live in countries where domestic violence is not considered a crime

61

countries severely restrict abortion rights for women

50

countries have a lower legal age of marriage for women than men

2.6bn

women live in countries where marital rape is not a criminal offence

28

countries have reached or exceeded 30% of women in the national parliament; 23 of them used quotas

17

countries have a women as head of government, head of state or both

16.7%

of ministers in the world's governments are women as of 2012; up from 14.2% in 2005

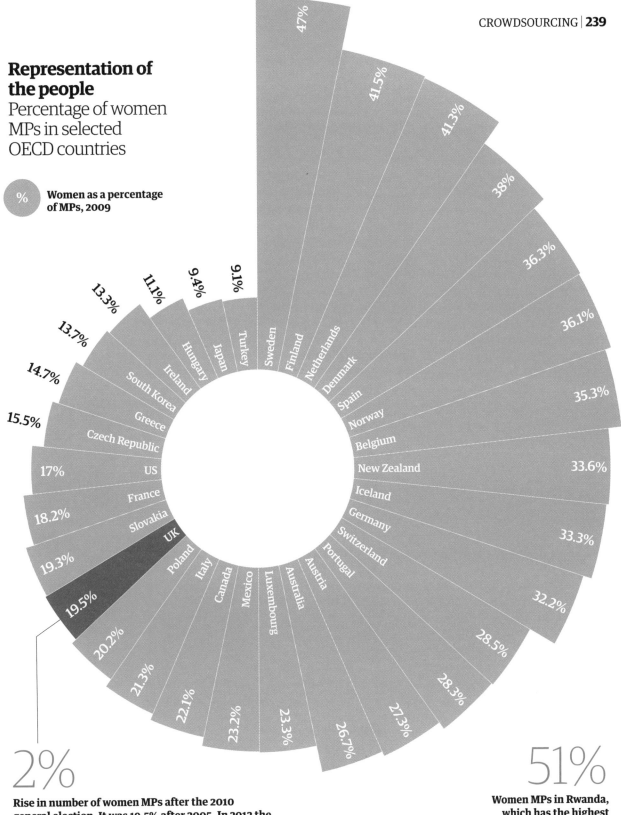

Representation of the people

Percentage of women MPs in selected OECD countries

% Women as a percentage of MPs, 2009

Sweden 47%
Finland 41.5%
Netherlands 41.3%
Denmark 38%
Spain 36.3%
Norway 36.1%
Belgium 35.3%
New Zealand 33.6%
Iceland 33.3%
Germany 32.2%
Switzerland 28.5%
Portugal 28.3%
Austria 27.3%
Australia 26.7%
Luxembourg 23.3%
Mexico 23.2%
Canada 22.1%
Italy 21.3%
Poland 20.2%
UK 19.5%
Slovakia 19.3%
France 18.2%
US 17%
Czech Republic 15.5%
Greece 14.7%
South Korea 13.7%
Ireland 13.3%
Hungary 11.1%
Japan 9.4%
Turkey 9.1%

2%

Rise in number of women MPs after the 2010 general election. It was 19.5% after 2005. In 2012 the percentage dropped again with the resignation of Louise Mensch. A male MP was elected to her seat

51%

Women MPs in Rwanda, which has the highest percentage in the world

Women and the media

How male reporters and experts still dominate the media

Bylines on the front page

Based on analysis of nine national newspapers, Monday to Saturday, over the course of four weeks, the research found that men continued to dominate newspaper front pages to an overwhelming degree, with almost 80% of front page articles having male bylines. The figure exactly echoes byline research conducted by the Guardian last year

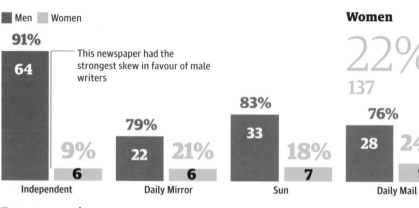

■ Men ■ Women

91%
64

This newspaper had the strongest skew in favour of male writers

9%
6

Independent

79%
22

21%
6

Daily Mirror

83%
33

18%
7

Sun

76%
28

24

Daily Mail

Men

78%
493

Women

22%
137

Front page pictures

How many are predominantly or exclusively of women or men?

Daily Express — 22 / 27

Daily Mail — 7 / 25

Daily Mirror — 58 / 51

FT — 51 / 13

Guardian — 51 / 32

Independent — 73 / 38

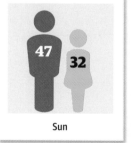

Sun — 47 / 32

Daily Telegraph — 38 / 43

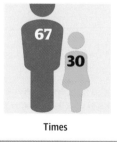

Times — 67 / 30

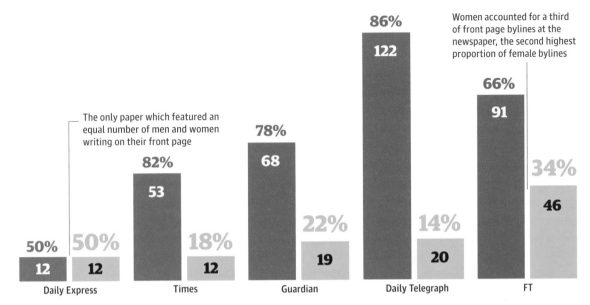

50% **50%**
12 12
Daily Express

82%
18%
53
12
Times

The only paper which featured an equal number of men and women writing on their front page

78%
22%
68
19
Guardian

86%
14%
122
20
Daily Telegraph

66%
34%
91
46
FT

Women accounted for a third of front page bylines at the newspaper, the second highest proportion of female bylines

ont page quotes

...unt of all those quoted or mentioned by name in newspaper lead stories found that 84%
... men and 16% were women. We then undertook a more detailed analysis of the first
...on mentioned in each lead story, looking at who was quoted most and in what capacity

Experts and victims

A detailed analysis of the first person mentioned or quoted in each lead story found that where an expert was quoted it tended to be a man and where a victim was quoted it tended to be a woman

... person quotes

...n **Women**
0.3% **69.7%**

Overall total quotes

Men **Women**
84% **16%**

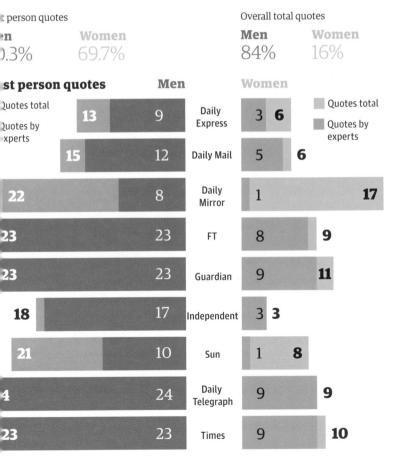

st person quotes **Men** **Women**

Quotes total
Quotes by experts

	Men			Women	
Daily Express	13	9		3	6
Daily Mail	15	12		5	6
Daily Mirror	22	8		1	17
FT	23	23		8	9
Guardian	23	23		9	11
Independent	18	17		3	3
Sun	21	10		1	8
Daily Telegraph	4	24		9	9
Times	23	23		9	10

Quotes total
Quotes by experts

Quotes from experts

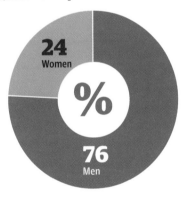

24 Women

76 Men

Quotes from victims

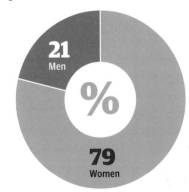

21 Men

79 Women

Energy from the natural world
Wind farms, operational and planned, 2012

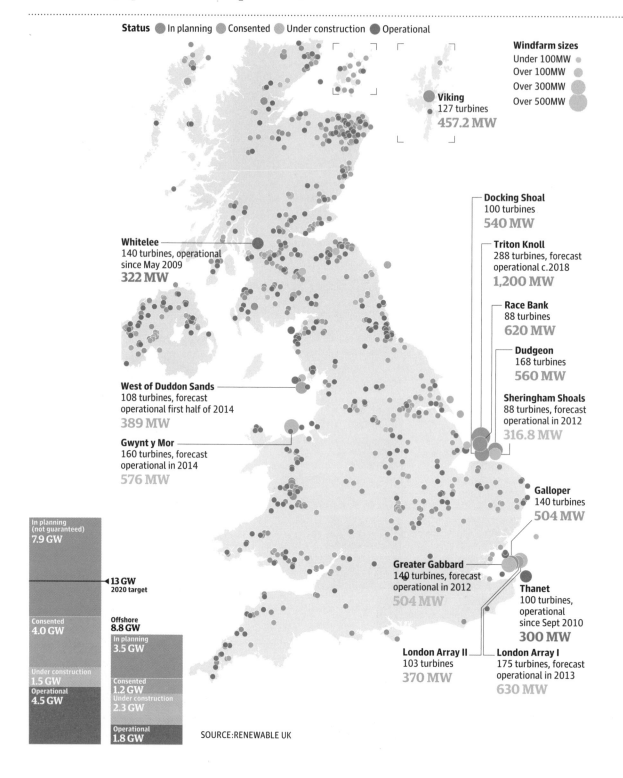

Status ● In planning ● Consented ● Under construction ● Operational

Windfarm sizes
Under 100MW ·
Over 100MW ●
Over 300MW ●
Over 500MW ●

Viking
127 turbines
457.2 MW

Docking Shoal
100 turbines
540 MW

Triton Knoll
288 turbines, forecast
operational c.2018
1,200 MW

Race Bank
88 turbines
620 MW

Dudgeon
168 turbines
560 MW

Sheringham Shoals
88 turbines, forecast
operational in 2012
316.8 MW

Whitelee
140 turbines, operational
since May 2009
322 MW

West of Duddon Sands
108 turbines, forecast
operational first half of 2014
389 MW

Gwynt y Mor
160 turbines, forecast
operational in 2014
576 MW

Galloper
140 turbines
504 MW

Greater Gabbard
140 turbines, forecast
operational in 2012
504 MW

Thanet
100 turbines,
operational
since Sept 2010
300 MW

London Array II
103 turbines
370 MW

London Array I
175 turbines, forecast
operational in 2013
630 MW

**In planning
(not guaranteed)
7.9 GW**

◄ **13 GW**
2020 target

**Consented
4.0 GW**

**Offshore
8.8 GW**

**In planning
3.5 GW**

**Under construction
1.5 GW**

**Operational
4.5 GW**

**Consented
1.2 GW**

**Under construction
2.3 GW**

**Operational
1.8 GW**

SOURCE:RENEWABLE UK

In practice: don't mess with the Doctor

I f you really want to wind people up, don't write about budget cuts or school buildings or the world economy. Ask readers to help you compile a list of every Doctor Who villain. Ever. I know, because that's what the Guardian's Datablog and Datastore website did – with dramatic results.

Doctor Who is made for data. It's the longest-running sci-fi show in Britain, possibly the world. The good doctor has battled monsters and aliens in 769 episodes since William Hartnell's first appearance in 1963. Our project was inspired by a user on the "data visualisation website" Many Eyes. @xxnapoleansolo had compiled a list of every Doctor Who villain since the programme was relaunched in 2005. But that wasn't completist enough for us. So we tried asking the BBC for a list. "Good God," a spokeswoman replied. Another press officer came back with the suggestion that if we really wanted to get this done, we needed to ask the fans. So we did.

I'm not sure the Guardian Datablog has ever had an article retweeted on Twitter more than 200 times in 10 minutes before. It spread around the Doctor Who web faster than a cyber battle fleet; the comments on the article now read like the ultimate distillation of Doctor Who knowledge. "Being strictly accurate, although they appear, the Ice Warriors don't turn out to be the enemy in the Curse of Peladon," observed @croydon-slacker.

"Do the Ogrons count as villains in their own right, or because they were always the Big Villain's stooges, are they sort of subsidiary baddies?" piped up @Venebles. "Not that I'm sad, or anything."

The result, inevitably, is still evolving, although no prizes for guessing that the Daleks are number one (32 stories), followed by the Cybermen (24) and The Master (22).

As another user noted: "You do realise you will retire with this list uncompleted, don't you?"

The trials of a Time Lord
The eleven Doctors and the foes they have faced since 1963

Proportion of TV stories featuring Daleks, Cybermen or the Master as major villains

SOURCE: BBC

29 stories
5
1

1. William Hartnell 1963-66

21 stories
4
2

2. Patrick Troughton 1966-69

24 stories
8
3

3. Jon Pertwee 1970-74

46 stories
2 1 3

4. Tom Baker 1974-81

20 stories
5
2
1

5. Peter Davison 1982-84

11 stories
2
1
1

6. Colin Baker 1984-86

12 stories
1 1
1

7. Sylvester McCoy 1987-89

1 story
1

8. Paul McGann 1996

10 stories
2

9. Christopher Eccleston 2005

36 stories
4
3
3

10. David Tennant 2005-2010

28 stories so far
2
3

11. Matt Smith 2010-present

34 stories feature Daleks as major villains, six of them with their creator, Davros.

1963 to present

24 stories feature the Cybermen

1966 to present

22 stories feature the Master, in four incarnations

1971-2010 (so far)

433 villains have appeared in Doctor Who since it began in 1963, according to Guardian readers*

9 stories feature the Sontarans

1973 to present

6 stories feature the Silurians

1970 to present

6 stories feature Ice Warriors

1967 to 1974

4 stories feature Autons

1971 to present

3 stories feature Weeping Angels

2008 to present

*FIGURES COVER UP TO 2012'S ANGELS IN MANHATTAN

Case study
Reading the
Riots

PHOTOGRAPH: KERIM OKTEN/EPA

It took the world by surprise. For five days in August 2011, following the shooting of a young man in London, riots spread from Tottenham, across the capital, as far as the north of England, Manchester and Liverpool.

They were an echo of the disturbances of two decades earlier in 1981 in Brixton, London, Moss Side, Manchester and Toxteth, Liverpool. But those took place in an age without Twitter or instant communications – and without access to the data which allowed us to tell a new story about the riots in 2011.

In 1981, an official board of inquiry was set up into the causes of the disturbances under Lord Scarman, who produced a report which influenced social policy for a decade. In the aftermath of 2011, there was to be no official verdict; instead the causes have been pronounced on by every politician and commentator. That environment is one where data journalism can start to provide real answers, based on evidence rather than assertion. And, this time around, there is no shortage of that data.

For the Guardian it meant instant data journalism. Firstly, it was filling the hole of knowledge for anyone wanting to know what was happening where. We compiled a list of every incident where there was a verified report, then mapped it with Google Fusion Tables, and allowed people to download the data behind it – possibly the simplest but most popular thing we did.

Timeline: the August 2011 riots
How a north London protest exploded into violence across England

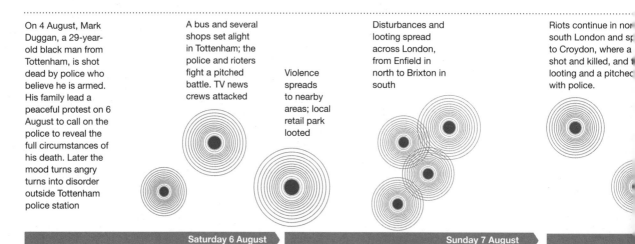

On 4 August, Mark Duggan, a 29-year-old black man from Tottenham, is shot dead by police who believe he is armed. His family lead a peaceful protest on 6 August to call on the police to reveal the full circumstances of his death. Later the mood turns angry turns into disorder outside Tottenham police station

A bus and several shops set alight in Tottenham; the police and rioters fight a pitched battle. TV news crews attacked

Violence spreads to nearby areas; local retail park looted

Disturbances and looting spread across London, from Enfield in north to Brixton in south

Riots continue in nor south London and sp to Croydon, where a shot and killed, and looting and a pitche with police.

Saturday 6 August

Sunday 7 August

This was just a small part of a much bigger project: Reading the Riots – a unique look at the riots as experienced by those who were there. Under the project, led by Paul Lewis at the Guardian and Professor Tim Newburn at the London School of Economics, a specially recruited team interviewed around 270 people about the riots and why they had been involved. The project was the first time such a major attempt had been made to forensically examine the motivations behind a riot since the work in Detroit in 1967.

1,984

people were tried after the English riots in August 2011. A quarter of them were juveniles, aged 10–17, which compares to **16%** of cases in 2010

SOURCE: MINISTRY OF JUSTICE

In addition to the qualitative data of the interviews, we would also have quantitative responses to a set of questions each person interviewed would answer.

Plus, for the first time, we would have access to 2.57m tweets sent around the riots themselves, to help us try to establish the truth about the role of social media.

As the riots wound down and the police began to make arrests, hundreds of people started appearing in magistrates' courts charged with riot-related offences. Security vans were queuing up outside courts across the country and judges were drafted in to man special night courts as they struggled to process all the defendants.

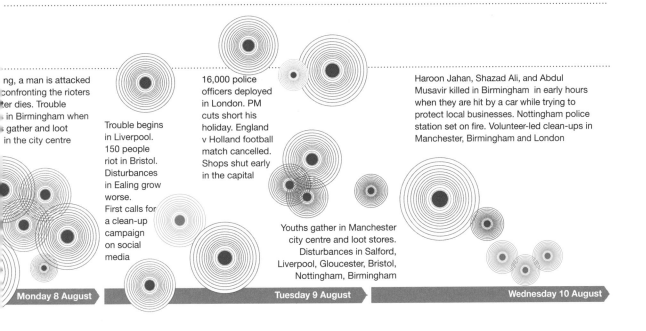

ng, a man is attacked confronting the rioters er dies. Trouble in Birmingham when gather and loot in the city centre

Trouble begins in Liverpool. 150 people riot in Bristol. Disturbances in Ealing grow worse. First calls for a clean-up campaign on social media

16,000 police officers deployed in London. PM cuts short his holiday. England v Holland football match cancelled. Shops shut early in the capital

Haroon Jahan, Shazad Ali, and Abdul Musavir killed in Birmingham in early hours when they are hit by a car while trying to protect local businesses. Nottingham police station set on fire. Volunteer-led clean-ups in Manchester, Birmingham and London

Youths gather in Manchester city centre and loot stores. Disturbances in Salford, Liverpool, Gloucester, Bristol, Nottingham, Birmingham

Monday 8 August

Tuesday 9 August

Wednesday 10 August

Reading the Riots project
How researchers built their picture of the 2011 violence and its aftermath

270
people who admitted to being involved in the rioting were interviewed

1.3m
words were produced in this first phase of research

2.57m
riot-related tweets were analysed, showing how Twitter spread but also countered rumours about the violence

130
police officers of all ranks were interviewed in the second phase of the research

40
victims of the riots, some of whom had lost their businesses or homes, were interviewed

75
lawyers – 50 defence lawyers and 25 from the Crown Prosecution Service – were interviewed in phase two

Where interviewees live

Salford
7
Liverpool **16** **29** Manchester

Nottingham **3**

30
Birmingham

London
185

85% thought poverty was an important or very important factor in causing the riots

35% of adult were claimin benefit

42% of children in court were on free school meals

65% of 10-17 year-olds lived in the poorest areas

33% Were unempl

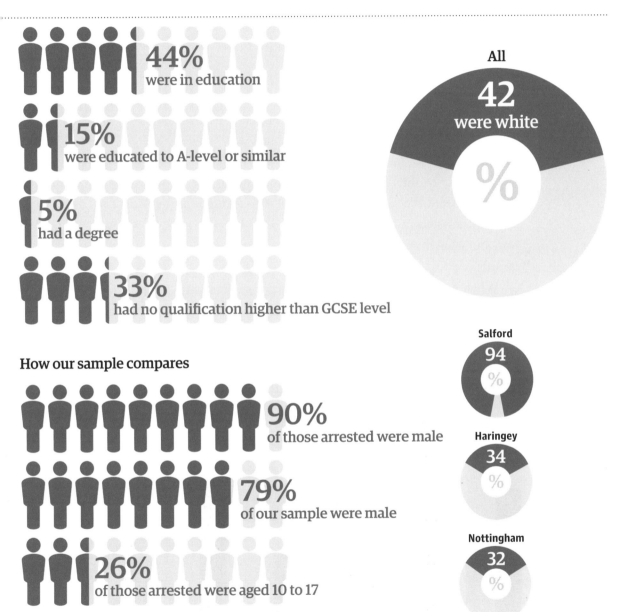

44% were in education

15% were educated to A-level or similar

5% had a degree

33% had no qualification higher than GCSE level

How our sample compares

90% of those arrested were male

79% of our sample were male

26% of those arrested were aged 10 to 17

31% of our sample were aged 10 to 17

All

42 were white

%

Salford

94 %

Haringey

34 %

Nottingham

32 %

Under UK law, the name and address of someone appearing in court is public information – it just can't be revealed by the media if the defendant is aged under 18. Each day in every court a detailed record of each case is compiled, extracts of which are given to court reporters after the cases are finished. This is the magistrates' court register and, although it's stored on computer, it's given to reporters normally as a printout, and not necessarily for every case – just the ones they're interested in. In the aftermath of the riots this meant the only court cases that were being reported were the unusual, newsworthy ones, not the everyday typical cases. If we were to work out what the riots meant and what happened, we would need those records.

When we requested these registers we were met with stony silence by the courts themselves. "I don't understand what you need it for," said

25%

longer sentences on average were meted out by magistrates to defendants accused of riots-related crimes, according to Guardian analysis of the first 1,000 cases to be dealt with. **70%** of defendants were remanded in custody to await Crown court trial, swelling the prison population by more than **600**

SOURCE: FOIA REQUEST

Did courts treat rioters more harshly?
Average custodial sentence for public order offences, 2011

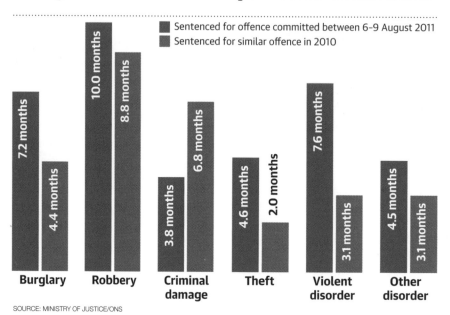

■ Sentenced for offence committed between 6–9 August 2011
■ Sentenced for similar offence in 2010

- Burglary: 7.2 months / 4.4 months
- Robbery: 10.0 months / 8.8 months
- Criminal damage: 3.8 months / 6.8 months
- Theft: 4.6 months / 2.0 months
- Violent disorder: 7.6 months / 3.1 months
- Other disorder: 4.5 months / 3.1 months

SOURCE: MINISTRY OF JUSTICE/ONS

Mapping the violence
Using Google Fusion Tables as a reporting tool

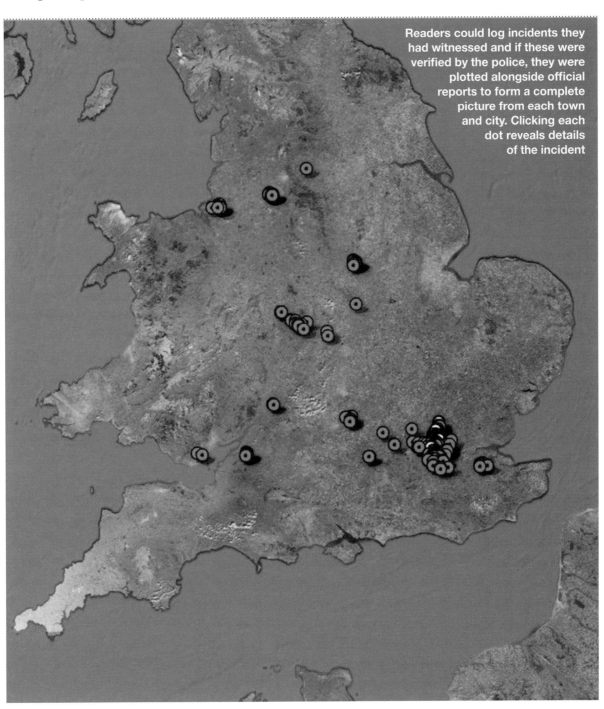

Readers could log incidents they had witnessed and if these were verified by the police, they were plotted alongside official reports to form a complete picture from each town and city. Clicking each dot reveals details of the incident

Mapping the violence 2
How interactive reporting allowed us to create a more detailed graphic for print

Each night covers from 6pm until 6am the next morning

- Saturday night, 6 August
- Sunday night, 7 August
- Monday night, 8 August
- Tuesday, 9 August

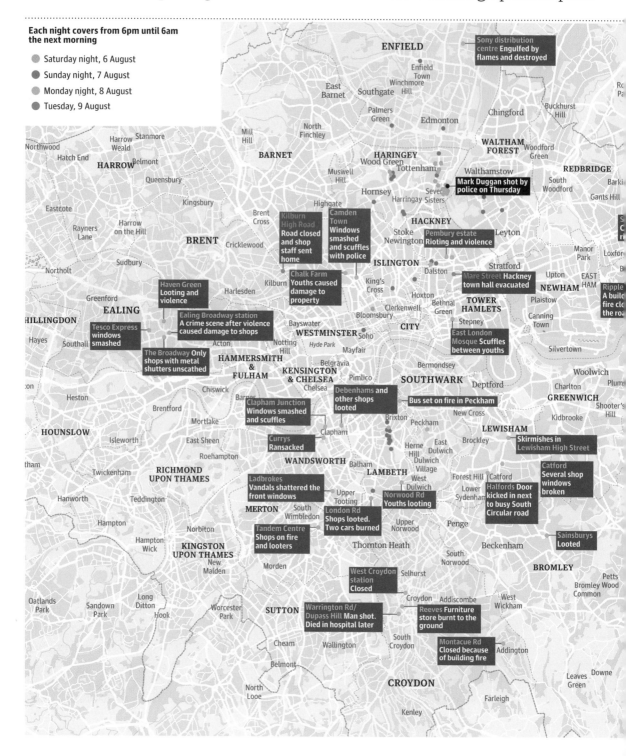

Sony distribution centre **Engulfed by flames and destroyed**

ENFIELD

Enfield Town
Winchmore Hill
East Barnet
Southgate
Palmers Green
Edmonton
Chingford
Buckhurst Hill

Mill Hill
North Finchley

BARNET

WALTHAM FOREST
Woodford Green

HARINGEY
Wood Green
Tottenham
Walthamstow
Mark Duggan shot by police on Thursday
South Woodford

REDBRIDGE
Barking
Gants Hill

Northwood
Harrow Weald
Stanmore
Hatch End
Belmont
HARROW
Queensbury
Kingsbury

Muswell Hill
Highgate
Hornsey
Harringay
Seven Sisters

HACKNEY
Stoke Newington
Pembury estate Rioting and violence
Leyton

Manor Park
Loxford

Eastcote
Rayners Lane
Harrow on the Hill

BRENT
Cricklewood

Brent Cross

Kilburn
High Road
Road closed and shop staff sent home

Camden Town
Windows smashed and scuffles with police

Northolt
Sudbury

Kilburn

Chalk Farm
Youths caused damage to property

ISLINGTON
Dalston
Stratford
Mare Street Hackney town hall evacuated
Upton
EAST HAM

NEWHAM
Ripple
A buil... fire clo... the roa...

Greenford

EALING
Haven Green
Looting and violence

Harlesden

King's Cross
Hoxton
Clerkenwell
Bethnal Green

TOWER HAMLETS
Stepney

Plaistow
Canning Town

HILLINGDON
Hayes
Southall

Ealing Broadway station
A crime scene after violence caused damage to shops

Acton

Bayswater
Bloomsbury

WESTMINSTER
Notting Hill
Hyde Park
Mayfair
Soho

CITY

East London Mosque **Scuffles between youths**

Silvertown

Tesco Express **windows smashed**

The Broadway **Only shops with metal shutters unscathed**

HAMMERSMITH & FULHAM
Chiswick

KENSINGTON & CHELSEA
Pimlico
Belgravia
Chelsea

Bermondsey

SOUTHWARK
Deptford
Charlton

Woolwich
Plum...

GREENWICH
Shooter's Hill

Heston

Barnes
Brentford
Mortlake

Clapham Junction
Windows smashed and scuffles

Debenhams and other shops **looted**

Bus set on fire in Peckham

New Cross

Kidbrooke

HOUNSLOW
Isleworth
East Sheen
Roehampton

Currys
Ransacked

Clapham

Brixton
Peckham

Herne Hill
East Dulwich
Dulwich Village
West Dulwich

LEWISHAM
Brockley

Skirmishes in **Lewisham High Street**

Twickenham

RICHMOND UPON THAMES

WANDSWORTH
Balham

LAMBETH

Forest Hill
Catford
Several shop windows broken

Hanworth
Teddington

Ladbrokes
Vandals shattered the front windows

Upper Tooting

Norwood Rd **Youths looting**

Lower Sydenham
Halfords **Door kicked in next to busy South Circular road**

Hampton

MERTON
South Wimbledon

London Rd
Shops looted. Two cars burned

Upper Norwood
Penge

Sainsburys **Looted**

Hampton Wick

KINGSTON UPON THAMES
New Malden

Norbiton

Tandem Centre
Shops on fire and looters

Thornton Heath

South Norwood
Beckenham

BROMLEY
Petts Wood
Bromley Common

Oatlands Park
Sandown Park
Long Ditton
Hook

Worcester Park

Morden

West Croydon station
Closed

Selhurst

Croydon
Addiscombe
West Wickham

SUTTON

Warrington Rd/ Dupass Hill **Man shot. Died in hospital later**

Reeves **Furniture store burnt to the ground**

Montacue Rd **Closed because of building fire**

Addington

Leaves Green
Downe

Cheam
Wallington
South Croydon

Belmont

North Looe

CROYDON

Kenley
Farleigh

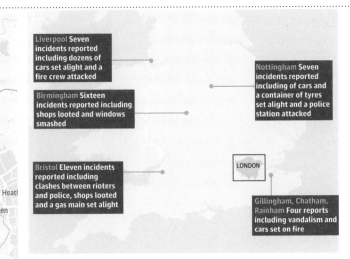

Liverpool **Seven** incidents reported including dozens of cars set alight and a fire crew attacked

Birmingham **Sixteen** incidents reported including shops looted and windows smashed

Bristol **Eleven** incidents reported including clashes between rioters and police, shops looted and a gas main set alight

Nottingham **Seven** incidents reported including of cars and a container of tyres set alight and a police station attacked

LONDON

Gillingham, Chatham, Rainham **Four reports** including vandalism and cars set on fire

This map, produced for the print version of the Guardian which went to press on 9 August, shows how granular the detail on the rioting incidents was becoming, with information right down to street level, thanks to police reports, Twitter and help from the readers.

It also shows that the reporting team already had one eye on trying to determine why a peaceful protest about a controversial shooting had turned into such a flashpoint and why waves of violence spread so rapidly across the capital and then across the country. Was it, as some claimed, a reaction to poverty, cuts in youth services and unemployment?

These were some of the questions that the Reading the Riots project would seek to answer.

Of London's 32 boroughs (excluding the City), here's how these six rank. In each measure 1st is best and 32nd is worst

Income (median household)	NEETS (Age 16-18 not in Education, Employment, or Training)	Free school meals (secondary school students)	Unemployment (rate)

Croydon — 15th
Ealing — 17th
Enfield — 22nd
Haringey — 25th
Southall — 29th
Hackney — 30th

11th
10th
14th
16th
18th
19th
22nd
=23rd
24th
25th
24th
25th
=26th
=28th
28th
30th
32nd

ONE MILE

one court. "You'll have to go to the Ministry of Justice," said another. It was only when the Ministry of Justice sent an instruction to every court in the country that they released the data – as PDFs. These were particularly tricky to extract, except by hand, and we wanted to record addresses and case outcomes. Literally thousands of defendants' details were involved so we persisted. We wanted to be able to create a picture of who was in court, what happened to them and where they came from, and this data would tell us addresses, ages, gender, what they were charged with and where it happened. Soon we had over 1,000 cases – an unprecedented criminology database which has given us a unique set of data.

Our quick analysis of 1,000 cases – and one of the first detailed studies of the data – showed us what many lawyers had feared: the courts were handing down prison sentences to convicted rioters that were on – average 25% longer than normal. As more cases came in, even this stark figure proved to be an underestimate of the justice facing people involved.

243

people jailed for riots-related offences were released after serving half their sentence or less, and tagged: home detention curfew in the official parlance. The majority of these – 162 – had been convicted of burglary

SOURCE: FOIA REQUEST

The first results
Initial findings from the courts after the riots

Early data obtained from the courts in August 2011, based on a sample of 123 cases

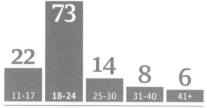

| 11-17 | 18-24 | 25-30 | 31-40 | 41+ |
| 22 | 73 | 14 | 8 | 6 |

Sex of defendants

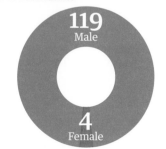

119 Male

4 Female

Remanded to jail

60 %

Referred to the crown court

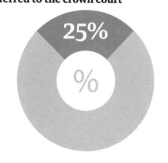

25 %

The response to the riots was so strong that three major pieces of research were also carried out inside government. The Ministry of Justice, Department for Education and Home Office have all published comprehensive guides to what went on and who was involved – but only of those arrested and processed by the courts. This is what we have learned so far from both our research and the official figures.

What do we know about the five nights? The most comprehensive research has been conducted by the Home Office. It found that there were a total of 5,112 individual riot-related crimes across ten police force areas. Most were recorded by London's Metropolitan Police, with 68% (3,461) of the total, followed by Greater Manchester Police (11%, 581), West Midlands (10%, 495) and Merseyside (4%, 195). There were over 4,000 arrests as a result of the riots.

7m

Twitter users saw the #riotscleanup and other message about the volunteer efforts to clean up London, Manchester, Birmingham and other cities – far in excess of any incitement messages. Some clean-up messages were retweeted more than a thousand times

SOURCE: GUARDIAN RESEARCH

Some types of crimes happened more often than others. Just over half (51%) of all crimes were committed against commercial premises – shops being the main target, especially electrical and clothing shops. Car crime, assaults and robberies also happened. But the picture varied across the country. In London, Manchester and the West Midlands, what the Home Office calls "acquisitive" crimes were the most common. Everywhere else, criminal damage was the first type of offence. The worst violent crime was in London and the West Midlands, where collectively four men were murdered.

So, who were the rioters?

What we do know is that people accused were predominantly young and male (the official figures are that 90% were men or boys). Just under half were aged 18 to 24, with 26% aged between 10 and 17 years old – children, in the eyes of the law. In West Yorkshire, 44% of those arrested were kids. Interestingly, men were more likely to be arrested for disorder and violent crimes; women for theft and burglary.

We also asked our sample about their education. Of the adults, 33% had no qualification higher than GCSE level, while the highest

What caused the riots?
Reading the Riots interviewees vs the general population, 2011

Respondents who said listed item was an "important" or "very important" cause of the riots, %

■ Rioters ■ Guardian/ICM

	Rioters	Guardian/ICM
Poverty	86%	69%
Policing	85%	68%
Government policy	80%	65%
Unemployment	79%	79%
Shooting of Mark Duggan	75%	51%
Social media	74%	64%
Media coverage	72%	73%
Greed	70%	77%
Inequality	70%	61%
Boredom	68%	67%
Criminality	64%	86%
Moral decline	56%	82%
Racial tensions	54%	56%
Poor parenting	40%	86%
Gangs	32%	75%

qualification of another 15% was A-level or similar. Only 5% of rioters said they had a degree, compared to around 20% of the UK population as a whole (based on 2001 census data), though around 44% of rioters were in education.

Race was certainly an issue for the media, with the assumption that a huge number of rioters were non-white. In fact, numbers were more evenly split than that. The Ministry of Justice data revealed that where ethnicity was recorded, 33% of those appearing in the courts on riot-related charges were white, 43% were black and 7% Asian. However, these figures varied significantly from area to area, often closely resembling the ethnic makeup of the local population: in London, 32% of defendants were white. In Merseyside, the figure was 79%. Similarly, the data from Reading the Riots found the majority of interviewees in London were of black or mixed race, while in Manchester, Salford or Liverpool, interviewees were overwhelmingly white.

Integration
"I feel I am part of British society"

■ 2008-09 citizenship survey   ■ Reading the Riots respondents

Strongly agree
53%
14%

Tend to agree
39%
37%

All agree
92%
51%

Stop and search
Police tactics and their impact on rioters

Have you been stopped and searched in the past 12 months?

No   27%
Yes   73%

Stop and search in London, 2009-10

Black people as...
% of London population   % of people stopped and searched

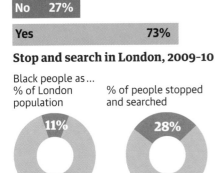

11%   28%

One of the defining features of the response to the riots is the pronouncement of causes before there was any data. One example is poverty. "These riots were not about poverty," said David Cameron. "That insults the millions of people who, whatever the hardship, would never dream of making others suffer like this."

But the question is: how do we know? If poverty affects health, education and crime, could it be a factor?

The Home Office research found that those appearing at court tended to be from more deprived circumstances than the wider population of England: 35% of adults were claiming out-of-work benefits (compared to 12% of the

SOURCES FOR THE GRAPHICS ON THIS PAGE: ICM/BCS/GUARDIAN RESEARCH/POLICE POWERS AND PROCEDURES BULLETIN

Poverty and the riots: Manchester
Deprivation and the addresses of suspects

Poverty indicator

- Richer area
- Poorer area
- ● Riot location
- • Suspect address

PRESTWICH

PENDLEBURY

BLACKLEY

BROUGHTON

NEWTON HEATH

SALFORD

BRADFORD

GREATER MANCHESTER

TRAFFORD

OLD TRAFFORD

STRETFORD

REDDISH

WITHINGTON

HEATON MERSEY

M60

SOURCE: GUARDIAN DATA,
DCLG INDICES OF MULTIPLE DEPRIVATION

working age population); 42% of young people brought before the courts had free school meals, only available in England to the 16% of secondary school pupils from the poorest backgrounds.

First, we showed where people accused of rioting lived in relation to where the riots took place. This showed how Manchester's arrested all came from the suburbs, while in London the riots were closer to home.

We wanted to know what would happen if we overlaid those addresses with the poverty indicators mapped by England's Indices of Multiple Deprivation (IMD), which map poverty in very small areas across the country. We had already done this with the riot locations themselves, but knowing where people came from seemed a better indicator, especially if people were travelling.

Liverpool University urban planning lecturer Alex Singleton took a look at the postcode data we had to recorded to work out exactly what links can be shown so far by mapping people to IMD areas. He found that:

7%

of participants in the first phase of Reading the Riots thought that the police in their area generally do an "excellent" or "good" job. In contrast, **56%** of respondents to the British Crime Survey think the police generally do an "excellent" or "good" job

SOURCE: GUARDIAN RESEARCH

● 58% of those appearing in court identified their residential location as being within the 20% most deprived areas in England – which matches what the Home Office found

● For 60% of those addresses appearing in the sample, these areas had not changed; however 14% had got worse between 2007 and 2010

Of course, riots are complex things and all sorts of elements play a part, shown by the cases where reasonably well-off people were involved. But what if poverty matters, whatever the prime minister says?

As Singleton wrote for us at the time: "Rioting is deplorable; however, if events such as this are to be mitigated in the future, the prevailing conditions and constraints affecting people living in areas must form part of the discussion. A 'broken society' happens somewhere, and geography matters."

Total officers deployed in London

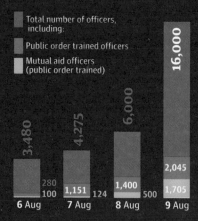

■ Total number of officers, including:
■ Public order trained officers
■ Mutual aid officers (public order trained)

3,480 — 6 Aug — 280 — 100
4,275 — 7 Aug — 1,151 — 124
6,000 — 8 Aug — 1,400 — 500
16,000 — 9 Aug — 2,045 — 1,705

Mutual aid officers deployed to police forces nationwide during riots*

To the Metropolitan Police	1,250
350	To Greater Manchester
350	To West Midlands
125	To Nottinghamshire
75	To Avon & Somerset
75	To Gloucestershire

* assuming 25 officers per Police Supply Unit (one inspector, three sergeants , 21 constables)

SOURCE: HMIC REPORT

offence
home
male
female

An ITO World projection showing how some defendants travelled to the scene of trouble. They went further in south and west London than in north London where the trouble began

Did rioters commute in for the looting? That is a theory being explored by police and politicians. And as hundreds of suspected looters were pushed through the magistrates' courts, what information did it tell us about how the events of those nights in early August 2011 unfolded?

£300m

Estimated total cost to the economy or riots-related insurance claims in London alone. London's policing costs were put at **£74m** during a hearing by the Commons home affairs select committee

SOURCE: GUARDIAN RESEARCH

An analysis of one day's court hearings found that 70% of those accused of riot-related crimes had travelled from outside their area. The Communities Secretary, Eric Pickles, has called it "riot tourism", and it is part of the argument used by those who want to withdraw benefits and council housing from those accused of rioting, even in a different borough.

Similarly, the then-housing minister, Grant

Shapps, said: "If someone has travelled for those riots, then the fact you have committed it in the next-door borough or somewhere else should count equally."

We wanted to know the answer to this and brought in transport data specialists ITO World to help show the distances between people's home and the riots themselves.

How far did people actually travel? Now we have the first answer: 2.2 miles.

The average distance from home to where defendants were accused of a riot offence was just over two miles, or a half-hour walk. If the most likely road route was taken into account, that distance rose to 2.6 miles.

That varies between cities. In Manchester, the average distance from home to offence location was 2.8 miles. In Birmingham, the average was 2.9 miles and in Nottingham 2.6 miles.

In London, people were closer to home: 1.5 miles in Peckham and 2.2 miles in Brixton. But those accused of riot-related offences in suburban Ealing and Croydon were 2.7 miles and 2.3 miles away.

The Home Office also looked at how significant gangs were in the riots. They found that 13% were "reported to be affiliated to a gang" in London. Outside London, fewer than 10% of those arrested were

61%

of the **2,278** commercial premises hit by the riots (for which data was available) were retailers. Of these, **12%** were shops selling electrical goods, mobile phones, computer games and DVDs; **10%** sold clothing and sportswear; **10%** were restaurants and cafes; **9%** small independent retailers; and **8%** supermarkets

SOURCE: GUARDIAN RESEARCH

An ITO World projection for Birmingham, where the average distance travelled by rioters was 2.9 miles

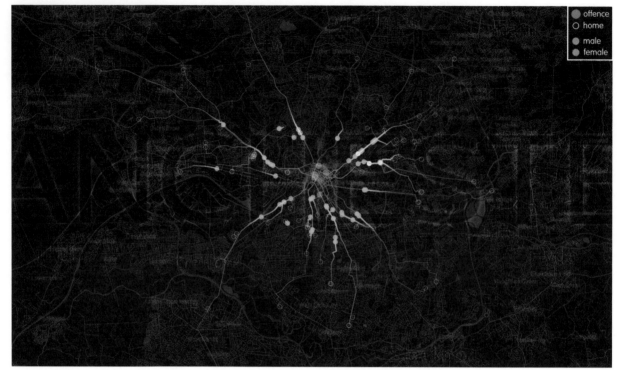

● offence
○ home
● male
● female

An ITO World projection for Manchester showing flows of rioters into the city centre

identified as gang members. But in two areas, West Yorkshire and Nottinghamshire (17%), the figures are a lot higher.

Many believed the rioters to be existing criminals and the official stats do back up the idea of an "underclass of convicts". According to the MoJ, 76% had a previous caution or conviction, 26% had more than ten previous offences and 26% had been in prison before.

The Guardian/LSE's own statistics supported this to an extent, but suggested that among rioters not caught by police previous conviction rates may be lower. 63% of Guardian/LSE respondents had previously received a caution or reprimand and over 70% had been previously arrested – significantly higher than the population as a whole, but lower than the averages for typical court defendants.

But what about the role of social media? Did

81%
of the rioters interviewed said they believed there would be riots again. Only **12%** disagreed. **37%** of those who expected more said there would be none for four or more years, **34%** expected more violence in the next three years, and **29%** expected riots in 2012

SOURCE: GUARDIAN RESEARCH

Twitter or Facebook actually incite the riots themselves? The Metropolitan Police considered switching off social networks during the worst events in London and politicians called for censorship of Twitter, Facebook and the BlackBerry messenger system. But the first proper analysis of Twitter – thanks to 2.57m tweets seen by the Guardian's data team – seemed to show that the opposite happened, and that it was mainly used to react to riots and looting.

In fact, it showed how extensively Twitter was used to co-ordinate a movement by citizens to clean the streets after the disorder. More than 206,000 tweets – 8% of the total – related to attempts to clean up the debris left by four nights of rioting and looting.

James Ball wrote on Comment is Free that: "The lessons of the experience are several. The most obvious is that social networks are simply tools: when used for activities of which we approve – like riot clean-up, or the Arab Spring – their power seems unambiguously positive. When used for other causes, they are portrayed as sinister. There's no way to embrace the immense good such tools can use without learning to live with, and mitigate, their downsides."

65%
of those interviewed would not get involved in similar events again
SOURCE: GUARDIAN RESEARCH

If data journalism is traditionally a long, drawn-out affair – resulting in analysis of only marginal interest – the riots highlighted a new type of data work: instant data journalism which helps to make an evolving news story clearer.

But what made this compelling is what came next: a rigorous, academically significant piece of social research, which brought together the Guardian's best journalists and dedicated researchers to create a comprehensive picture of what really went on. It had data behind it, of course, but at its heart were real stories told by real people.

Data has too often been seen as abstract to real lives. Not any more.

Chasing rumours
How Twitter tracked the riots and the clean-up, 2011

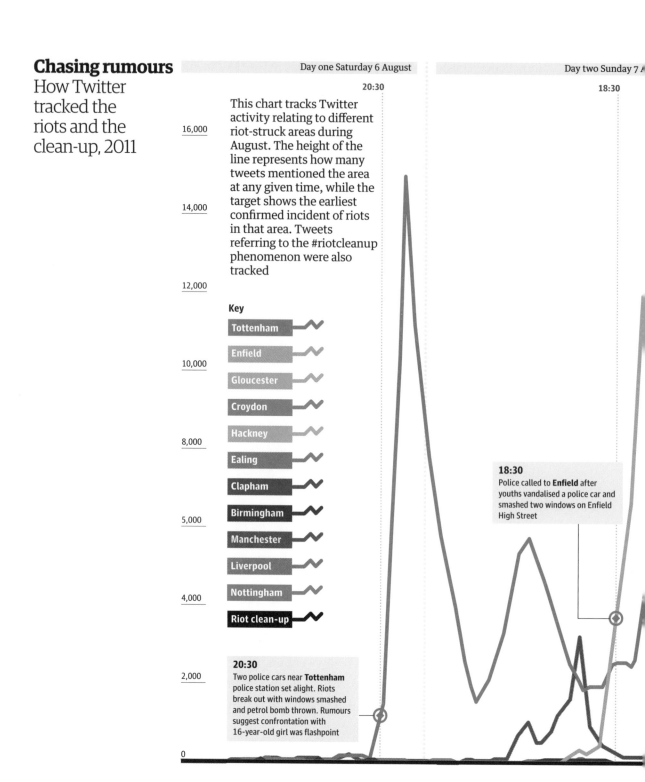

Day one Saturday 6 August

Day two Sunday 7 A

This chart tracks Twitter activity relating to different riot-struck areas during August. The height of the line represents how many tweets mentioned the area at any given time, while the target shows the earliest confirmed incident of riots in that area. Tweets referring to the #riotcleanup phenomenon were also tracked

Key

Tottenham
Enfield
Gloucester
Croydon
Hackney
Ealing
Clapham
Birmingham
Manchester
Liverpool
Nottingham
Riot clean-up

20:30
Two police cars near **Tottenham** police station set alight. Riots break out with windows smashed and petrol bomb thrown. Rumours suggest confrontation with 16-year-old girl was flashpoint

18:30
Police called to **Enfield** after youths vandalised a police car and smashed two windows on Enfield High Street

RESEARCH: JOHN BURN-MURDOCH, PAUL LEWIS, JAMES BALL
GRAPHIC: CHRISTINE OLIVER, MICHAEL ROBINSON

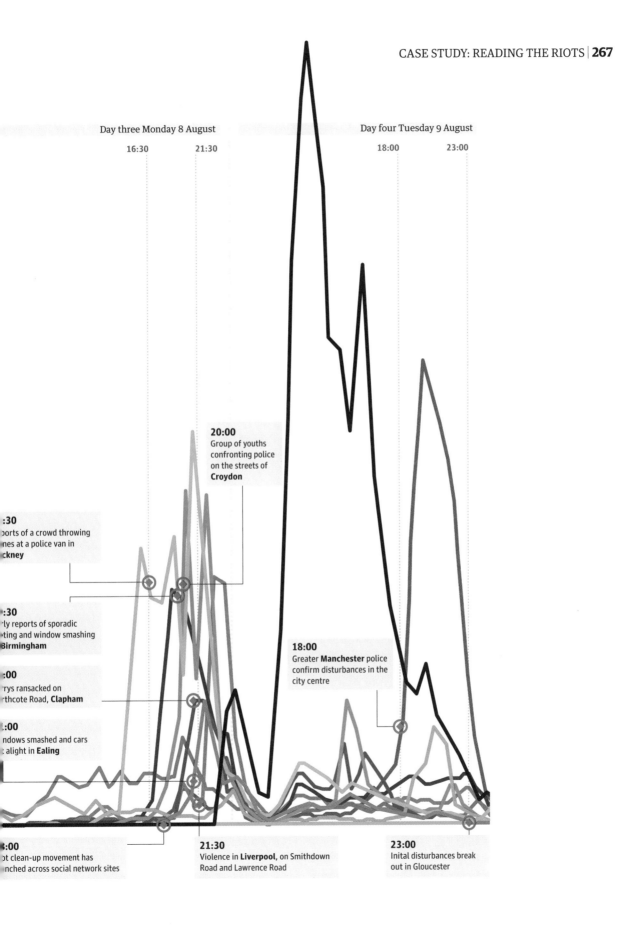

Day three Monday 8 August

16:30   21:30

Day four Tuesday 9 August

18:00   23:00

20:00
Group of youths
confronting police
on the streets of
Croydon

:30
orts of a crowd throwing
nes at a police van in
ckney

:30
ly reports of sporadic
ting and window smashing
Birmingham

:00
rys ransacked on
rthcote Road, **Clapham**

:00
ndows smashed and cars
alight in **Ealing**

18:00
Greater **Manchester** police
confirm disturbances in the
city centre

:00
t clean-up movement has
nched across social network sites

21:30
Violence in **Liverpool**, on Smithdown
Road and Lawrence Road

23:00
Inital disturbances break
out in Gloucester

Reading the 1967 Detroit riots

Guardian columnist Gary Younge on how the deadliest riots in US history spawned a landmark study by the Detroit Free Press, which was the inspiration for the Reading the Riots project

Early in the morning on Sunday 23 July 1967 the Detroit police raided an after-hours drinking establishment where more than 80 black men and women were celebrating the return of two Vietnam veterans. This in itself was hardly rare. Police used to raid "blind pigs" all the time.

What was extraordinary was what came next: an outpouring of protest, violence, looting, police brutality and, ultimately, full-scale federal military intervention. Before the week was out there were 43 dead, 467 injured, more than 7,200 arrests, and more than 2,000 buildings destroyed: the deadliest riots in US history.

Nathan Caplan, a psychology professor at the University of Michigan's institute for social research (ISR), was unconvinced by his colleagues' claims that the riots were simply an expression of immaturity and social deviancy. So he went to the affected neighbourhoods with one of his graduate students to conduct some field research.

At the same time, Philip Meyer, a national correspondent for Knight Newspapers, which owned the Detroit Free Press, was also trying to break out of the constraints of his discipline. Just a few weeks earlier Meyer had returned from a career break as a Nieman fellow at Harvard, where he had studied social research methods. When the riots in Detroit started he saw an opportunity to apply academic rigour to journalistic reportage. "It struck me like a bolt of lightning," says Meyer. "The University of California had just released their report into the Watts riots and I thought, we could do this too. But people wouldn't have to wait two years for the results. With journalists we could do it faster."

>
> 'It struck me like a bolt of lightning,' says Meyer. 'The University of California had just released their report into the Watts riots and I thought, we could do this too. But people wouldn't have to wait two years for the results'

And so they did. Caplan and Meyer got together, drafted a question-
naire and then trained 30 black interviewers to go into the affected areas
and gather information. The next week the interviewers went into the
field, sending each day's interviews back to the university. In the third
week Meyer and Caplan analysed the data and Meyer started writing it
up. Just a month after the disturbances had started, the Free Press
published its findings.

Entitled The People Beyond 12th Street: A Survey of
Attitudes of Detroit Negroes After the Riot of 1967,
the report's methodology and language are very
much of their time. Nonetheless, even though by
modern standards the sample was small and only
a minority of those they spoke to were rioters, its
data was revelatory.

The data was revelatory ...
there was no correlation
between economic status
or educational levels and
propensity to riot. The main
grievances were police
brutality, overcrowding, poor
housing and lack of jobs

It showed that, contrary to popular belief,
there was no correlation between economic status or
educational levels and propensity to riot. Nor had the
riots been the work of recent immigrants from the South. The
main grievances were police brutality, overcrowded living conditions,
poor housing and lack of jobs.

The overwhelming majority of black people in Detroit at the time
(84%) thought the riots could happen again. Only a quarter believed they
had more to gain than lose by resorting to violence. But, explained Meyer
at the time, "Even those who think the long-term effects of violence are
likely to be bad see some compensating benefits." "They know we mean
business now," one 31-year-old told him.

The Kerner Commission, set up by the president, Lyndon Johnson,
to examine the cause of the riots in Detroit and elsewhere, used the data
from the Detroit Free Press/ISR survey in reaching its findings. "What
white Americans have never fully understood – but what the Negro can
never forget – is that white society is deeply implicated in the ghetto," it
argued. "White institutions created it, white institutions maintain it, and
white society condones it."

Famously it concluded: "Our nation is moving towards two societies,
one black, one white – separate and unequal."

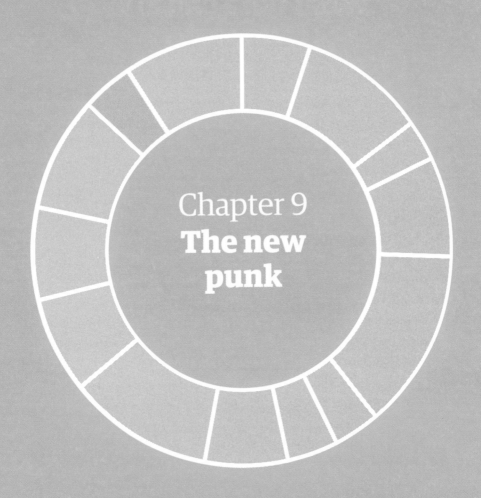

Chapter 9
The new punk

What data can and cannot do

Jonathan Gray of the Open Knowledge Foundation argues that aspiring data journalists and civic data hackers should strive to cut back on data-driven hype and to cultivate a more critical literacy towards their subject matter

In the early days of photography there was a great deal of optimism around its potential to present the public with an accurate, objective picture of the world. In the 19th century pioneering photographers (later to be called photojournalists) were heralded for their unprecedented documentary depictions of war scenes in Mexico, Crimea and across the US. Over a century and a half later – after decades of advertising, propaganda, and PR, compositing, enhancement and outright manipulation – we are more cautious about seeing photographs as impartial representations of reality. Photography has lost its privileged position in relation to truth. Photographs are just a part of the universe of evidence that must be weighed up, analysed, and critically evaluated by the journalist, the analyst, the scholar, the critic, and the reader.

The current wave of excitement about data, data technologies and all things data-driven might lead one to suspect that this machine-readable, structured stuff is a special case. The zeitgeist at times bears an uncanny resemblance to the optimism of a loose-knit group of scientists, social scientists, and philosophers at the start of the 20th century, who thought they could eschew value-laden narratives for an objective, fact-driven model of the world.

"Facts are sacred," says the Guardian Datablog and "for a fact-based worldview," says Gapminder. The thought of tethering our reportage, analyses and reflection to chunks of data-given truth is certainly consoling. But the

> ❝ The zeitgeist bears an uncanny resemblance to the optimism of ... scientists, social scientists, and philosophers at the start of the 20th century, who thought they could eschew value-laden narratives for an objective, fact-driven model of the world ❞

notion that data gives us special direct access to the way things are is – for the most part – a chimera.

Data can be an immensely powerful asset, if used in the right way. But as users and advocates of this potent and intoxicating stuff we should strive to keep our expectations of it proportional to the opportunity it represents. We should strive to cultivate a critical literacy with respect to our subject matter. While we can't expect to acquire the acumen or fluency of an experienced statistician or veteran investigative reporter overnight, we can at least try to keep various data-driven myths from the door. To that end, here are a few reminders for lovers of data:

> " Data can be an immensely powerful asset, if used in the right way. But as users and advocates of this potent and intoxicating stuff we should strive to keep our expectations of it proportional to the opportunity it represents "

Data is not a force unto itself. Data clearly does not literally create value or change in the world by itself. We talk of data changing the world metonymically – in more or less the same way that we talk of the print press changing the world. Databases do not knock on doors, make phonecalls, push for institutional reform, create new services for citizens, or educate the masses about the inner workings of the labyrinthine bureaucracies that surround us. The value that data can potentially deliver to society is to be realised by human beings who use data to do useful things. The value of these things is the result of the ingenuity, competence and (perhaps above all) hard work of human beings, not something that follows automatically from the mere presence and availability of datasets over the web in a form which permits their reuse.

Data is not a perfect reflection of the world. Public datasets (unsurprisingly) do not give us perfect information about the world. They are representations of the world gathered, generated, selected, arranged, filtered, collated, analysed and corrected for particular purposes – purposes as diverse as public sector accounting, traffic control, weather prediction, urban planning, and policy evaluation. Data is often incomplete, imperfect, inaccurate or outdated. It is more like a shadow cast on the wall, generated by fallible human beings, refracted through layers of bureaucracy and official process. Despite this partiality and imperfection, data generated by public bodies can be the best source of information we have on a given topic and can be augmented with other data sources, documents and external expertise. Rather than taking them at face value or as gospel, datasets may often serve as an indicative springboard, a starting point or a supplementary source for understanding a topic.

Data does not speak for itself. Sometimes items in a database will stand by themselves, and do not require additional context or documentation to help us interpret them – for example, when we consult transport timetables to find out when the next train leaves. But often data will require further research and analysis in order to make sense of it. In many ways official datasets resemble official texts: we need to learn how to read and interpret them critically, to read between the lines, to notice what is absent or omitted, to understand the gravity and implications of different figures, and so on. We should not imagine that anyone can easily understand any dataset, any more than we would think that anyone can easily read any policy document or academic article.

> Official datasets resemble official texts: we need to learn how to read and interpret them critically, to read between the lines, to notice what is absent or omitted, to understand the gravity and implications of different figures

Data is not power. Data may enable more people to scrutinise official activities and transactions through more detailed, data-driven reportage. In principle it might help more people participate in the formulation of more evidence-based policy proposals. But the democratisation of information is different from the democratisation of power. Knowing that something is wrong or that there is a better way of doing things is not the same thing as being in a position to fix things or to effect change. For better or for worse, flawless arguments and impeccable evidence are usually not sufficient in themselves to effect reform. If you want to change laws, policies or practices it usually helps to have things like implacable advocacy, influential or high-profile supporters, positive press attention, hours of hard graft, bucketloads of cash and so on.

Being able to see what happens in the corridors of power through public datasets does not mean you can waltz down them and move the furniture around. Open information about government is not the same as open government, participatory government or good government.

Interpreting data is not easy. Furthermore there is a tendency to think that the widespread availability of data and data tools represents a democratisation of the analysis and interpretation of data. With the right tools and techniques, anyone can understand the contents of a dataset, right? Here it is important to distinguish between different orders of activity: while it is easier than ever before to do things with data on computers and on the web (scrape it, visualise it, publish it), this does not necessarily entail that it is easier to know what a given dataset means. Revolutionary content management systems that enable us to search and browse legal documents don't mean that it is easier for us to interpret the law. In this sense it isn't any easier to be a good data journalist than it is to be a good journalist, a good analyst, a good interpreter. Creating a good piece of data journalism or a good data-driven app is often more like an art than a science. Like photography, it involves selection, filtering, framing, composition and emphasis. It involves making sources sing and pursuing truth – and truth often doesn't come easily. Amid all of the services and widgets, libraries and plugins, talks and tutorials, there is no sure-fire technique to doing it well.

I'm sure as time goes by we'll have a more balanced, critical appreciation of the value of data, and its role within our information environment. As former BBC journalist Michael Blastland writes in the recently published Data Journalism Handbook: "We need to be neither cynical nor naive, but alert."

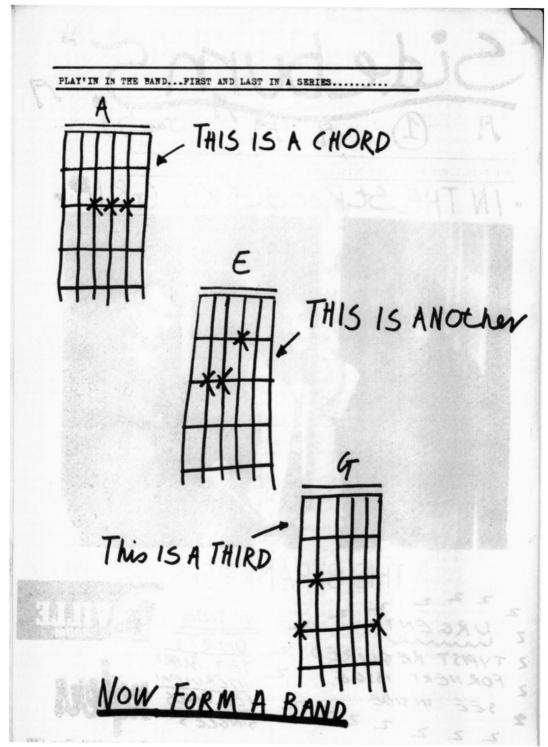

A page from the January 1977 punk fanzine Sideburns

Is data journalism the new punk?

This is a chord … this is another … this is a third. NOW FORM A BAND. So went the first issue of British punk fanzine Sideburns in 1977 in the "first and last part in a series".

It might be 35 years old, but this will do nicely as a theory of data journalism now.

Why? Arguably punk was most important in its influence, encouraging kids in the suburbs to take up instruments, with little or no musical training. It represented a DIY ethos and a shake-up of the old established order. It was a change.

Crucial to it was the idea: anyone can do it.

Is the same true of data journalism? Do you need to be part of a major news operation, working for a big media company to be a data journalist?

Now is the time to examine this – in May 2010, we forecast that reporters would soon be flooded with a "tsunami of data". Crime, health, education, the economy: every aspect of our lives is measured by the government, which has become very good at collecting data. But, traditionally, that data has been made as inaccessible as possible. Published on PDFs rather than spreadsheets; jargonised so much as to make it meaningless; aggregated into such big geographical areas that it tells us nothing about where we live.

The Big Society declaration published by Downing Street in 2010 included a key line: "We will create a new 'right to data' so that government-held datasets can be requested and used by the public, and then published on a regular basis." This meant local crime statistics, full details of all government contracts and quangos spending more than £25,000, local government spending of more than £500 and full salary details of senior civil servants.

Two years on and data journalism is part of the fabric of what we, and many other news organisations, do. What is it? I would say data journalism is such a wide range now of styles – from visualisations to long-form articles. The key thing they have in common is that they're based on numbers and statistics – and that they should aim to get a "story" from that data. The ultimate display of that story, be it words or graphics, is irrelevant, I think – it's more about the process.

> Data journalism is now such a wide range of styles ... the key thing they have in common is that they're based on numbers and statistics - and that they should aim to get a 'story' from the data

There are even different streams now – short-form, quick-and-dirty data visualisations of the kind done every day on the Guardian's Datablog site, right through to complex investigations and visualisations such as our riots data analysis.

So, can we still say that anyone can do data journalism, in the first and last part in a series. Would this work? ▶

The ageing world
Using multiple datasets to paint a picture of the future

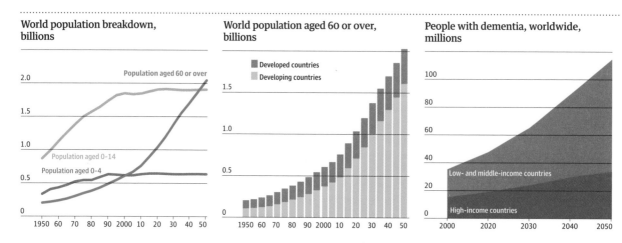

World population breakdown, billions

World population aged 60 or over, billions

People with dementia, worldwide, millions

SOURCE: UNFPA REPORT: AGEING IN THE TWENTY-FIRST CENTURY: A CELEBRATION AND A CHALLENGE

This is a dataset

Data summary

London knife crime 2010-11
Click heading to sort table. Download this data

Local authority	Total reported crime	Knife crimes	% of all crime
Barking & Dagenham	19,149	36	0.19
Barnet	25,670	31	0.12
Bexley	13,754	8	0.06
Brent	29,433	47	0.16
Bromley	22,002	23	0.1
Camden	34,168	26	0.08
Croydon	32,228	67	0.21

Here's another

Data summary

2011/12 offence rate by borough
Click heading to sort

	Violence Against The Person	Sexual Offences	Robbery	Burglary	Theft & Handling	Fraud & Forgery	Criminal Damage	Drug offences	Other Offences
Barking & Dagenham	21.05	1.38	5.3	12.11	31.58	6.24	10.58	5.32	1.84
Barnet	10.89	0.79	3.04	12.86	26.34	4.87	6.33	2.83	0.7
Bexley	11.02	0.66	1.28	5.99	15.81	2.57	6.7	3.64	0.64
Brent	26.2	1.2	7.88	14.05	32.01	5.08	8.53	16.23	1.6
Bromley	13.55	0.73	2.09	9.85	22.6	4.2	7.69	3.06	0.59
Camden	21.71	1.47	5.5	12.93	73.03	4.25	8.29	10.47	1.33
Croydon	17.64	1.29	4.76	12.1	28.94	4.95	9.43	6.47	1.13

Here are some free tools

Datawrapper

An open source tool helping everyone to create simple, correct and embeddable charts in minutes.

Login / Sign Up   Try it now!

Easy to use

This little tool reduces the time needed to create a correct chart and embed it into any website from hours to seconds. It makes charting easy, and helps you avoiding common errors.

Full control

Datawrapper is 100% free software. You can use our free hosted service, or install it on your own server for maximum control. Written in PHP, Datawrapper is easy to install, modify and extend.

Customizable

We encourage you to customize the charts layout, fonts and colors to make them integrate nicely in your website. Strengthen your own brand, not ours.

now be a data journalist

OK, it lacks a certain 1976 grittiness, but the theory is there. You don't have to be a developer or a coder to be a data journalist.

We asked our Twitter followers what they thought was required. A couple stand out to me:

> Maybe everyone can do it, but not everyone can do it well. Like so many other things, done well is a mix of art & science

@BrettBernstein

> Mutual disregard for shared constructs of authority? Shared overarching aim of revealing reality away from the facade?

@EdThink

But is that enough? The thing about data journalism is that there are so very many "chords" – just the free ones could fill several training manuals: Google Fusion Tables, Tableau, Gephi, OutWit Hub, Google Refine … Can anyone really do it?

Dan Sinker knows about both data and punk: he heads up the Knight-Mozilla News Technology Partnership and is a former editor of Punk Planet.

He says there are some parallels – with a crucial difference.

"While I agree with the premise – it's never been easier to do this stuff than it is right now – I think there are a few steps beyond just learning three chords when doing data journalism. For one, Legs [McNeil, who coined the word 'punk'] didn't really say a band needed to be *good* but I'd like to think we'd require that for data journalism."

> " I think there are a few steps beyond just learning three chords when doing data journalism. For one, Legs McNeil didn't really say a band needed to be *good* but I'd like to think we'd require that
>
> **Dan Sinker, Knight-Mozilla News Technology Partnership**

The theory goes that the punk bands we remember best are the ones that were good – but there needed to be a whole lot of kids experimenting and sounding awful before they got there.

For what it's worth, I like the fact that there

are many just trying stuff out, even if it is forgettable – because some of it will be amazing.

In fact, data journalism is a great leveller. Many media groups are starting with as much prior knowledge and expertise as someone hacking away from their bedroom. Many have, until very recently, had no idea where to start and great groups of journalists are still nervous of the spreadsheets they are increasingly confronted with.

It's rare for the news site reader to find themselves as powerful as the news site editor, but that's where we are right now – and that power is only increasing as journalists come to rely more and more on their communities for engagement and stories.

> Data journalism is a great leveller. Many media groups are starting with as much prior knowledge and expertise as someone hacking away from their bedroom

Says Sinker: "Where I think there are more parallels are in the fact that this is a young community (in years if not always age), and one that's actively teaching itself new tricks every day. That same vitality and excitement that motivated punk, it's motivating news hackers right now."

Meanwhile, more and more news teams are discovering that data equals stories and bulking up their teams. Some would say it's just an extension of work they've always done, but that's to ignore the huge shift in power the web has created.

"Some people think that this stuff is instant," says Sinker. "Even though there are incredible tools now, there is still a learning curve." Out there in the world, there are lots of people who have just formed a band and got on with it – despite the obstacles.

Take the data team at the Argentinian newspaper La Nación, recently shortlisted for the Data Journalism Awards for their work on transport subsidies, which uncovered that the government had spent more than £21bn in less than a decade to prop up the operation of private buses in Argentina – and revealed the companies which benefited most.

When the team started, it was sparse, to say the least, says Florencia Coelho, who is a head of research and training in new media at the organisation.

"We had no web programmer or CAR [computer-assisted reporting] people in our newsroom. We gathered an interactive designer and we self-taught Tableau with their free training videos in what we called our Tableau days, in a Starbucks at a shopping mall in Buenos Aires."

The team is still not exactly huge – but it is easily the best data journalism site in South America and one of the most innovative around. You can read more about it on the website produced by the Neiman Journalism Lab at Harvard University (**www.niemanlab.org**).

It's not all about investigative reporting. First, all reporting probably counts as investigative journalism, but if you want to play semantics, then I will see your "investigative" and raise you "analytical". Not all data journalism has to bring down the government – it's often enough for it to shine a light in corners that are less understood, to help us see the world a little clearer. And if that's not investigative, what is?

> We had no computer-assisted reporting people in our newsroom. We gathered an interactive designer and we self-taught Tableau with their free training videos, in a Starbucks at a shopping mall in Buenos Aires
>
> **Florencia Coelho, La Nación**

There's a great democratisation of data going on. Rather than the numbers belonging to the experts, they belong to all of us, and data journalism is part of that reclaiming of the facts. Even at the OECD, users' voices are part of the process, making up the core analysis that lies at the heart of the Better Life Index on well-being.

And, just to be clear, data journalism doesn't have to mean data visualisation. It is not about producing charts or intricate graphics – the results of data journalism just happen to lend themselves to that. Sometimes a story is best told in images and infographics, other times it works as words and stories. It's the ultimate in flexible formats.

But, when it comes to visualisations, sometimes the simplest things can flood the web and turn viral.

Single charts are likely successful because they are easy to consume; the viewer only needs to learn how to read one "chunk" of visualisation to get the whole story. Simplicity lends itself to quick understanding and sharing, whereas complexity can prevent a viewer from reaching those points. Curiously, mixed charts, which form what we commonly think of as the typical infographic, are the least successful here, perhaps because they take more mental work to consume completely. It underlines the point that simplicity and brevity are huge strengths in visual communication.

Sometimes things done messily can still be hits – it's the information that's vital. People are willing to forgive a lack of perfection; they are much less forgiving to those who get the facts wrong.

Data visualisation experts will always say: allow the data to choose the visualisation, that it's crucial for the visualisation to fit the numbers – and not the other way around. That approach equally applies itself to whether something needs a visualisation in the first place.

Of course, for some people, this will never be journalism. But then, who cares? While they're worrying about the definitions, the rest of us can just get on with it.

Punk eventually turned into new wave, new wave into everyday pop and bands that just aren't as exciting. But what it did do is change the climate and the daily weather. Data journalism is doing that too.

In the words of Joe Strummer:

"People can do anything."

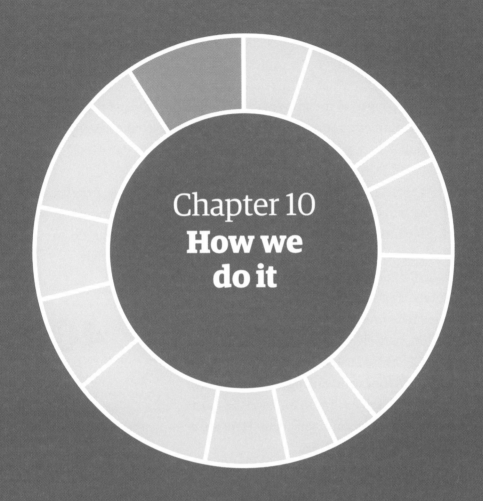

Chapter 10
**How we
do it**

**What you'll find out
in this chapter:**
» Where to find datasets
and what to do with
them » The revolution
the internet has sparked
in Africa » The most
dangerous countries,
according to the murder
map of the world

Behind all our data journalism stories is a process. It's changing all the time as we use new tools and techniques. But this is – roughly – how it goes. It's not rocket science – the biggest part of the discussion comes in the creation of the stories rather than the process, which is time-consuming but simple.

Some people say the answer is to become a sort of super hacker, write code and immerse yourself in SQL. You can decide to take that approach. But a lot of the work we do is just in Excel.

1 We locate the data or receive it from a variety of sources, from breaking news stories, government data, journalists' research and so on. Sourcing the data is a much undervalued skill. You can do worse than start with http://www.guardian.co.uk/data – we've already done the hard work of identifying and cleaning up hundreds of datasets from carbon emissions, via crime rates to Bafta winners.

Alternatively, I have a Delicious feed where I link to datasets – you can find that at **www.delicious.com/smfrogers**. But broadly, the general approach is to look for the most authoritative place for your data. Here are a few very specific examples:

400
Radiation in milliseiverts received by workers at the Fukushima nuclear power plant in Japan after the Tsunami caused the station's reactors to overheat. By contrast, the dosage from a dental x-ray is 0.01mSv

● **GDP** from the Office for National Statistics. There are loads of different definitions of GDP. You probably want inflation-adjusted, which has the label: ABMI. It should be pointed out that the ONS has incredible information on this site – but it is also the world's worst website

● **Carbon emissions** from the US Energy Information Agency. A fantastic resource and has every country in the world on it

● **UK immigration statistics** from the Home Office. These stats also cover asylum and come out annually but also every few months. They offer Excel downloads and data for where applications come from.

And here are a couple of general Guardian resources that you might find useful:

● **guardian.co.uk/world-government-data** World government data

Immigration and employment
Who comes to Britain to work, 2010

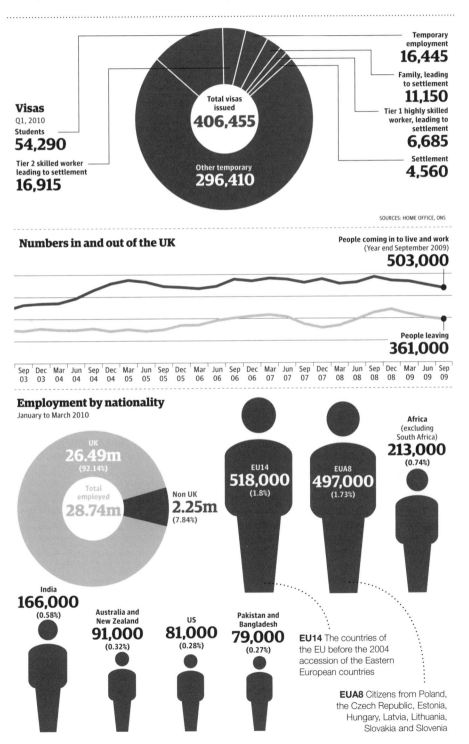

Visas
Q1, 2010
Students
54,290

Tier 2 skilled worker
leading to settlement
16,915

Total visas
issued
406,455

Other temporary
296,410

Temporary
employment
16,445

Family, leading
to settlement
11,150

Tier 1 highly skilled
worker, leading to
settlement
6,685

Settlement
4,560

SOURCES: HOME OFFICE, ONS

Numbers in and out of the UK

People coming in to live and work
(Year end September 2009)
503,000

People leaving
361,000

Sep 03 | Dec 03 | Mar 04 | Jun 04 | Sep 04 | Dec 04 | Mar 05 | Jun 05 | Sep 05 | Dec 05 | Mar 06 | Jun 06 | Sep 06 | Dec 06 | Mar 07 | Jun 07 | Sep 07 | Dec 07 | Mar 08 | Jun 08 | Sep 08 | Dec 08 | Mar 09 | Jun 09 | Sep 09

Employment by nationality
January to March 2010

UK
26.49m
(92.14%)

Total
employed
28.74m

Non UK
2.25m
(7.84%)

EU14
518,000
(1.8%)

EUA8
497,000
(1.73%)

Africa
(excluding
South Africa)
213,000
(0.74%)

India
166,000
(0.58%)

Australia and
New Zealand
91,000
(0.32%)

US
81,000
(0.28%)

Pakistan and
Bangladesh
79,000
(0.27%)

EU14 The countries of
the EU before the 2004
accession of the Eastern
European countries

EUA8 Citizens from Poland,
the Czech Republic, Estonia,
Hungary, Latvia, Lithuania,
Slovakia and Slovenia

How the data journalism process works
From retrieving information to publishing the results

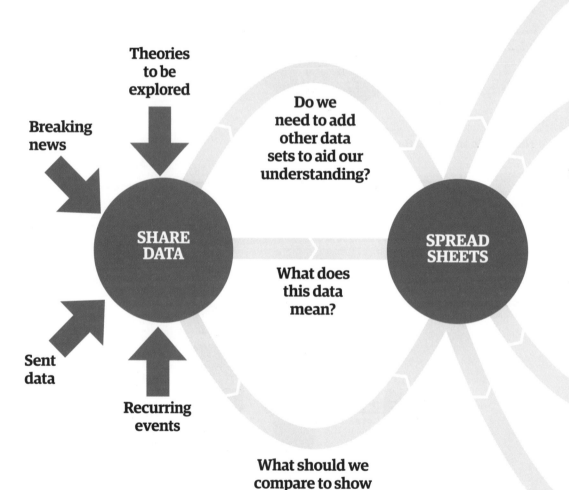

Theories to be explored

Breaking news

Sent data

Recurring events

SHARE DATA

Do we need to add other data sets to aid our understanding?

What does this data mean?

What should we compare to show change?

SPREAD SHEETS

Putting data into comparable units

Getting rid of unnecessary columns of data

Merging cells

Changing data into correct format

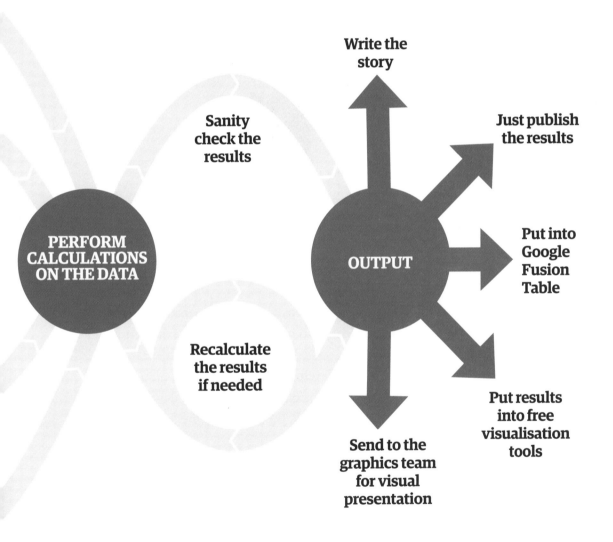

PERFORM CALCULATIONS ON THE DATA

Sanity check the results

Recalculate the results if needed

OUTPUT

Write the story

Just publish the results

Put into Google Fusion Table

Put results into free visualisation tools

Send to the graphics team for visual presentation

Parenthood across the world
Changing fertility rates, 2005-10

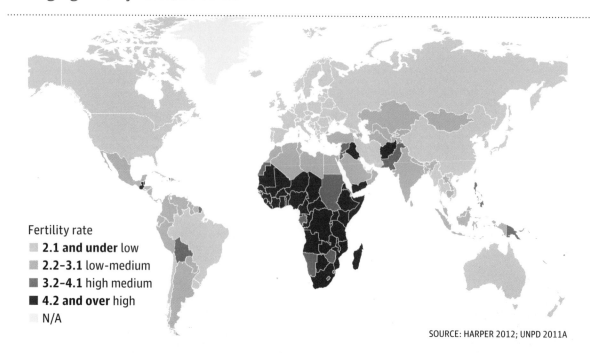

Fertility rate
- **2.1 and under** low
- **2.2–3.1** low-medium
- **3.2–4.1** high medium
- **4.2 and over** high
- N/A

SOURCE: HARPER 2012; UNPD 2011A

search, which amalgamates government data from many different countries such as crime, geo data and health – over 15,000 datasets are available

● **guardian.co.uk/data/global-development-data/search** Global aid and development data search. This brings together aid and development data from the UN, OECD, World Bank, the IMF and others - and covers over 3,200 datasets

2 We then start looking at what we can do with the data – do we need to mash it up with another dataset? How can we show changes over time? Those spreadsheets often have to be seriously tidied up – all those extraneous columns and weirdly merged cells really

28m
children of primary school age are out of school in poor countries affected by conflict. From 1999 to 2008, an additional **52m** children enrolled in primary school. But in 2008, there were still **67m** primary school age children out of school around the world

SOURCE: UNESCO

don't help. And that's assuming it's not a PDF, the worst format for data known to humankind. Tables on pages can sometimes be extracted using Adobe Professional (which has an option if you highlight the table and control-click it). Often it's simpler to use a basic programme like Text Wrangler to access the data. If a table's published on a web page, one thing worth trying is saving the web page as html – and then opening it in Excel, which then opens its as a table.

3 And even when data is published in spreadsheet (or CSV) form, it often comes in from respected sources in a state. The Office for National Statistics, for instance, is fond of inserting hidden columns and blank lines into Excel that serve no purpose but to make the data harder to analyse. Data from the US Census Bureau can be similarly opaque and the Bureau for Labor Statistics' unemployment figures are very tricky to clear up.

The answer is to copy the data out, open a new Excel window and "paste special" the data into it as "values" – then you can work out where those troublesome lines are. Another important thing to do is keep the codes.

Often official data comes with the official codes added in – for instance, each school, hospital, constituency and local authority has a unique identifier code. Countries have them too (the UK's code is GB, for instance). They're useful because you may want to start mashing datasets together and it's amazing how many different spellings and word arrangements can get in the way of that. There's Burma and Myanmar, for

18%

Increase in energy use by UK households in the last 40 years. Despite greener homes, and campaigns on insulation and energy use, domestic energy use is up from **37m** tonnes of oil equivalent (mtoe) in 1970 to **44** mtoe in 2009, up **18%**. We prefer our homes hotter now, up from an average of **14°C** in 1971 to **17°C** in 2008

Gas and electricity
Wholesale prices vs energy bills, 2012

Typical annual customer bill, £

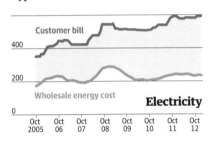

Breakdown of typical dual fuel bill*, %

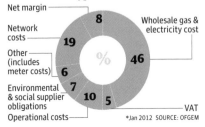

Second homes

What second homes tell us about the North–South divide, 2012

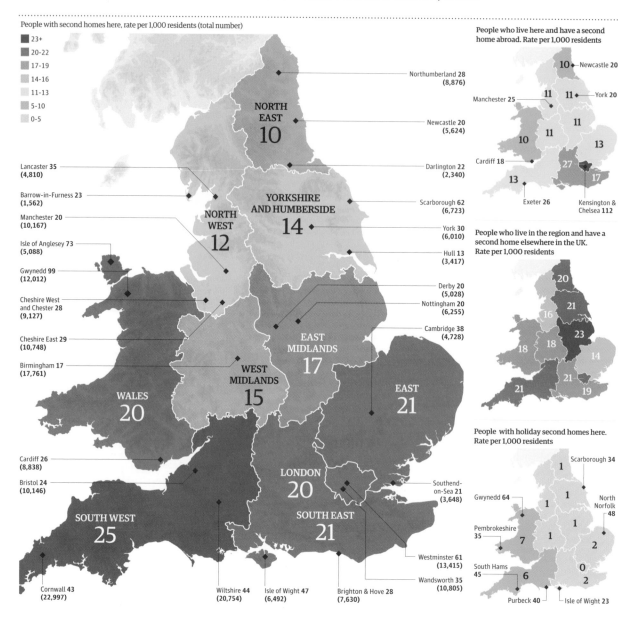

People with second homes here, rate per 1,000 residents (total number)

- 23+
- 20-22
- 17-19
- 14-16
- 11-13
- 5-10
- 0-5

Northumberland **28** (8,876)

Newcastle **20** (5,624)

Darlington **22** (2,340)

Scarborough **62** (6,723)

York **30** (6,010)

Hull **13** (3,417)

Derby **20** (5,028)

Nottingham **20** (6,255)

Cambridge **38** (4,728)

Southend-on-Sea **21** (3,648)

Westminster **61** (13,415)

Wandsworth **35** (10,805)

Brighton & Hove **28** (7,630)

Isle of Wight **47** (6,492)

Wiltshire **44** (20,754)

Cornwall **43** (22,997)

Bristol **24** (10,146)

Cardiff **26** (8,838)

Birmingham **17** (17,761)

Cheshire East **29** (10,748)

Cheshire West and Chester **28** (9,127)

Gwynedd **99** (12,012)

Isle of Anglesey **73** (5,088)

Manchester **20** (10,167)

Barrow-in-Furness **23** (1,562)

Lancaster **35** (4,810)

NORTH EAST **10**

YORKSHIRE AND HUMBERSIDE **14**

NORTH WEST **12**

WALES **20**

EAST MIDLANDS **17**

WEST MIDLANDS **15**

EAST **21**

LONDON **20**

SOUTH WEST **25**

SOUTH EAST **21**

People who live here and have a second home abroad. Rate per 1,000 residents

Newcastle **20**
York **20**
Manchester **25**
Cardiff **18**
Exeter **26**
Kensington & Chelsea **112**

10 11 11 11 10 11 13 27 17 18 13 26

People who live in the region and have a second home elsewhere in the UK. Rate per 1,000 residents

20 16 21 18 18 23 14 21 19 21

People with holiday second homes here. Rate per 1,000 residents

Scarborough **34**
North Norfolk **48**
Gwynedd **64**
Pembrokeshire **35**
South Hams **45**
Purbeck **40**
Isle of Wight **23**

1 1 1 1 1 1 7 1 2 6 0 2

instance, or Durham, City of compared to City of Durham. Codes allow you to compare like with like. There's a useful function that will help you with this: VLOOKUP in Excel allows you to bring datasets together. It looks for the value in one sheet and brings in the results from another. Pivot table reports in Excel also allow users to count the number of times something comes up, aggregate data or work out averages. It's really useful and we used it a lot with the WikiLeaks data.

4 Now we're getting there. Next up we can actually start to perform the calculations that will tell us if there's a story or not – and then sanity-check them to see if it just sounds wrong. The most common are the simplest – percentage change or rate per 100,000 people.

5 At the end of that process is the output – will it be a story or a graphic or a visualisation, and what tools will we use? Our top tools are the free ones that we can produce something quickly with – with the more sophisticated graphics produced by our development team.

Which means we commonly use Google Charts for small line graphs and pies, or Google Fusion tables to create maps quickly and easily. We used it to show the WikiLeaks Iraq death figures.

But the best option of all is to find a designer you can work with. Designing a graphic and analysing data are two different jobs.

93%

Drop in turtle doves in the UK since 1970. Also down are starlings, tree sparrows and corn buntings – by **80%**. Some birds are up – species like the blue tit, robin and blackbird, which can live in gardens and other human-dominated environments. Ornithologists say global warming may be playing a part

SOURCE: BRITISH TRUST FOR ORNITHOLOGY

In defence of bad graphics

Are most online data visualisations ... well ... just not very good? It's an issue we grapple with a lot – and there has been a recent backlash against many of the most common data visualisations online.

Poor Wordle – it gets the brunt of it. It was designed as an academic exercise that has turned into a common way of showing word frequencies and (yes, we are guilty of using it) an online sensation. There's nothing like ubiquity to turn people against you.

New York Times senior software architect Jacob Harris has called for an end to word clouds, describing them as the "mullets of the Internet". (Although the NYT has used them to great effect.)

While on Poynter, the line is that "People are tired of bad infographics, so make good ones."

Grace Dobush has written a great post explaining how to produce clear graphics, but can't resist a cry for reason:

> "What's the big deal? Everybody's doing it, right? If you put [Infographic] in a blog post title, people are going to click on it, because they straight up can't get enough of that crap. Flowcharts for determining what recipe you should make for dinner tonight! Venn diagrams for nerdy jokes! Pie charts for statistics that don't actually make any sense! I have just one question – are you trying to make Edward Tufte cry?"

Oh, and there has also been a call for the annihilation of online data visualisers, from Gizmodo's Jesus Diaz:

> "The number of design-deficient morons making these is so ridiculous that you can fill an island with them. I'd do that. And then nuke it."

A little extreme, no?

MOST POPULAR INFOGRAPHICS YOU CAN FIND AROUND THE WEB

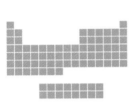

PERIODIC TABLE OF SOMETHING

CREDIT CRISIS VISUALIZED
WITH NUMBERS THAT ARE
NOT EXPLAINING ANYTHING

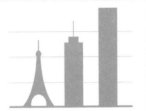

WORLD'S TALLEST BUILDINGS PLUS
SOMETHING THEY ARE BUILDING IN DUBAI

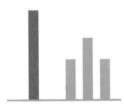

WATER, GAS, OIL OR WHATEVER
UNITED STATES CONSUMES
MORE THAN ANY OTHER COUNTRY

TUBE MAP OF SOMETHING

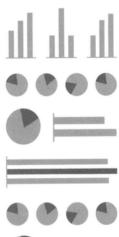

VENN DIAGRAM OF SOMETHING

TAG CLOUD WITH RANDOM WORDS
IN THE SHAPE OF SOMETHING

A CRAPLOAD OF IRRELEVANT DATA
PUT TOGETHER IN A BIG VERTICAL IMAGE

The Italian designer Alberto Antoniazzi skewers the most popular infographic forms to be found on the web.
You can see more of his work at **www.albertoantoniazzi.com**

There has definitely been a shift. A few years ago, the only free data visualisation tools were clunky things that could barely produce a decent line chart, so the explosion in people just getting on and doing it themselves was liberating. Now, there's a move back towards actually making things look … er, nice.

Calling for better graphics is also like calling for more sunshine and free chocolate. Who's going to disagree with that? What the critics do is ignore why people produce their own graphics. We often use free tools because they are quick and tell the story simply.

But when we have the time, nothing beats having a good designer create something beautiful – and the Guardian graphics team produce lovely visualisation for the Datablog all the time.

What is the alternative online for those who don't have access to a team of trained designers? Many Eyes was the big hope, but it hasn't been meaningfully updated since its genius creators, Martin Wattenberg and Fernanda Viégas, skipped off from IBM to Google's "Big Picture" data visualisation group. Outside of Google tools and fusion tables the major player is Tableau Public, which has the advantage of being simple to use and looks good.

And there's a lot of snobbery around. After all, William Playfair was arguably better qualified in direct action than graphic design (he stormed the Bastille) when he invented the line, bar and pie chart in the 18th century.

It must be challenging for people who have spend years in design school to have some punk waltz in with a bit of nous and Illustrator on their machine to produce stuff that people, y'know, like

Nevertheless, it must be challenging for people who have spent years in design school to have some punk waltz in with a bit of nous and Illustrator on their machine to produce stuff that people, y'know, like.

Witness the 2010 face-off (or spectacles-off) between the data journalist David McCandless and graphic designer Neville Brody on Newsnight.

McCandless, the designer behind the book Information is Beautiful, argued that data visualisations were a valuable tool for understanding difficult issues involving big numbers in an increasingly visual culture.

Brody, best known for his work as a typographer and his ground-breaking designs for The Face and Arena magazines in the 80s, criticised a tendency to make information "beguiling and seductive". He argued that making information "pretty" obscured the importance of the news. The resulting confrontation remains essential viewing on YouTube.

Maybe there's a feeling out there that more should have resulted from the explosion of interest in visualising data. Creative Review sums it up as the inevitable disappointment that maybe visualisations haven't changed the world, after all. "Data visualisation is no more inherently neutral than any other form of statistical analysis ... The great hope of some data visualisers runs into the buffers of reality. Yes, graphical invention can be used to explain complex ideas and present detailed data in digestible form in the cause of an argument or political position, but this will not necessarily aid understanding. As newspapers have known for decades, a graph is just another way of telling a story. But whose story?"

For what it's worth, I think having loads of people out there producing graphics is nothing to worry about. Even Wordles. It shows that data analysis is part of all our lives now; not just the preserve of a few trained experts handing out pearls of wisdom. Witness our Flickr group: 1,200 people producing graphics every day of completely different styles and – to be honest – variable quality. Bring it on, I say.

No one likes bad graphics, but in the end the good visualisations will shine through.

177

Different names for products trademarked by Apple by 2011, including **57** for applications

SOURCE: APPLE

An atlas of pollution
The world in carbon dioxide emissions

Latest data published by the US Energy Information Administration provides a unique picture of economic growth – and decline. China has sped ahead of the US, as shown by this map, which resizes each country according to CO_2 emissions. And, for the first time, world emissions have gone down

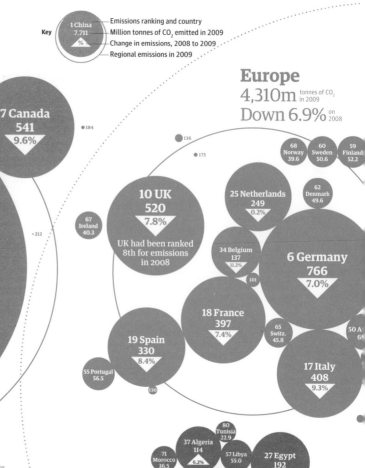

Key
1 China
7,711 — Emissions ranking and country
— Million tonnes of CO_2 emitted in 2009
% — Change in emissions, 2008 to 2009
— Regional emissions in 2009

7 Canada
541
9.6%

2 US
5,425
million tonnes
7.0%

US emissions are down for the second year in succession – after almost uninterrupted year on year increases since these records began in 1980. The decline has matched the country's economic woes which have seen it only just emerge from recession. Since 2000 the country's CO_2 emissions have fallen by 7.5%

Europe
4,310m tonnes of CO_2 in 2009
Down 6.9% on 2008

68 Norway 39.6
60 Sweden 50.6
59 Finland 52.2

136
175

10 UK
520
7.8%
UK had been ranked 8th for emissions in 2008

25 Netherlands
249
0.2%

62 Denmark 49.6

67 Ireland 40.3

34 Belgium 137 11.2%

6 Germany
766
7.0%

101

19 Spain
330
8.4%

18 France
397
7.4%

65 Switz. 45.8

50 A 6

17 Italy
408
9.3%

55 Portugal 56.5

130

North America
6,411m tonnes of CO_2 in 2009
Down 6.9% on 2008

184
212
179

13 Mexico
444
1.9%

76 Cuba 30.4
122
213
74 Puerto Rico 33.3
208
150
83
95
94
194
181
210
211
146
187
188
160
201
195
98
171
105
119
129
113
169
96
88
30 Venezuela 162 1.4%
64 Trinidad & Tobago 47.8

149

49 Colombia 70.1
157
151
168

77 Ecuador 28.7
70 Peru 38.2

14 Brazil
420
0.3%

90
132
110

Central & South America
1,273m tonnes of CO_2 in 2009
Up 3.6% on 2008

35 Chile 119 74.1% Biggest % increase

214

29 Argentina 167 3.2%

193

Africa
1,122m tonnes of CO_2 in 2009
Down 3.1% on 2008

80 Tunisia 22.9
37 Algeria 114
57 Libya 55.0
27 Egypt 192 3.5%
71 Morocco 36.5 6.2%
192
143
117
177
199
190
186
185
164
180
163
115
104
46 Nigeria 77.7
162
176
91
112
155
173
107
97
141
134
125
126
116
152
189
114
78 Angola 24.0
144
165
100
148
131
128
161
206
216
205
159

12 South Africa
450
6.7%

138
142
127
200

World
30,452m tonnes of CO_2 in 2009
Down 0.1% on 2008

Detailed data
Full list of each country's CO2 emissions in 2009
Rank/country/emissions in million tonnes

#	Country	Emissions	#	Country	Emissions	#	Country	Emissions	#	Country	Emissions	#	Country	Emissions	#	Country	Emissions	#	Country	Emissions
1	China	7,711	16	Indonesia	413	31	Singapore	161	46	Nigeria	77.7	61	Hungary	50.0	76	Cuba	30.4	91	Sudan	13.0	106		
2	US	5,425	17	Italy	408	32	Malaysia	148	47	Philippines	72.4	62	Denmark	49.6	77	Ecuador	28.7	92	Sri Lanka	12.8	107		
3	India	1,602	18	France	397	33	Pakistan	140	48	Israel	70.5	63	Oman	49.0	78	Angola	24.0	93	Burma	12.5	108		
4	Russia	1,572	19	Spain	330	34	Belgium	137	49	Colombia	70.1	64	Trinidad and Tobago	47.8	79	Yemen	22.9	94	US Virgin Islands	12.5	109		
5	Japan	1,098	20	Taiwan	291	35	Chile	119	50	Austria	69.2	65	Switzerland	45.8	80	Tunisia	22.9	95	Jamaica	12.1	110		
6	Germany	766	21	Poland	286	36	Uzbekistan	115	51	Qatar	66.5	66	Bulgaria	44.5	81	Croatia	21.5	96	Netherlands Antilles	11.6	111		
7	Canada	541	22	Ukraine	255	37	Algeria	114	52	Belarus	60.6	67	Ireland	40.3	82	Jordan	20.0	97	Kenya	11.5	112		
8	South Korea	528	23	Thailand	253	38	Iraq	104	53	Syria	56.9	68	Norway	39.6	83	Dominican Republic	19.9	98	Guatemala	11.3	113		
9	Iran	527	24	Turkey	253	39	Greece	100	54	Turkmenistan	56.8	69	New Zealand	39.1	84	Bosnia & Herz.	18.3	99	Armenia	11.2	114		
10	UK	520	25	Netherlands	249	40	Vietnam	98.8	55	Portugal	56.5	70	Peru	38.2	85	Estonia	17.5	100	Zimbabwe	10.6	115		
11	Saudi Arabia	470	26	UAE	193	41	Czech Republic	95.3	56	Bangladesh	55.1	71	Morocco	36.5	86	Slovenia	17.4	101	Luxembourg	10.6	116		
12	South Africa	450	27	Egypt	192	42	Hong Kong	86.0	57	Libya	55.0	72	Azerbaijan	36.2	87	Lithuania	15.8	102	Cyprus	9.4	117		
13	Mexico	444	28	Kazakhstan	185	43	Kuwait	84.9	58	Serbia	52.3	73	Slovakia	35.8	88	Panama	15.5	103	Latvia	8.5	118		
14	Brazil	420	29	Argentina	167	44	Romania	80.5	59	Finland	52.2	74	Puerto Rico	33.3	89	Lebanon	14.8	104	Ghana	8.1	119		
15	Australia	418	30	Venezuela	162	45	North Korea	79.5	60	Sweden	50.6	75	Bahrain	31.1	90	Bolivia	13.9	105	Honduras	7.9	120		

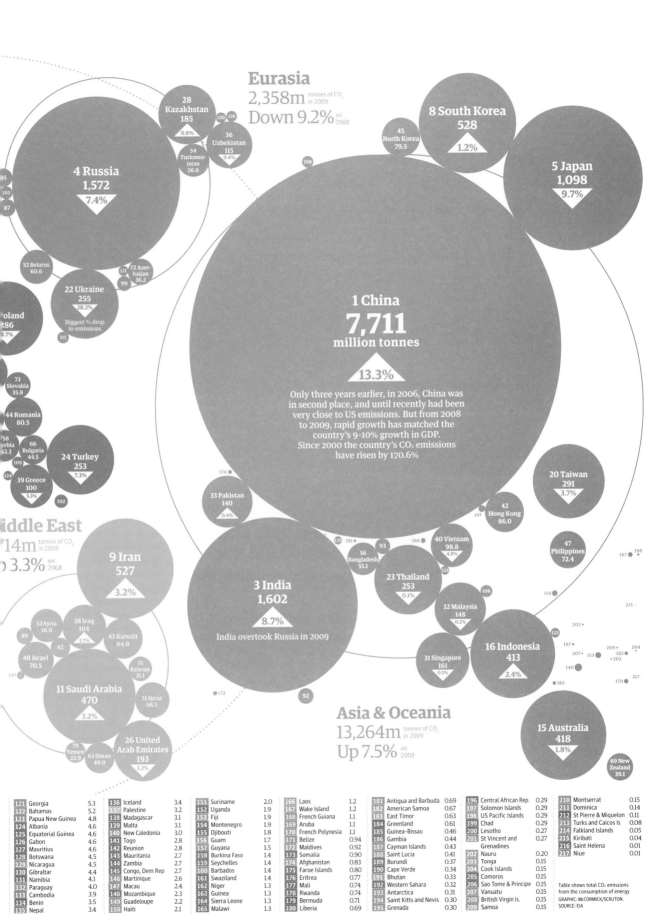

In practice: reporting Superstorm Sandy

When a big crisis happens, the first thing to disappear is often a sense of perspective: what's really going on, where is it happening and how bad is it? Sitting in London, 3,500 miles away, it felt like that for us with Hurricane Sandy. We weren't short of information – constant breaking news and social media saw to that – but we were short of the key information. The noise becomes greater than the basic facts. That seemed to me like somewhere we could do something useful: provide the basic information about what was going on. What did Sandy actually do?

The tools

Our approach was pretty basic: I'm not a developer and my first port of call was a free tool: Google Fusion Tables. We needed something we could just update simply and easily as the news rolled in, and I needed to be able to make the whole thing without having to wait for development time; the news was moving too quickly for that.

We use Fusion Tables a lot on the data desk – mostly for that ease of use. But we also have the code to make the map the way we like it now. There's increased functionality thanks to Guardian developer Chris Cross, including a location search and a button to "share view", which creates a zoom-specific URL for sharing on Twitter and Facebook.

The style is the result of a lot of trial and error to create a map look I like (it's a very personal process, this), mainly using the Google Maps API wizard, which is a neat playground. So, by the time Sandy came along, we had some tools we could use again, rather than start from scratch.

Fusion Tables has two things that make that simple: the "add row" function means that myself

29.1%

The fall in New Orleans' population after Hurricane Katrina, which made landfall in August 2005, during the most active Atlantic hurricane season in record history. More than 1,800 people are thought to have died

SOURCE: US CENSUS;
NATIONAL HURRICANE CENTRE

Tracking Sandy
Using Google Fusion Tables to track the storm

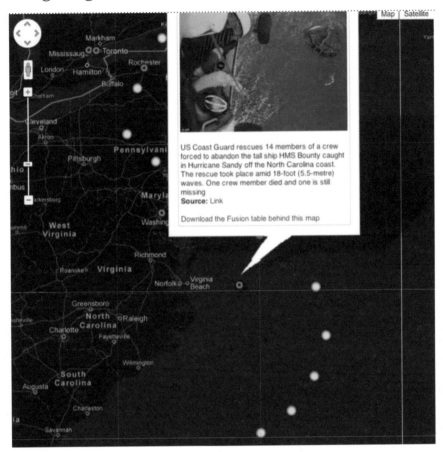

US Coast Guard rescues 14 members of a crew forced to abandon the tall ship HMS Bounty caught in Hurricane Sandy off the North Carolina coast. The rescue took place amid 18-foot (5.5-metre) waves. One crew member died and one is still missing
Source: Link

Download the Fusion table behind this map

The path of the storm was tracked in white; incidents in red. Clicking on red dots brings up a short report on the incident and a link to the relevant news story

and my colleague John Burn-Murdoch could just add events to the map as we got them. Importantly, the geocode function works in the same way as Google Maps – enter an address and it will find it for you, with a high degree of accuracy. It's flexible too, so where we had really detailed geo info, such as road junctions, we could get the lat and long, and they would appear in exactly the right place.

Customising the info windows to include links and pictures is simple too. That just left getting the info: the reporting work. And that was what took the time.

Superstorm Sandy
Reporting the biggest storm of the century so far, 2012

NYC evacuation zones

Zone A - Potential flooding from any hurricane near NYC

Zone B - Potential flooding from a category 2+ hurricane

Zone C - Potential flooding from a category 3-4 hurricane hitting just south of NYC

● **Evacuation centres**

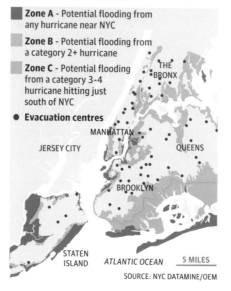

SOURCE: US NATIONAL WEATHER SERVICE

SOURCE: NYC DATAMINE/OEM

Above, an image from the National Oceanic and Atmospheric Administration's GEOS-13 satellite shows the vast scale of the storm which hit the US east coast. Even though it had been downgraded to a tropical cyclone as it made landfall, other weather fronts, strong winds, already high tides and a storm surge made Sandy a superstorm. Left, graphics showing the path of the hurricane and its impact on New York City

The information

We decided to focus on the after-effects: not the closures and evacuations, but the resulting destruction and casualties. Our starting point was the wire feed that all news organisations have. But that was just a starting point.

Take the case of the heroic off-duty police officer Arthur Kasprzak who rescued his family but died in his basement on Staten Island. The initial report we saw was on AP, but with very few details. So we had the basic story but none of the detail. But it gave us a place to look, and we then found this report on SILIVE a local site for Staten Island. That gave us address details such as the road so we could locate it on the map.

Another great source was the NY Daily news live blog – which had a lot of detail for us to then look elsewhere to find more information.

15

Female Nobel Peace prize winners in the award's 110-year history. In fact there have been more institutions than women – **24**. The vast majority are men: **85**, and **29** winners are from the US. Nearly half of all winners have to share their prize – only **52%** get to keep it all to themselves

Crowdsourcing and outputs

We knew that we would miss stuff, so we called on the best resource we have: our readers. We had a form below the map for anyone to submit information. This wasn't going to automatically make it to the map; we needed to check each one before adding.

The whole process meant that we had a dataset we could analyse. The "Filter" on Fusion Tables allows you to embed a map showing just part of the data, and we did that for this post on deaths during the storm.

We wanted to be transparent and let people could see where we'd got our information, so every event has a source link that is there for anyone to download – and hopefully produce something more sophisticated that we can then showcase on the site.

A version of this article originally appeared on Source, an online magazine about code and data visualisation in journalism

8.5m

The number of people who were without power in the eastern United States, in the immediate aftermath of Hurricane Sandy. The 14ft storm surge inundated New York and New Jersey's electricity stations, many of which are underground

SOURCE: CBS

The last word: why we need open data journalism

Data is everywhere: from governments publishing billions of bytes of the stuff, to visual artists creating new concepts of the world, through to companies building businesses on the back of it.

And everyone wants to be a data journalist too – the barriers for entry have never been lower as free tools change the rules on who can analyse, visualise and present data. Truly, anyone can do it.

At the same time, journalism has undergone a transformation; it's not that long ago that the only way to get a story published by a major news organisation involved years of training and interning and generally slaving away until you get noticed and published.

Now, the power has shifted and the days when journalists could shut themselves away from the world in order to hand out gems of beautiful writing have vanished.

These are the days of open journalism, and reporters who can use the power of the web can produce stronger, better stories. Open journalism involves the person reading and commenting on the story as much as the

The attainment gap
How private education enhances life chances

Numbers of pupils, thousands

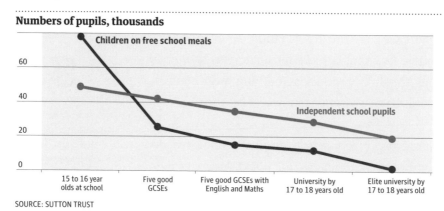

SOURCE: SUTTON TRUST

Private security
Size of security firm G4S and the sectors in which it operates, 2012

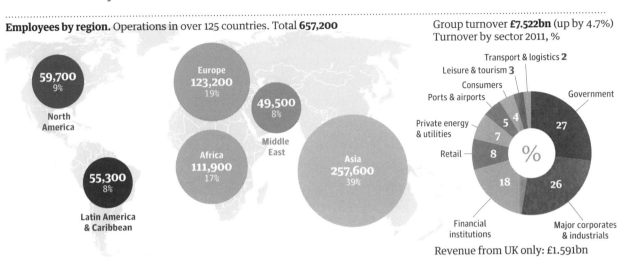

Employees by region. Operations in over 125 countries. Total **657,200**

59,700
9%
North America

55,300
8%
Latin America & Caribbean

Europe
123,200
19%

49,500
8%
Middle East

Africa
111,900
17%

Asia
257,600
39%

Group turnover **£7.522bn** (up by 4.7%)
Turnover by sector 2011, %

Transport & logistics **2**
Leisure & tourism **3**
Consumers
Ports & airports
Private energy & utilities
Retail
Government
5
4
7
27
8
%
18
26
Financial institutions
Major corporates & industrials

Revenue from UK only: £1.591bn

original reporter, and with the power to shape and influence the news they see in front of them.

But how does that connect to data journalism? These are two segments of the same pie chart – and for data journalism to develop beyond a mere new fad, it has to engage and involve not just the people creating the news but also the people reading it.

Data journalism is not (just) about being clever and then showing the world how clever you are. It has to be about more than that.

It's important because data journalism has its roots in publicly available data. As soon as data.gov launched in 2009 it didn't matter how good or bad it was – the principle had been set: all government data must be public, and available in a form you can use. Since then, the world has been deluged in open data, with cities, states and regions around the globe publishing everything from detailed crime statistics to the locations of public toilets.

But having an open data portal doesn't automatically make you a haven of freedom;

6,535
Abortions for non-British citizens visiting the UK for the procedure in 2010. **4,402**, came from Ireland, and the second largest contingent from Northern Ireland. There were **158** women from Middle Eastern countries, such as the UAE, Bahrain, Qatar and Egypt. **189,574** abortions were carried out in 2010, up **0.3%**

SOURCE: DEPARTMENT OF HEALTH

even Bahrain and Saudi Arabia now have open data portals. In a prescient article for Slate, David Eaves writes: "For many of us who have campaigned for the right to access and reuse government information, it would be easy to pause and relish the sweet victory. We have the ammunition, so now, believe the most techno-utopian advocates, open data will fundamentally change politics – depoliticizing debates and eliminating irresponsible positions. But that would be a mistake."

This is where data journalists come in: by exposing and interrogating the data, we can test how accurate it is, mash it up with other datasets and produce results that tell you something new about the news.

Traditionally, journalists treated data with a kind of breathless trust which they would never accord a human source. Numbers are trusted because investigating them is too scary. The former BBC reporter Michael Blastland examined the norovirus – or winter vomiting bug – outbreak of 2008, showing exactly how easy it is to get the numbers wrong.

The story was that three million people had gone down the previous year with the disease. He looked at the confidence intervals – the guide to how reliable these numbers were – and realised that the number could just as easily be 280,000. Or even 34 million. The truth was that no one knew but the story had been written up anyway.

There are early examples of great journalists adopting data too, of course: pioneers like Philip Meyer, the American reporter whose investigation of the causes of the 1967 Detroit riots inspired our Reading the Riots project. He used survey data and a computer to create a new kind of journalism.

But this is no longer a niche form of reporting. The people that care about the numbers are out there in the world:

Single lives
The growing percentage of people who live alone

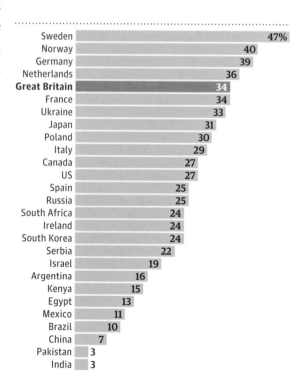

Country	%
Sweden	47%
Norway	40
Germany	39
Netherlands	36
Great Britain	**34**
France	34
Ukraine	33
Japan	31
Poland	30
Italy	29
Canada	27
US	27
Spain	25
Russia	25
South Africa	24
Ireland	24
South Korea	24
Serbia	22
Israel	19
Argentina	16
Kenya	15
Egypt	13
Mexico	11
Brazil	10
China	7
Pakistan	3
India	3

our readers. Arguably, most of the million or so people who read the Datablog each month are predominantly general interest readers; not developers, designers or even other journalists. They want the numbers because they want to trust the report, to test its veracity and sometimes to see what else they can find in the data.

Because everyone is an expert in something, that engagement can mean fascinating results – for example, the way we were able to improve the map colours on the blog with the help of our readers.

70m

Passenger movements at Waterloo, Britain's busiest rail station, in 2009–10, reflecting its position as a major commuter destination. But if you look at interchanges instead, i.e. the stations where people change trains, Clapham Junction is way in the lead, with over **20m**

SOURCE: OFFICE FOR RAIL REGULATION

However, plenty of data is still closed, and we in the media are part of this process. Often the data will be alluded to in a story or interactive and you will not get to see it. It's as if to say: "Look – we made this fantastic interactive guide; you couldn't possibly have anything to offer. So long, and thanks for looking!"

The raw data of key national and international events is often withheld in favour of snazzy presentations of the information without letting you download the data to examine it for yourself.

Immediate and detailed election data is one example: it is supplied by a paid-for feed and certainly not available for immediate download. Or there's live Olympic results – you might be able to see an athlete winning a gold before your eyes, but is that raw data available for you to visualise and experiment with?

News organisations may be campaigners for open information but by withholding that data, become complicit in a system which essentially keeps data private until it's no longer commercially valuable. It's all very well calling for governments to throw open the doors of their data vaults, but if you are not willing to be open too, what is that worth?

Open data assumes the readers are an integral part of the story – open data journalism does the same. By publishing the data in an accessible form, making it available to whoever wants it, suddenly our journalism is stronger and better. So, what follows is our ten-point guide to how it can work:

Open data journalism: how it can work best

The best journalism reveals something new about the world – and feels timely. Data journalism works best when it forces itself into the agenda and makes the news. Timely means people will care about it enough to try and become part of the story.

1
Expose the data behind the story

2
Provide the key data people need

It's a mess out there. As a reader, how can you find the key dataset you need and make sure it's neither out of date nor unreliable? That's where data journalism's role in curating the key numbers can come in. Research is a vital part of a reporter's job and an editor selects the most important data. Combining these skillsets means you can help readers find what they are looking for. Journalists can be the bridge between the providers of data and the consumers – testing, checking and interpretting the data, but also bringing it alive.

All data is personal at some level, and the best interactives and visualisations allow users to see how the numbers reflect their lives where they live. As more and more granular data is released we can bring it to life by making it personal.

3
Make it personal

4
Anyone can do it

They really can – knowing whether something is a story or not is the key skill. There are enough free tools out there to ensure that visualising and analysing the data is easy.

5 Make our data open

What is open data? It is data published in a machine-readable format that anyone can use. That excludes the near-unusable PDFs. By making our data open we mean producing it in a form people can use, whether it's CSV, Excel or even RDF.

6 "Do what you do best, and link to the rest"

The American journalist Jeff Jarvis said that and the principle is simple: there's bound to be someone out there doing something amazing - why not be open enough to embrace that?

7 Free data now

It's not enough to just aggregate data any more - what about the raw, real-time live data behind everything from public transport to election results?

8 We're not the experts

We can't be experts in every aspect of life - why not try and engage those who are, so we can make them part of our process?

9 Make big data accessible

As the datasets that we can explore get bigger, it's our job to make them smaller and simpler to understand.

10 Engage

At the end of the day, it's all about the stories.

Credits

The graphics in this book were created by the Guardian graphic team, in association with the Guardian news and news design teams, between 2006 and 2012.

Michael Robinson

Michael has worked at the Guardian for the past 12 years as a graphic consultant and as the Head of Graphics since 2004. He has been a freelance graphic consultant specialising in information graphics, an illustrator and art director for a number of international magazines, books, private clients and major corporations for which he has been awarded by the D&AD and other international awards.
As Head of Graphics at the Guardian Michael and his team have won gold, silver and bronze medals at the SND Malofiej International Infographics awards, SND US awards and their work has been exhibited at the Design Museum in the Best of British Exhibition.
Michael can be contacted at:
michael@mridesign.co.uk,
michaelrobinsoninfodesign@gmail.com
www.mridesign.co.uk

Garry Blight

Garry joined the Guardian's editorial team in 2010, having previously worked in the Guardian's commercial and marketing departments. He originally trained as an illustrator but subsequently found himself drawn to the world of digital media. His work was awarded a Prix Italia Special prize in 2011. He can be contacted by email at garry.blight@guardian.co.uk

Paddy Allen

Paddy Allen builds news interactives for the Guardian

Guardian research team

John Burn-Murdoch

John graduated from City University's interactive journalism course in 2012. He is a researcher and was part of the Reading the Riots team

Paul Scruton

Paul joined the Guardian graphics team in 2005 following a nine-year stint at Reuters news agency. Originally a technical illustrator, he works mostly in Adobe Illustrator and the 3D modeling package Cinema 4D, as well as Photoshop and Flash. He enjoys getting to grips with a difficult concept and the challenge of bringing clarity to it within the tight deadlines demanded by a busy news room. Paul is contactable by email at paul.scruton@guardian.co.uk

Mark McCormick

Mark studied graphic, editorial & information design at the School of Art and Design in Newcastle, graduating in 2004. He freelanced at various design practices before he joined the Guardian graphics team in 2005. Mark designs for all platforms of the Guardian using Illustrator, Photoshop and Cinema 4D. He has recently become more involved in animation, HTML and After Effects. When not at the Guardian, he has a flourishing freelance career creating graphics, branding, apps, magazines and screen printing.
See more of his work at typeindication.co.uk and get in touch with him at mark@typeindication.co.uk

Kari-Ruth Pedersen

Kari worked as a reporter, sub-editor and designer on local newspapers in Manchester and Sheffield before joining the Guardian. She is the art director (news) of the Guardian. She designed this book. She can be contacted at kari.pedersen@guardian.co.uk

Ami Sedghi

Ami graduated from the University of Westminster's journalism course in 2012, and is now a researcher and writer across the paper

Jenny Ridley

After working as a theatre sister in the UK and Canada for eight years, Jenny retrained as a graphic artist at St Martins in the 1980s. Following stints at the Sunday Correspondent and the Independent, she joined the Guardian's graphics-led education supplement, eG, in 1990. Over the last 17 years Jenny has worked as an information graphic artist on the paper and also the website. Jenny now works as a freelance artist and is contactable by email at ridley.jenny@gmail.com

Christine Oliver

Christine studied Information graphics and page layout design before setting out on a career in news graphics. She worked for The Times, Sunday Times and Independent before joining the Guardian in 2005, where she is equally at home producing interactive content for web and mobile devices as she is with tackling the paper's breaking news. Working predominantly with the Adobe programs Illustrator, Flash and Edge, she enjoys the wide range of serious, fun and quirky subjects she gets to illustrate. Christine is contactable by email at christine.oliver@guardian.co.uk

Finbarr Sheehy

Finbarr has worked in the graphics department of the Guardian for 21 years. Before this he studied at Kingsway Princeton Art College and spent four years at the design group Line + Line. He specialises in technical illustration and infographics of all kinds, and can be contacted at avalon1803@yahoo.com

Quick graphic index

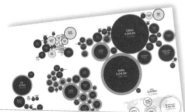

World population
14

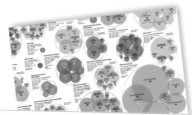

Whitehall's rarefied circles
20

The cost of bringing up baby
40

IED attacks in Afghanistan
74

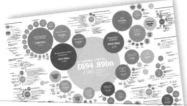

Public spending
96

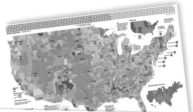

The US 2012 election
130

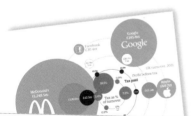

Tax and major corporations
154

How we die
170

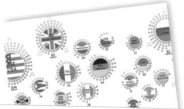

Olympic medals
188

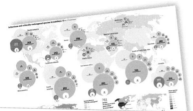

Endangered species
226

How British do you feel?
234

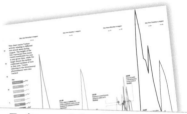

Twitter and the 2011 riots
266